PARENT, STUDENT AND TEACHER COLLABORATION: THE POWER OF THREE

Parent, Student and Teacher Collaboration:
The Power of Three

Peter Coleman

CORWIN PRESS, INC.
A Sage Publications Company
Thousand Oaks, California

P·C·P
Paul Chapman
Publishing Ltd

For information address:

Paul Chapman Publishing
A SAGE Publications Company
6 Bonhill Street
London EC2A 4PU
United Kingdom

Corwin Press, Inc.
A Sage Publications Company
2455 Teller Road
Thousand Oaks, California 91320
E-mail: order@corwin.sagepub.com

British Library Cataloguing in Publication Data
Coleman, Peter
  Parent, student and teacher collaboration : the power of three
  1. Education – Parent participation 2. Home and school
  3. Parent-teaching relationships 4. School improvement programs
  I. Title
371.1'92

ISBN 1 85396 407 7
ISBN 1 85396 399 2 (Pbk)

Typeset by Dorwyn Ltd, Rowlands Castle, Hants
Printed and bound in Great Britain

A B C D E F 3 2 1 0 9 8

Contents

Acknowledgements

Many people contributed to this book. A large group of graduate students (over 30 in all) participated in the initial development of the data collection instruments, and in various later project activities. Many of them subsequently used data from the project for their theses (16 MA, MEd., and PhD. studies drew in some way upon the Coproduction Project).

Two students in particular were important participants. Yvonne Tabin took charge of all the project data for several years; her care and tending of the data was vital. She was also an active participant in the analysis of data, and the preparation and presentation of some of the papers. Her own doctoral dissertation will be based on the project data.

Joan Collinge also contributed in the preparation and presentation of some of the papers, and played an important continuing role as 'critical friend' of the project. She also participated in the development and presentation of some of the papers, and used project data for her doctoral dissertation; her analysis of collaborative and less collaborative teachers was the basis for Chapter 6.

More generally, the Social Sciences and Humanities Research Council of Canada funded the project; I am grateful for their support, without which the work would not have been possible.

My university, and my Faculty, provided support of a different kind. Many of my colleagues, past and present, are fine exemplars of the 'academic ethic'; they model scholarly behaviour in many ways. My nearly 20 years as an academic at Simon Fraser University has been immensely enriched by their presence in the university community.

Beyond this university, many other friends and colleagues have helped indirectly. In particular Ben Levin at the University of Manitoba is consistently stimulating on many of the topics discussed in this book – very few preconceived notions survive his challenge unscathed.

1

Introduction

Everything is the sum of its edges

(Jonathan Gash)

OUTLINE OF KEY ELEMENTS

Davies (1987) described parents and teachers as being co-producers of education when they are **consciously working together on instructional matters**, either in the home or at the school, and are doing so on the basis of shared conceptions of student needs with respect to learning and development. We began with this general notion as the label for the research project, The Coproduction of Learning. However, we added a third important component, the attitudes and actions of students as partners in the enterprise. Hence our work was guided by the notion of the classroom triad, and this book based upon the research is entitled *Parent, Student and Teacher Collaboration: The Power of Three*. Since many other people worked on various aspects of the study, I use 'we' throughout to acknowledge the group effort. However, this book is based upon my own interpretation of data which we collected together.

The triad conception

The triad idea is a simple one. Within the classroom setting **there are in fact three actors ever present** – the teacher, the student, and the parent(s), who are 'present' in the sense that the beliefs, attitudes, and habits of mind of the family are thoroughly embedded in the mind of the child. The interactions amongst these three actors largely determine the student's willingness and readiness to learn; predict student satisfaction and commitment to school and schooling; and hence largely shape both the attitudes towards school and learning, and the level of achievement of the child.

The 'teachability' of the student (in the eyes of the teacher), the collaboration in learning between student and teacher (in the eyes of the student), and the effectiveness of the classroom (in the eyes of the parent) are all largely derived from interactions within the triad.

Furthermore, these interactions **are all alterable**, largely but not exclusively through the initiatives of teachers. In general, educators hold decisive power in interactions with parents and students. Thus anyone who wishes to understand

1

how and why children learn more or less in school needs to understand the range of possibilities within triad interactions. Anyone who wishes to improve student learning or the functioning of a classroom or school needs to know what kinds of triad interactions are most productive, and are to be encouraged.

Parent involvement

For our purposes, parent involvement is concerned with parent engagement in learning activities, mostly although not exclusively in the home. Involvement is not limited to actual learning tasks. It includes the notion of the 'curriculum of the home' – the 'patterns of habit formation and attitude development that prepare a child for academic learning and (that sustain) the child through the years of schooling' (Redding, 1992, p. 1). This is the parent's main contribution to the student's willingness and readiness to learn.

This kind of parental involvement has been shown to yield direct benefits to students (Fullan, 1982; McLaughlin, 1987). Additionally, scholars have found quite consistently that parents prefer to be involved in student learning rather than in school governance or other activities that focus on the school in its entirety (McGeeney, 1980; Tizard and Hughes, 1984).

Multiple methods

Throughout this book we reduce discussions of methods of investigation to a minimum; much of this minimum is placed in the Appendix. But since our findings are often at odds with what other scholars, educators, and parents believe to be true, and since we make recommendations for action, we feel an obligation to show that we have given much attention to issues of reliability (that is, the extent to which the results are likely to hold true in other places like the ones we worked in). Hence we include some discussion of the social science methods used. This runs contrary to current practice in books, in which scholars often simply report findings without reference to how they arrived at their conclusions.

We assumed from the start that in order to try to capture the nature of triad interactions we would need to rely heavily upon case study research methods. However, our work also hopes to contribute to school improvement. Telling stories, even truthful ones, about the experiences of families in schools cannot contribute to policy change. Thus we needed to supplement our cases with quantitative studies, which test the generalizability of our case study findings.

Given this understanding, we needed a methodology that would capture as great a range of triad interactions as possible, with a high degree of reliability. Given our view that these interactions were alterable, we also needed a methodology that would be sensitive to changes in the interactions. A combination of case studies and surveys seemed likely to accomplish these purposes.

Figure 1.1 provides an overview of the basic design that guided the collection of data. The classroom triad constitutes the central element in that design.

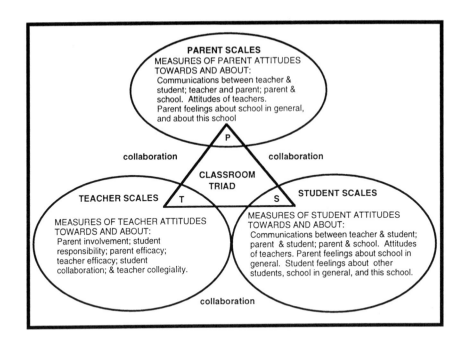

Figure 1.1 The basic research design

Each member of the triad – student, parent, teacher – establishes an **instructional relationship** with each of the others. Each set of instructional relationships affects the others. By instructional relationship we mean simply a set of attitudes and values about teaching and learning, and the practices that reflect these.

For example, the parent who says to a child 'I can't help you with that math homework; I was never any good at math' is shaping an instructional relationship by conveying at the same time some anxiety about learning, some hostility towards mathematics, and an assessment of the value of formal education in her own life. She is reducing the probability of a further request for help from the student, and hence of an active and effective instructional relationship in the future. Since 'math anxiety' is common amongst students and limits teacher success with them, the example also illustrates how classroom instructional relationships can be affected by home instructional relationships.

Within the circles representing roles of the actors are listed the attitudinal variables or 'constructs' that we thought might be important. We developed surveys intended to provide scales to measure the 'constructs' listed in the diagram. ('We develop scales when we want to measure phenomena that we believe to exist because of our theoretical understanding of the world, but which we cannot assess directly.' DeVellis, 1991, pp. 8, 9). We wished to measure general attitudes to school and schooling held by triad participants.

We also collected interview data from all teachers and from a randomly selected sub-group of those volunteer parents and students in their classrooms who had completed the surveys, to allow individual beliefs and attitudes to be analyzed in more depth, and especially to try to discover causal connections between attitudes held by participants.

The pilot analysis

Using the survey data from the first year of the study we developed a pilot analysis to guide subsequent work. The process is described in the Appendix. The result was a flow chart of influences, for parents and students (Figure 1.2).

The flow chart suggests that for students, the basic element in the series leading to satisfaction with school (measured by the rating) is communication with parents about school issues (Scale A, on the right-hand edge). This communication predicts sense of personal efficacy (self-confidence as a learner)

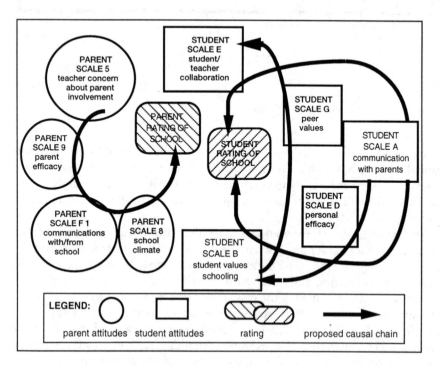

Figure 1.2   A model of causal relationships

with respect to schooling, and student valuing of school and schooling. The latter directly predicts the student's overall rating of the school. **How the student has been prepared for schooling by the parents influences the extent to which he or she is satisfied with the school.**

The other main impact of Scale A is upon student/teacher collaboration (Scale E), as viewed by the student. The higher the level of communication with parents, the higher the level of perceived collaboration with the teacher. **The level of collaboration between student and teacher is shaped by how he or she has been prepared for schooling by the parents.** This collaboration too has a direct impact upon the student's rating of school.

On the parent side, the basic element is the parent's perception that the teacher is concerned about parent involvement. This leads to increased feelings of parental efficacy with respect to schooling, more satisfaction with communications, a more positive perception of the climate of the school, and a more positive rating of the school.

Our most general conclusion from the chart is that two kinds of changes in teacher practices are critical to improving student and parent attitudes to school:

1. **any teacher activity that raises the level of parent/student communication is highly desirable;**
2. **any teacher practice change that strengthens the student perception of collaboration with the teacher in a learning partnership is also highly desirable.**

It is ironic that the set of influences which shape student judgments about the school begin with a home variable (Communication with Parents). For parents the set begins with a school variable (Teacher Concern for Parent Involvement). This suggests a vital feature of school improvement – **it must start with a reconsideration of school effects upon the home, and home effects upon the school, and treat these interactive effects as essential alterable variables.**

This first model guided our case study work in the project. We reassess the model of relationships conveyed in Figure 1.2 often in the case studies that follow.

Research processes

One vital point about our teacher, student, and parent participants should be emphasized. Universities in Canada, and scholars working within them, are bound by very stringent ethical rules and guidelines. Hence every participant in our work was a true volunteer, who had given active initial consent to participation, and **continued to consent throughout the process.** This requirement affected our work significantly – often we lost important data because participants withdrew during the study period. The reader is cautioned: **the sample upon which all our work is based is in one sense biased – all our students and parents are sufficiently convinced of the importance of formal education to wish to participate helpfully in a research project.**

Similarly, all our teachers are sufficiently convinced of the importance of parents in the educational process to think the study worth doing, and to wish to participate helpfully.

The point should not be overstated – our overall sample of families is broadly representative of the population of the province of B.C. with respect to level of education, income, family composition, and other social characteristics. Our work then describes the typical school population.

Similarly, our volunteer teachers are typical rather than unusual. We have some young and beginning teachers, some older and very experienced teachers, and many between these extremes. The schools in which we worked are also representative of B.C. schools; many are in rural locations, although none are 'remote' from urban centres by B.C. standards (more than 30 miles from a town).

Readers outside North America will need to be particularly careful in drawing inferences about their own schools and classrooms, which may differ considerably. However, in the course of making presentations of the work at international (and particularly European) conferences, it has become clear that the interactions between parents, students, and teachers which we describe are recognizable to educators in many countries.

SCOPE AND ORGANIZATION

Each of the subsequent chapters contains a sub-study that makes use of the database in different ways to investigate different issues. The particular approach taken will be discussed within each chapter. The more general issues raised will be discussed in the final section of the book.

This book is based upon work conducted over six years in a wide range of classrooms. The emphasis was on diversity of settings rather than consistency since we intended to produce generalizable research, rather than 'thick description' of a few instances. However, on occasion individual classrooms illustrate very important practices and relationships, and become central to a chapter.

On the basis of Finn's (1989) review of the drop-out literature we reasoned that teacher/family collaboration was particularly important during the transition from elementary to junior high (Grades 4, 5, 6, and 7; between the ages of 10 and 14 in British Columbia). Since student attitudes to and valuing of school is a most important element for us, we chose to study such 'middle school' students.

Organization of the book

We treat the data we collected from interviews with and surveys completed by the triad participants as a set of information which could be used to find responses to a variety of questions about the importance of triad relationships in schools and schooling. Each of Chapters 3 to 10 contributes an analysis of an important sub-topic. The final section of each chapter describes the significance

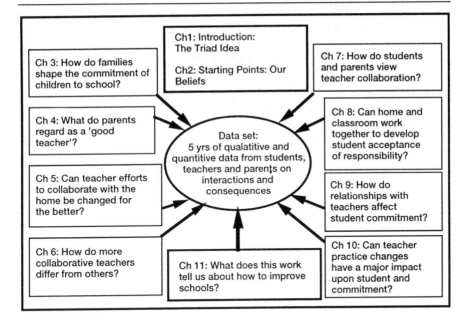

Figure 1.3 Overview of the book

of the chapter findings, and draws implications for educators, as well as for parents and students.

Figure 1.3 provides an overview of the topics addressed. It shows the basic question we posed to the database in each chapter. By the end of the book, each chapter will have contributed some understanding of the importance of the triad relationship and its consequences. The final chapter will re-examine our findings, and describe their significance for parents, teachers, and policy-makers interested in school improvement.

In essence we hope to convince the reader that 'the sum of the edges' of the school experience for students must include the daily influence of the family in the schoolroom. To ignore this 'hidden link' is to remain ignorant about students' lives and motivations, and makes it very difficult for educators to improve schools and schooling for students.

Audience for the book

We see the audience for the book as wide, including school administrators, teachers, parents, and certainly policy-makers in governments at all levels. There are also implications for teacher training to be drawn. Although the work was done in a Canadian province, British Columbia, we believe it has wide relevance, to the US, the UK, and Australia in particular.

The book is intended for the general reader. However, Chapter 2 is introductory and technical and may be avoided by readers more concerned with what we found out than with our initial assumptions based upon the scholarly literature. The Appendix and Chapter Notes contain technical details likely to be of concern primarily to scholars and students of scholarship.

Parents who are likely to be concerned about schools and schooling are those for whom formal education is seen as a potential gateway to a better life than they or their own parents enjoyed. In the small towns and cities outside the metropolitan area of Greater Vancouver, where much of our work was done, most of our volunteer parents fell into this category. Such parents are one part of the intended audience for this book. Educators concerned about the future lives of the children they work with are the other main group to whom the book is addressed.

2

Starting Points: Our Beliefs and Assumptions

Teacher to student *(on an assignment – 'My Goals in Life'):*
It is a wild, unattainable dream. That is why I gave it a failing grade.

Mother: *I think you should consider turning the paper back in just the way it is. If you think it is unattainable, then you can change it yourself. I don't think it is for a high school instructor to set a limit on your hopes and dreams.*

(Monty Roberts (the student), *The Man Who Listens to Horses*)

For the researchers, this work was undertaken in the belief that unless educators and parents reconsider family involvement in formal education, schools and schooling will continue to be an unsatisfactory experience for some, perhaps most, of our students. The surest route to better schools lies through involving parents in the learning activities of students.

There are several important differences between our work and that of others with an interest in school improvement. These differences derive from value differences. We will summarize these in a series of 'imperatives', the beliefs and assumptions with which we began the research study, and that guided our work. Readers who are concerned only with the substance of our findings may wish to avoid this chapter, which describes and analyzes a large body of research.

We consider three main topics: school effectiveness and parent involvement, the political and social context of public schooling, and the internal politics of schools.

PARENT INVOLVEMENT AND EFFECTIVE SCHOOLS

Measuring school effectiveness: tests and alternatives

First, we are less impressed with the importance of test scores than other scholars, and more concerned with the overall place of schooling in the lives of families. Citizens when consulted prefer broader school goals than those measured by tests. Goodlad (1984) has described these goals, saying that 'we want it all', that is not only higher test scores but also happier and more committed

9

children, better prepared in many ways to lead satisfying and productive lives. He uses the term 'general satisfaction' to summarize the preferences of parents and others. More recently, Newmann and colleagues have argued that 'the most immediate and persisting issue for students and teachers is not low achievement, but student disengagement' (1992, p. 2).

Typically, school practices supporting parent involvement have been justified on the basis of parent contributions to student achievement (see for instance the enormous body of work summarized by Wang, Haertel, and Walberg, 1993). Such parental effects upon achievement have usually been measured by the family education level (years of formal schooling of the mother, most often). This measure typically predicts about 5 times as much variance in student achievement as all school factors combined. That is, if you know the education level of the family, you can predict the achievement of the child and get it right most of the time. However, family education and income levels are only 'proxies' (that is simple, available, and roughly accurate measures) for 'family environment', a cluster of values, attitudes and home practices with respect to education (Marjoribanks, 1989).

James Coleman and colleagues (Muller, 1993) have shown that one element of family environment, the presence of conversations at home between parents and children about 'current school experiences' (a measure similar to Student Scale A in the previous chapter), is a better predictor of student achievement than either family income or family education. It is 'family environment', what another scholar calls the 'curriculum of the home' (Redding, 1992), that is vital, not the proxies which represent this curriculum. It is not **who parents are** but **what the parents do** to encourage and facilitate learning that makes a difference to students (Kellaghan *et al.*, 1993).

High test scores are not achieved in an emotive vacuum by student automatons. Scores reflect the importance that schooling assumes in the lives of young people, and their consequent 'engagement' (Newmann, 1992).

Looking at less successful students reveals a similar pattern. A longitudinal study of student drop-outs, which followed 194 families for 19 years, concludes that

> dropping out of high school is a complex chain of events that begins with children's experiences within the early family environment. The strongest direct predictors of dropping out are family factors in addition to adolescent behaviors.
>
> (Garnier, Stein, and Jacobs, 1997, p. 414)

The most successful families 'offered more of a sense of meaning, purpose, and valued cultural goals to their children' (p. 415).

The family effect on achievement, and the family factors influencing dropping out, are almost certainly mediated through student engagement or commitment to schooling: the impact of conversations in the home must be first upon student attitudes and values. Only through these attitudes can the family influence learning outcomes. School practices that support parent involvement **are justified primarily on the basis of their contribution to student commitment.**

The relationships between achievement and commitment which are important to our argument are as follows:

1. commitment is linked to achievement in interactive ways – each influences the other;
2. parent influence is largely upon commitment; and
3. this influence is exercised through 'the curriculum of the home', those attitudes and activities of parents which reveal their educational values.

Furthermore, we believe that what parents do is an **alterable variable** that can be influenced by teacher practices (as suggested by the model described in Chapter 1). This leads to our first imperative:

1. **Student commitment to schooling (or engagement in learning) is primarily shaped by parents through the 'curriculum of the home'; but this parent involvement is an alterable variable which can be influenced by school and teacher practices.**

In Figure 2.1 we summarize what we believe to be the relationship between what parents value and what schools do, focusing on the most important aspects of schooling. The chart illustrates both outcomes and general influences upon students, with the family as main and most continuous influence. We use student commitment to school as a generally useful measure of school quality.

We assert that the proper purpose of schools is not to serve as an arm of government, pursuing public policy objectives, but to provide a service to families. The most important outcomes of a good school are not social leveling, or supporting the expansion of the national economy, but rather student commitment to education and learning, resulting in later 'success' as defined by the family and the student. This usually includes 'career success' – a broadly satisfying series of jobs; what we call 'life enhancement' – the learned ability to enjoy a wide range of recreational, civilizing, and enriching activities; and 'citizenship' – a commitment to the traditional civic virtues. (For the astonishingly strong and persistent connection between schooling and quality of later life, see Hyman, Wright, and Reed, 1975, and Hyman and Wright, 1979.)

It may well be that schools pursuing their proper tasks, as we see them, will also contribute indirectly to social benefits; the outcomes for individuals which we value certainly have social dimensions. But we wish to emphasize the decision-making roles of students and parents as active participants in learning, as an essential element in school improvement. This leads to our next imperative:

2. **Schools should be judged, in the first instance, by assessing how well they serve the interests of individual students and their families. Student commitment to schooling (or engagement) is a useful measure of this schooling outcome.**

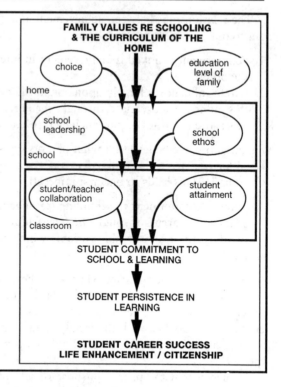

PROPOSITIONS

1. the outcome of interest to parents is student success after schooling is over, based upon schooling.

2. the prime cause of success is family environment, that is the values, like achievement orientation (desire to succeed) and other similar values making up the 'curriculum of the home'; such elements are variable, not fixed, and can be shaped by parental education levels, and by opportunities to choose a school reflecting these values.

3. the school must build upon the eagerness to learn that children bring from home to school on the first day. The school can accomplish this by creating a positive ethos, that is by providing challenging classrooms in which every student has some success, thus sustaining the commitment of all students.

4. in accomplishing these purposes for each individual student the home is an essential partner, especially through home learning activities.

Figure 2.1   The outcomes of schooling

SCHOOLS AS ORGANIZATIONS IN CONTEXT

The dominant view of educational organizations held by organizational theorists has been that they are 'loosely coupled' (Weick, 1976), organizations in which 'goals are ambiguous, hierarchies of authority are not closely integrated, technologies are unclear, participation is fluid, and organizational units are partially autonomous from their environments' (Corwin and Borman, 1988). That is to say, **schools are places where no one knows what is happening or why.**

We visualize schools, and the classrooms within them, as caught up in a web of influences, some external. Although the classroom and school boundaries can be effective insulators against external influence, more often the web is sensitive, and reacts to a wide variety of outside pressures. Teachers in particular spend enormous quantities of time and energy in responding to demands from government, many of which are forgotten by bureaucrats even before teachers have been able to implement them.

Influence of the family

There are two ways in which the family can influence the school: one, by involvement in governance; and two, through its influence on student learning (Fullan, 1982). Those who become involved in governance may wish to see school improvement occur within the existing structure. Alternatively, they may be convinced that 'schools are no longer in accord with their political environments – that is, with the desires of the parents and the communities they presumably serve and with the political system whose procedural principles public institutions are obligated to reflect' (Raywid, 1990, p. 152).

In this work, we rarely address governance issues at all. Rather, we describe parent influence upon instructional relationships that impact directly on student commitment to and success in school. Epstein's summary of this aspect of parent involvement is comprehensive:

> The evidence is clear that parental encouragement, activities, and interest at home and participation in schools and classrooms affect children's achievements, attitudes and aspirations, even after student ability and family socioeconomic status are taken into account. Students gain in personal and academic development if their families emphasize school, let the children know that they do, and do so continually over the school years
> (1987, p. 120)

Although parent involvement in instruction certainly contributes to student success, teachers and administrators often fail to establish strong links between home and school. Lightfoot (1979) comments that: 'families and schools are engaged in a complementary sociocultural task and yet they find themselves in great conflict with one another' (p. 20).

One cause for such conflict is that, while the family focuses on the child as individual, the school focuses on the child as a member of a group (Katz, 1964, p. 441). The needs of the individual versus those of the group are often at issue in parent–teacher confrontations regarding instructional opportunities afforded individual children. The typical shorthand for such parent concerns is 'fairness'; teachers are often perceived to be unfair by parents. Conversely, the highest praise a student can confer upon a teacher is to say 's/he is fair', meaning that the teacher balances the needs of individuals in the class with those of the whole group.

Teachers as professionals

Another cause for such conflict between family and school emerges when members of the teaching profession dismiss parents, either explicitly or implicitly, from the process of educating their child. For parents, the message that the task should be 'left to the professionals' negates the value of the family's contribution to a child's progress and disenfranchises the parent.

Yet for the professional the exclusion of parents is often seen as a vital kind of empowerment: it is an element in professional autonomy. Professional language and the body of knowledge associated with a profession is used to distance members of the profession from clients. Sykes argues that teachers 'must share responsibility with parents, and this means reducing social distance and demystifying school knowledge' (1990, p. 81).

The evaluation of students, that is the social sorting role of the school, is another conflictual area in teacher/parent relationships. Teachers feel some obligation to speak for the 'rational, predictable and stable social system with visible and explicit criteria for achievement and failure' (Lightfoot, 1979, p. 39). Their relationships with students reflect the 'preparatory, transitional and sorting functions performed by schools' (Lightfoot, 1979, p. 39). The classroom is the young child's first encounter with notions of success and failure: home is 'where they always have to take you in', and status is a birthright; but in schools and classrooms 'school membership' is more available to some students than others (Newmann, 1992), and status is earned in competition.

Lightfoot describes the processes of socialization and accommodation required when children move from the family environment in which they are considered 'special' into one in which they are members of a collective. But it is clear that 'conflict emanates from real differences in the sociocultural function of families and schools' (Lightfoot, 1979, p. 44). Teachers feel this keenly, and all too often 'expected the institution to support their interests against those of parents' (Lightfoot, 1979, p. 44). Administrators often feel pressure to convert real wants of parents into demands acceptable to teachers.

Parents and teachers each have the power to cause the other distress. Some teachers, for instance, are concerned about the parents' power to question their authority and professional competence, an understandable concern, given Power's (1985) finding that parents 'felt that teachers were less competent than teachers believed themselves to be' (p. 75) and the chronic anxiety about professional efficacy felt by teachers (Lortie, 1975). To limit their contact with parents limits the opportunities afforded parents to question the teachers' professional status. Unfortunately, this often creates or exacerbates the very conditions of mutual distrust both parents and teachers wish to avoid.

Baskwill notes that parents too confront questions of competency and efficacy:

> teachers have a great deal of power over the lives not only of the children we teach but of their families as well. We have the power to make the best of parents doubt their own abilities. We have the power to create feelings of guilt or frustration, to confuse, anger or reduce to tears even the most stalwart. We have the power to impose – or simply allow – an unbalanced relationship that puts too much guilt on one party, too much authority and responsibility on the other, so that no real communication, no real sharing of ideas and information can occur.
>
> (1989, p. 5)

Each group, then, has concerns regarding the power the other can wield. These concerns affect feelings of personal and professional competency.

Collaboration and the school as 'learning community'

The collaborative approach benefits all concerned. Teachers who actively encourage parent involvement enjoy an increased sense of professional efficacy

(Dye, 1989), the belief that 'they are effective in teaching, that the children they teach can learn, and that there is a body of professional knowledge available to them when they need assistance' (Hoover-Dempsey, Bassler and Brissie, 1987, p. 421). Increased efficacy is an outcome of confidence gained in their ability to 'demonstrate their professional skill and gain the confidence of parents' (Dye, 1989, p. 27). Another factor contributing to increased efficacy is the tendency of parents to rate such teachers more positively than those who do not promote collaborative relationships (Epstein, 1985).

By involving parents in their classrooms, teachers not only learn more about the children they teach and their families, but also provide themselves with informal opportunities to acquire new knowledge and skills of a general sort (Dye, 1989). Such teachers place themselves in the position of 'learner' and empower those around them by granting them an opportunity to teach, an act that demonstrates respect for the parent and a willingness to establish a rapport that cuts across the boundaries that traditionally separate school and home. Parents also benefit from the collaborative relationship. Dye reports that parents involved in her study 'showed an increased understanding and enjoyment of life at school' (1989, p. 27).

In summary, then, the attitudinal benefits to students, parents, teachers, and schools from collaboration (or co-production, in our terminology) are clear. All of these benefits depend upon genuine collaboration, which requires the abandonment of the kind of professionalism that thrives on mystification, and the conscious decision by teachers to empower parents through sharing vital curricular and instructional knowledge.

Both teachers and parents become learners, although what is learned differs. Teachers learn more about home influences on children and about the impact the teachers are having upon the children in the eyes of parents; parents learn more about school programs and practices and about ways in which they can help the child. Oakes and Lipton summarize parental responsibilities thus: 'When parents support learning at home, their children are almost guaranteed to do well at school . . . what really matters is the values you communicate and the consistent encouragement you provide your child' (1990, p. 233). Co-production is the strongest form of such encouragement.

Our next imperative follows from these points:

3. **The most important external influence upon the classroom, that of the family, is at least potentially alterable and, hence, must be incorporated into models of school effectiveness and improvement.**

INFLUENCES WITHIN EFFECTIVE SCHOOLS

Internal influences upon school quality are comprised of such things as instructional programs and practices, school climate (which includes the views of students and parents) and professional ethos, shaped by teacher collegiality and administrator actions (Mackenzie, 1983). These elements interact and may combine to form a 'particular ethos, or set of values, attitudes, and behaviors . . . characteristic of the school as a whole' (Rutter *et al.*, 1979, p. 179). For Rutter and his colleagues, this 'ethos' explained the differences between successful and unsuccessful schools.

School effectiveness studies (these studies typically examine these differences) have now been conducted in many countries. The findings of such studies are often quite consistent (Chrispeels, 1992). A brief review of some well-known studies will demonstrate that the family can affect school quality, as well as student learning.

Studies such as those of Rosenholtz (1989) and Mortimore *et al.* (1988) suggest, respectively, that the most effective teachers believe that 'teachers can make positive things happen, by eliciting parent involvement' (1989, p. 127) in classroom activities, and that parent involvement in the life of the school was 'a positive influence upon pupils' progress and development' (1988, p. 255). Effective schools are often characterized by a closer than normal relationship between parents and educators (Goodlad, 1984). Careful reviews of research such as those of Purkey and Smith (1983) and Davis and Thomas (1989) conclude that parent involvement practices which emphasize support for the academic goals of the school are important.

Much of what differentiates between schools must occur within classrooms. The connection between school improvement and classroom processes have not been much examined in the effective schools research (Bossert, 1988). One consistent difference has emerged, however: 'teachers in an effective school displayed almost double the mean percent of interactive teaching as that displayed by teachers at an ineffective school' (Teddlie, Kirby, and Stringfield, 1989, p. 3). Interactivity between the three central participants, teachers, students, and parents is the focus for this book.

School climate or ethos consists in part of shared beliefs and agreements about practice which can unite members of the school community and differentiate between schools. Several studies (e.g. Rosenholtz, 1989) have followed the lead of Rutter and colleagues, and examined the relationship between 'ethos' (or culture, as it is labelled by some scholars) and school effectiveness. There has been considerable emphasis upon the importance of 'cultural leadership' (Sergiovanni, 1987), the ways in which administrators can create and sustain an emphasis upon instruction (Leithwood and Montgomery, 1982), student engagement (Newmann, 1992), a cohesive work group (Blase, 1987), and positive school climate or ethos (Bossert *et al.*, 1982).

School climate is critical to triad relationships. Our measures of student and parent attitudes include attempts to assess their view of school climate.

School climate and power relationships

Systems of shared values, measured as climate, constrain and direct the actions of participants. This applies to parents and students just as much as it does to educators. But scholars have tended to overlook the effect of school values upon these participants, while emphasizing the 'professional culture of the school', and the empowerment of teachers.

But **issues of power are always important**: 'the failure to examine school systems in terms of the myriad of ways in which power suffuses them has rendered efforts at reform ineffective' (Sarason, 1990, p. 78). For example, the interests of students are subordinated to the interests of teachers in bad schools (Sizer, 1984; Sedlak *et al.*, 1986). 'The absence of student experience from current educational discourse seems to be a consequence of systematic silencing of the student voice. Most fundamentally, student experience goes unheard and unseen for what appears to be ideological reasons' (Erickson and Shultz, 1992).

It follows that classroom and school improvement cannot be attained without changing the power relationships between the three central figures – teacher, student, and parent. Many change models are 'outside-in', relying upon imposed technical changes (Huberman and Miles, 1984); our model is an 'inside-out' version of school improvement, in which classroom change and school improvement occur simultaneously as a consequence of changes in the fundamental relationships between the triad members. Newmann and colleagues have linked student engagement ('school membership') with school culture, including teacher collegiality, forms of instruction, and parent involvement, and shown how in an improving school these issues are attended to concurrently (1992).

But if the integrated school environment is to mean anything such collaboration should involve all three triad actors. The desirable form of parental involvement in instruction is in collaboration with teachers. One consequence of collaboration between parents and teachers is more out-of-school learning, via homework and project work, which essentially expands the school instructional day and week for students. One of the sharpest differences always observed between effective and ineffective schools is time use versus time waste (Davis and Thomas, 1989); the best way for teachers to improve student time use is through collaboration with parents.

The change in power relationships implicit in the triad model is consistent with other trends:

> the arguments that are being used to describe how schools should be managed are also being used to describe the education that students should receive and the skills they should acquire in the process. These skills include participation, discovery, innovation, creativity, adaptability, continuous self-generated improvement, the capacity to recognize and make choices, cooperation, mutual responsibility, and problem-solving. . . . What is done becomes what is taught. The implication, then, is obvious: If schools are to teach creativity and problem-solving and cooperation and involvement, they must practice them, not just in the classroom but at all levels of the system.
>
> (Shedd and Bacharach, 1990, pp. 193, 194)

With respect to teacher/student relations, for example, cooperative teaching models also constitute a change in relationship within classes, and between students and teachers.

Triad collaboration at classroom level will promote student bonding; this in turn increases the likelihood of student retention in school. Retention is likely to be particularly important for the students and families who are not well served by the schools at present, because they lack social capital (J. S. Coleman, 1987a), in particular knowledge of how to help their children learn. The collaborative triad described here promotes better, because more responsive, schools.

Sarason has pointed out that recent reform proposals in the USA 'do not require altering the nature of the relationships between those who make up the system' (1990, p. 14). Yet 'what you seek to change is so embedded in a system of interacting parts that if it is changed, then changes elsewhere are likely to occur' (1990, p. 16). In our view, the triad relationship we have sketched represents a fundamental change in schools, one which is supported by the empirical literature.

Leadership and school quality

In order to bring about this change in relationships, transformational leadership within the school is needed. The central task of such leadership is to create and sustain an **integrated school environment** in which students and parents are seen as full members of the school community. The most powerful and enduring lesson from all the research on effective schools is that the better schools are more tightly linked – structurally, symbolically, and culturally – than the less effective ones. They operate more as an organic whole and less as a loose collection of disparate subsystems (Murphy, 1990, p. 9).

4. **Triad collaboration at classroom level that promotes student bonding is the secret at the heart of school effectiveness. Better schools are necessarily both more responsive and more integrated. Leadership is vital to responsive and integrated school environments, in which all voices count.**

The beliefs with which we commenced the study on which this book is based are that:

1. **Student commitment to schooling (or engagement in learning) is primarily shaped by parents through the 'curriculum of the home'; but this parent involvement is an alterable variable which can be influenced by school and teacher practices.**
2. **Schools should be judged by assessing how well they serve the interests of individual students and their families. Student commitment to schooling is a useful measure of this schooling outcome.**
3. **The most important external influence upon the classroom, that of the family, is at least potentially alterable, and hence must be incorporated into models of school effectiveness and improvement.**
4. **Triad collaboration at classroom level that promotes student bonding is the secret at the heart of school effectiveness. Better schools are necessarily both more responsive and more integrated. Leadership is vital to responsive and integrated school environments, in which all voices count.**

3

The Hidden Link: Parent Influences upon Student Commitment

Only connect
(Joseph Conrad, *The Heart of Darkness*)

Here we examine the relationship between parents and students. Our original model (in Chapter 1) predicts that this influence is normally decisive in shaping the child's relationship with the school. The substantive question we pose here is:

How do families shape the commitment of children to school?

A secondary question is:

Do the educational expectations that parents hold, and the mediating and intervening activities in which they sometimes engage, play a part in the process of shaping commitment?

FRAMEWORK FOR THE ANALYSIS OF FAMILY INFLUENCE

We have argued that each member of the student, parent, and teacher triad influences each of the others. Each also influences the relationship between the other two. Here we will describe how parents influence children's commitment to school by shaping the relationship between student and teachers.

Our parents want the teacher to recognize the particularity of the child, while acknowledging that the child is a member of a classroom group and that 'getting along with others' is a vital capacity that the child must learn at school, as well as at home. When either teacher acceptance of the child as individual, or classroom integration of the child, seems absent, with effects upon the child's commitment or 'school membership' (Newmann, 1992), the parents become concerned. They see that this threatens the long-term interests of the child. They are likely to take some action, typically 'mediation' or 'intervention'.

Thus we will look at parents in two somewhat different relationships with the other triad members – sometimes as mediators between child and teacher, and sometimes as intervenors or catalysts.

As mediators the task of the parents is the typical 'getting to yes' familiar to us from various kinds of formal and informal negotiations; the 'yes' is the child's commitment to schooling. For the parent as mediator the task is to show the child why school is important, how to succeed in school while trying, and how to cope with the problems that school presents to the child almost daily.

While our work focuses on the middle school years, the importance of parent as mediator starts earlier. The relationship with the first teacher (kindergarten or daycare teacher) may be the child's first with an adult who is not a family member (Lightfoot, 1978). The concerned parent wants to make certain that the pattern the child establishes in forming this relationship is appropriate, productive, and repeatable – the relationship with the first teacher often shapes later student–teacher encounters. Early failure on the part of the child and the parent can have drastic and fairly immediate consequences; attitudes shaped early predict later problems; probable school drop-outs can be identified as early as the third grade (Lloyd, 1978). Parents intuitively understand this, and work very hard as mediators in the early years of school; many of the parents with whom we spoke had organized their lives so that they could spend time in the child's classroom during this period.

For the parent as catalyst the task is to intervene as needed to shape or reshape both the child's attitudes and responses to the school environment, and on occasion to try to reshape that environment. Usually responding to crises, the parental task is to change the school's perception of the child, which usually means helping the school understand the child's behavior. Reshaping the school in the eyes of the child usually means helping the child understand the school. (School here normally means teacher and classroom, that part of the school that most influences the child's perception and assessment of the institution.) For parents this task can seem impossible in some circumstances; at such times choice of school can be vitally important to parents (Raywid, 1990).

Theodore Zeldin points out that the chemical notion of catalyst, discovered in the nineteenth century, 'gives intermediaries a new status':

> Now we have discovered the power of intermediaries – conciliators who mend broken relationships, industrial relations arbitrators who produce mutually satisfactory working agreements, negotiators of international trade agreements who create wealth and opportunity, businessmen who forge new corporations with updated purposes out of old ones whose *raison d'etre* is fading. Forming productive coalitions is the new art of leadership.

(1994, p. 155)

Parents skilled as intermediaries are vital to the schools, as we will demonstrate.

Seeking answers in the interview data

Two main features of both home and school practices are considered vital to student achievement and commitment: pressure and support, 'stick' and 'carrot' (see Figure 3.1). These labels derive from the work of Huberman and Miles on change (*Innovation Up Close*, 1984). Other current labels for these

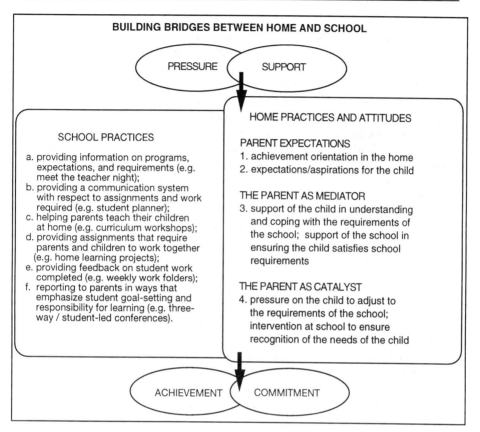

Figure 3.1 Supportive school practices and the parental contribution to student commitment

ideas are challenge and 'caring'. What is vital about these elements is their coexistence: pressure without support breeds resistance and eventually rebellion or apathy; support without pressure breeds baseless confidence likely to crumble at the first serious challenge.

Figure 3.1 lists both home and school practices that we have found to be associated with parent and student commitment to school and schooling. The school practices are the **routine** contribution (i.e. seen as normal practices by most teachers, even those who do not utilize them) that school people can make to the home practices that shape student commitment. (More detailed descriptions of common desirable school and classroom practices are given in later chapters. Other potential school contributions requiring special efforts are described in Kellaghan *et al.*, 1993.)

Three aspects of parent practice are listed in Figure 3.1 – establishing expectations for success in school; acting as mediator to help the child cope with school; and acting as intervenor to shape the child's behaviour and that of school or teacher. We expected to find reference to these in our interviews.

We emphasize the 'support' dimension because our parents almost universally believed that it is more directly associated with student commitment than is 'pressure'. (Parents of previous generations often emphasized 'stick' over 'carrot'.) Our parent and student interview data describe practices of 'support' in far greater detail than practices involving 'pressure'. Most of the parents acknowledged that their central task was building bridges between the 'worlds apart' (Lightfoot, 1978) of home and school. Both 'pressure' and 'support' are tools in this bridge-building. Parents are mediators and catalysts whose motto might well be 'only connect' the home and the school, to provide a consistent climate which elicits commitment from the child.

The climate of the classroom and school, and particularly its consistency with that of the home (J. S. Coleman, 1987b), influence the degree to which parents and students accept a particular school's values and participate in its activities (Finn, 1989), that is, exemplify commitment day by day. Such acceptance and participation, which at the classroom level teachers see as **student motivation to learn,** is vital to classroom and school effectiveness. In this respect school improvement is best understood as an upward spiral of more and more positive interactions between and amongst the centrally important partners in schooling – teachers, students, and parents.

Student (and to a lesser extent parent) ratings of school climate and school quality hence constitute a measure of **student commitment or bonding** with school. Bonding is the most effective anti-dropout vaccine (Finn, 1989). Understanding not only the home practices and attitudes that predict and shape such student commitment, but also the ways in which school and classroom activities can shape and support these home practices, contributes to the knowledge base for school improvement.

Family influences upon student commitment

It is not **who parents are** but **what the parents do** to encourage and facilitate learning that makes a difference to students (Kellaghan *et al.*, 1993). And what parents do is an **alterable variable** that can be influenced by school and teacher practices, as we have argued earlier.

Family effect on achievement is mediated through student attitudes. Only through these attitudes can the family influence learning outcomes. Thus levels of student commitment, like levels of student achievement, tell you more about the home than about the school. **Asking students to rate schools is to ask them indirectly to give a report about the educational influence of their homes.** Some of our early sub-studies support this view. For example, we know that the student rating of elementary school strongly predicts later adjustment to secondary school (Cairns, 1994); the rating is a measure of student commitment as well as a measure of school quality.

If what families do constitutes an alterable variable subject to influence by schools, efforts by schools to strengthen parent/student instructional relationships should result in more strongly motivated and more collaborative students.

To summarize, in this chapter we pose questions concerning the impact of pressure and support in the home on student commitment to school. We expect that home practices with respect to

(a) **shaping student expectations (attitudes towards achievement and aspirations); and**
(b) **mediating between student and school, by interpreting each to the other; and**
(c) **intervening to change attitudes and behaviour of student or school**

will support and sustain student commitment.

HOW WE SOUGHT ANSWERS TO THE QUESTIONS

We tried to find answers in two independent ways, using survey responses for the first attempt and interviews for the second. The results of the two analyses were then compared. This procedure contributes both to the reliability and to the usefulness of the findings.

The first step, using survey data from Year 5 of the study, was to develop a group of student cases for whom attitudes were very positive and a second group for whom they were quite negative. (See Note 1 in Chapter Notes for details.) The result of this step was a ranked list of 16 students; the rankings were kept confidential from the people carrying out the analysis of the interviews, the next step.

The second step was to examine the interviews for the 16 parents and students, who were from 14 different classrooms in 12 schools in two different school districts (Local Education Authorities in UK terms). The parent attitudes and practices, as exemplified in the interviews, were used to sort the 16 students from the homes of the parents we interviewed into high commitment/ low commitment, **based solely on what the parents said.** (The process of analyzing the content of interviews is described in Appendix A.) If the rankings of student commitment made on the basis of what the parents said were consistent with those derived from the survey data, our hypotheses about the importance of the parent linkage would be confirmed.

POSITIVE CATEGORIES:	
parent sees child as:	parent acts:
1. an able learner;	1. to support child;
2. collaborative with parent in school work;	2. in collaboration with school;
3. satisfied with school.	3. teacher facilitates parent involvement.
NEGATIVE CATEGORIES:	
parent sees child as	parent acts:
1. troubled learner;	1. reluctantly to support child;
2. uncollaborative with parent in school work.	2. without support from school or teacher.

Figure 3.2   Summary of content of parent interviews

Our results are shown in summary form in Figure 3.2. (A detailed listing is shown in the Chapter Notes as Figure 3.3).

PARENTS AS MEDIATORS AND CATALYSTS

We first report the findings of the qualitative analysis. In general we found that:

1. parent activities were much more often of the mediator than the catalyst type;
2. the positive codes were easier to categorize than the negative ones, which seemed very personalized; good student/parent/school relationships may be more patterned than bad ones; 'All happy families resemble each other, each unhappy family is unhappy in its own way' (Tolstoy);
3. some positive codes were nearly universal, appearing in all or nearly all of the sixteen cases; this makes non-appearance seem very significant;
4. the negative codes seemed significant when examined in conjunction with missing positive ones;
5. some codes seemed overwhelmingly convincing on their own; 'child not known to teacher', said in an interview in May, is an obvious danger signal, as are 'child in conflict with teachers' and 'child less committed to school' as descriptions of the child;
6. some codes are more subtle negative signals: 'child did homework in school' seems innocuous unless it is noted that codes labelled 'child finds school hard'; 'child cannot do homework'; 'child in conflict with teachers' and 'child not concerned about grades' occur in the same interview.

To provide a flavour of the cases, six portraits will be presented; three each from most positive and most negative cases. The portraits are organized with respect to the three elements of home practices and attitudes used in Figure 3.1 (expectations; mediator; catalyst or intervenor). Since some of the portraits are negative, they will necessarily describe **the absence of aspiration-building, mediations, and interventions.**

The interviews suggest that these three elements constitute a progression. Almost all parents describe basic positive expectations, fewer describe mediation activities, and fewer yet describe proactive intervention. However, all members of the last group are members of the other two groups. That is, any parent who intervenes has established expectations, and tried to mediate between child and school. In our sample, **intervention is the last resort of concerned parents**, not (as some believe) interference in school matters by pushy busybodies. (Briefer vignettes from the remaining cases appear in the Chapter Notes.)

Within the parent portraits, we have chosen to add material from interviews with that parent's child to shed more light on the student/teacher/parent relationships at the heart of our model.

SIX PORTRAITS

Case 1: The persistent parent

It's up to you, not to demand, but to, you know, make sure that you're persistent.

The first portrait illustrates all three parent activities. It is particularly illustrative of the intervention theme. (*Note:* FP stands for Female Parent; I for interviewer; MS for male student.)

Expectations
Basic expectations are expressed in beliefs about the child's capabilities:

> They are avid readers, they are all, well R. was reading before he went to kindergarten, and I have always encouraged reading.

Her son, R., is a good student; she accepts his particular work habits:

> FP: but when it comes to planning ahead, no he's not good at that. He's one of these people who like to just do it. He doesn't take a week or two, . . . He says for him it's better that way, so if it works. . . .

However, basic expectations are affirmed:

> I: So does he talk about plans for the future, what he's going to do after high school?
> FP: Yep. He does actually. He is going to be a brain surgeon.
> I: A brain surgeon. Do you sense he has any idea what that involves?
> FP: He does, ya
> I: So one of the things you do is talk about how important it is?
> FP: How important it is, ya, for them, not for, for nobody else but them, I tell them it's all up to them and all I can do is encourage them. They have to do their work.
> I: So he has a sense from you that it is very important to go on in school?
> FP: I hope he does, anyway, because I'd like him to.

Mediation
The parent has been actively engaged in the school, and uses this built-up stock of knowledge and contacts to mediate in her children's interests.

> I: You still would feel welcome to come [to the school]?
> FP: Oh, absolutely. I spent a lot of time here until I went back to work. . . . We had a little bit of a problem earlier on in the year when he wasn't doing, actually he wasn't doing all of his work and I spoke with his teacher and it did get better. . . . I kept in contact with her for a while to make sure that he was finishing his work.

Intervention
Rather than simply mediating between son and teacher, she intervenes to ensure good relations:

> FP: I spent a lot of time in school, especially when he first came here, I was always very involved in all their classes and I got to know all their teachers and the one thing I did do was ask that my kids be put in certain classes and Mr B. [principal] always did that.
> I: So you based those choices on . . .?
> FP: Well from what I see, see I like teachers that are stricter, I don't like this open concept, some teachers still adopt it and some don't and for my children, especially

for R., he needs someone who will keep on top of him because even though he's very bright, he's still just a kid, he likes to, if you don't keep on top of him he's going to goof off, you know, and in that respect I have been very lucky to have good teachers.
FP: Oh ya, I mean I wouldn't just say I want my child in this class, I have gone to Mr B., I have especially gone to the teacher they've had and said 'I would like them to go into this class, what do you think'? It has always been respected and usually the choices I've made have been good, so. . . .

When there was a problem she was quick and decisive in intervening:

FP: No, I've been right to the school . . . and I wouldn't let it go because it was important, and it was dealt with and looked after so I was quite pleased. . . . It is up to the parent though, you have to, you're just going to go and ask for something, and they say, 'well you know'. It's up to you, not to demand, but to, you know, make sure that you're persistent.

The student

Perhaps as a consequence of this parental activity, the child's view of the classroom is rosy:

I: So if I could make you the teacher for a week say, is there anything that you would change to make things run a bit differently?
MS: Hm, no.
I: No? So nothing you would change? Everything's just as you would like it?
MS: Ya, pretty much.

His plans for the future are ambitious and quite consistent with the parent's comments:

MS: I think I'm going to be a doctor, paediatrician.
I: What do you think you would need to do to be a paediatrician?
MS: Well, finish high school and go to university, . . . get a degree in it.
I: What about school, do you ever talk about careers or jobs at school?
MS: Uh huh. In the beginning of the year we had a big career day.
I: What do you think schools should be doing to help kids prepare for life after school?
MS: Help kids find out what they want to do, I guess.

Similarly his comments on parent activities are consistent with the parents:

I: Do they [parents] help you with your school work?
MS: Ya, if I'm having any trouble with my homework, they'll help me.
I: Do they ever talk just about education in general?
MS: Hm, I guess sometimes, they think it's important. They think it's good to get an education so ya.

On teacher–home communication he is also explicit:

I: Do you have a planner that you use?
MS: Ya.
I: And how does that get used?
MS: Well, every day like I write the homework down there and all the stuff I've got to do and then when I've got to get it done by and just when I've got to do it.
I: So it's something you do; does it have to be signed by anybody?
MS: My parents.

This case offers a positive view of triad relationships.

Case 3: The anonymous parent

It doesn't surprise me that he [the teacher] doesn't recognize me, but I would wish that he had.

The second case illustrates very different parent attitude and activity patterns. Two codes are used for this case that appear in no other: 'child not known to teacher' and 'parent does not know teacher'.

> FP: I have to say that R. is a fairly easy student so we don't really have a need [to talk to the teacher].
> I: would you say that R. takes responsibility for his own learning?
> FP: I think he does. I think he recognizes responsibility to study himself and learn things and he enjoys learning. He loves new information, likes to be involved in conversations and discussions at school and he's got something to share.

Expectations
Much of what is said seems quite positive:

> FP: I have never heard from the teacher. He gets fairly average grades. I have never heard that he's had a problem with his homework. So, he's the kind of kid that goes along so you never hear anything.
> FP: R. seems comfortable in his classroom. I mean like most kids, he will say something about the teacher doing something that he didn't like and then other times he'll talk about his teacher and something he said that day, so it's on a very positive note.

However, there is little commitment to high aspirations here:

> I: Does R. ever talk about the future, plans for the future, high school or anything?
> FP: No, he doesn't. That was on one of the questionnaires, I remembered that question. Because I didn't know if he should be or not. But he doesn't.

Mediation
The parent sees no need to act as link between child and school. She seems content not to know about R.'s progress, and not very much concerned about lack of information from the school. (This interview was conducted in May.)

> FP: No, R. has not gone back to being the student he was before last year, he has not. He lost some of the feeling he had at school and he hasn't gotten that back. Um, I'm not putting the emphasis on the education part, **the emphasis is on not looking for so much from school.** He really got a lot out of it before and he really liked it and he had some teachers that he really, really enjoyed.
> FP: So like when we talk about homework, they haven't been things he has mentioned so they haven't been things we have been part of. But he will mention it down the road a bit and I'll say 'when did you do that'?
> I: Do you have a sense that your child's teacher respects him?
> FP: I have no idea.
> I: You really haven't got a sense of the teacher?
> FP: No I don't. I've only spoken with R.'s teacher personally once this year and when I've gone back to the school he doesn't recognize me. It doesn't surprise me that he doesn't recognize me, but I would wish that he had.
> FP: We never get anything home from the teacher. There is never any notes sent home from the teacher or even a personal classroom handout. . . .

This is the most striking case we have of withdrawal by the parent; note the emphasis on reducing educational aspiration levels.

Intervention

The parent's intervention efforts at school are, like mediation efforts, minimal:

> FP: I tried a couple of times. I went to the school and we were there 20 minutes early and the teacher didn't show up until just before class started and R. had told him the day before that I would be there.
> I: So how were you received then do you feel?
> FP: He was very friendly but no time. And I mean not because he was not willing to listen but seriously because he didn't have the time because the class was ready to begin. I didn't feel he was prepared for me like I thought maybe he would be.

The student

The student's portrayal of the classroom environment is not particularly positive:

> MS: My friends say it is kind of dumb in the class . . . all Mr. B. talks about is funny stuff.
> I: Oh, so you'd like him to be a little more serious sometimes?
> MS: Oh, ya, sometimes.
> MS: Like in math and stuff, sometimes he makes fun of people, he makes them feel bad . . . if they do something that's really funny to other people he kind of makes a joke about it.
> I: But sometimes that upsets you and your friends?
> MS: Ya, because he's done it to one of my friends once.

He does get help with homework at home:

> MS: [re help with homework] Well, it's, it's fine. Um, there's no hassles or anything. Sometimes if my dad can't help me, like if he doesn't get it, my mom will.

His future plans are open, and in any event may not involve much more schooling:

> MS: My mom and dad keep saying that I'm a good cook so they keep on asking 'do you want to be a cook', so I just tell them I'll think about it.

The attitudes and actions of the parents here do not much resemble those in the previous case.

Case 8: Parent as home teacher

> [Learning] – a lot of times it's a family affair.

This case illustrates the mediator role, with the parent paying close attention to the child's schooling and acting as needed to support learning. Interventions focus on the child at home.

Expectations

The child is capable and hard-working, to the point of over-anxiety:

> FP: right now she always wants to do her best. She always wants to get the best mark and you know do well on tests and things. You know, I think she just has to learn to relax a little bit.

Mediation

In discussing the supportive role, the parent makes reference to her own childhood, and hopes for more from the schools for her own children.

> FP: My parents were good, but our homework was our homework and they didn't help a lot and I kind of missed that and I want my kids to do well in school.
>
> FP: There have been times when she has been frustrated with some stuff . . . sometimes we just have to take a big breath and sort of get through it and there have been times when there have been tears because she figures she won't learn it and. On the whole I think she has enjoyed it . . . but like I said that's about my only you know, concern as far as you know, approaching the teacher, and like I said I didn't approach her about that because we've managed to keep a handle on it so. . . .
>
> FP: She doesn't need a lot of help with certain areas. If she is unclear about something, she knows, like I mean she comes right away to ask either her dad or I about you know, to clarify something . . . I mean sometimes I think she asks a little bit too soon, and sometimes I'll say well read it over again and try and work out on your own . . . I want them, that they understand what they're learning and if they need help, you know I want us to be there to help.

Intervention

Despite the reluctance to intervene at school, the family has intervened in a teaching role. They have even developed specific techniques of teaching, which work for them:

> FP: With homework, trying to make it fun, trying to, you know, if there are areas that she doesn't understand, like putting it into relation to everyday, you know. They're having problems I think initially when they were learning about money, like 25 cents, and 5 cents and 10 cents, like if you add that together what it is. Well, we played store, you know, for an hour in the afternoon. I gave her real money and all of a sudden things started to click. . . .
>
> I: So do you generally then enjoy the experience?
>
> FP: Yes. I often joke, and say my husband and I will get an A on this project, you know, because, a lot of times it's a family affair.

She has various small ways of intervening at school and has been satisfied with the outcomes, which have had the effect of modifying the teacher's practices. That is, the parent has acted as catalyst:

> FP: [re the teacher] I know if there's a problem she'll give me a call or they have their daily planners and K. will show that to me if there's something and I will communicate back to the teacher with that . . . and that's sort of what was communicated right at the beginning of the school year, that if there were little things, like just to write in the planner, so I know to do that and K. is . . . is actually quite meticulous about showing me, you know, what's in that planner, so . . . I've written the note in the planner saying that there was an awful lot that she didn't manage to get done and like Mrs M. would say well that's fine or whatever.
>
> FP: Sometimes I will just go in and kind of explain, you know that K. does worry sometimes about certain things when I don't think she should have to . . . Mrs M. has told me well, you know, she will sort of broaden things for her, you know, like it doesn't have to be exactly this way. . . .

In general the parent is very happy with the school year that her daughter has had:

FP: I think this whole school year has been really good. I think she's learned and she's grown an awful lot this past year. Like I said, I love the school, I think it's a wonderful school.

Her grounds for this claim are revealing about what parents value in teachers:

FP: Generally with this school, like I mean it seems all the teachers know all the kids, even if they haven't had them. . . . they all, they have an interest in the kids. They look out for the kids and . . . that I think is a big thing, an interest in your kids.

The student

The student gives the common classroom description for British Columbia: too much noise, too many distracting students, too much teacher time spent in dealing with them.

FS: [comparing this year's teacher with a previous one] she doesn't like to put up with people that aren't on task . . . when she says 'may I have your attention please', you have to give her your attention in I think three seconds.
I: Do you ever feel that things could be done differently or better in your classroom?
FS: Sometimes, like if we could just work on the noise level or something.
I: If you could change one thing in your classroom, what would it be?
FS: Probably that people don't like distract others so that they can get their work done . . . sometimes it's hard because some of the trouble-makers in the class make like a lot of noise and one of them is in my group so it's kind of hard for me to work

The general portrait here is of considerable parent influence in mediator mode but slipping into catalyst mode quite easily – especially teaching the child material she had not grasped at school.

Case 10: Parent as ineffective advocate

I know he is unfair.

This case illustrates another set of parent attitude and activity patterns.

Expectations

The child is not comfortable at school, for good reason:

FP: Yes. Um, it's a new teacher, new to the school and the first parent/teacher interview which was I guess the first report card, I went . . . and T. just got really sort of average kind of marks . . . so when we were in the interview, because T. came with me, one of the first things Mr F. said to me was 'there's no hope for T. academically, he'll never make it to university, so I think you better start thinking about vocational or a trade for him because he doesn't have any academic skills'.
I: And T. is sitting right there?
FP: T. was sitting right there and T. piped up with tears in his eyes, and said 'Mr F. the first of the year I'm always kinda lazy'. He said 'I'm a really good student and I really try hard and I'll prove it to you how good my marks can be'.

Note that the details of this story do not need to be accurate for the impact on the child's commitment to school to be profound. Yet the child has ambitious plans, as the parent tells us:

I: Does he talk about his future plans at all?

FP: Oh, all the time. He's got a million things he wants to be and I think there's only two things that don't need a university degree, and we just look at him and say go for it, whatever you want to do, you gotta go for it . . . because my husband and I, neither one of us went to university and of course there's regrets because when you start raising a family, you can't afford to go to school, you know, it's like 'Oh no what am I going to do?' So, it's like go for it and I don't care what anybody thinks about his limitations, I don't think he has any limitations.

Mediation

The parent tries hard to mediate, but without success:

FP: We discuss everything and he hurts because he did a project with his friend who is a high achiever, an excessive high achiever, like he is a wonderful boy, he is one of T.'s best friends and they did a science project together. They got an A and T. got a C, so . . . he came home and said, 'Mom he is so unfair' and I said 'I know he is unfair' and I really believe he is doing those marks because we question him on his ability of giving T. the right credit and I really believe T.'s not getting the marks because we went and complained to the teacher and we complained to the principal.

The difficulties she faces in attempting to restore commitment are obvious:

FP: T. hasn't participated in any school activities. He feels no loyalty to go with the class or . . . . and T.'s attitude is – 'Mom, I don't even care' . . . but I really think it's his attitude towards Mr F. No matter how well he does, he is never going to get a good mark, so why bother?

I: How does T. feel about school this year?

FP: He can't wait until it's over. Like it amazes me that T. will still faithfully sit down and do his homework and do his projects.

FP: Yeh. He wants to achieve. He wants to do the best he can, you know . . . I have never known or met a child that has just set himself out to what he has to do, what his responsibilities are for homework and he just sits down and does it . . . T. is on his own from 2.30 until 7 o'clock at night because I work and R. usually does evening shifts so I just think he is an exceptionally wonderful responsible child . . . you know, he'll sit down and say 'I have already done my homework, mom, you don't have to worry I have already done it' so I think that's pretty responsible, you know.

Intervention

The parents attempted to intervene by going to see the principal, but without much success:

FP: So she just said, well we were blowing it out of proportion and that Mr. F. is a wonderful teacher and I am sure he has good reason why he said that.

To a large extent this case represents the failure of parent influence to mediate or intervene.

The student

The child's perspective here is sometimes consistent with the parent's, and sometimes not. On the teacher it is entirely consistent:

MS: When he explains something, he will like go on for a very long time, going on and on and on and you only get a short time to work on it.

MS: [On favourite teacher] Actually, it was Mrs O. She was more of a friend than a teacher. You could like joke around with her and say how you feel and stuff.

MS: [On present teacher] He doesn't mark me fair sometimes . . . like I will hand in a piece of work and my friend will hand in a piece of work and mine is like in my opinion and someone else's opinion, mine is way better and he gets a higher grade than me.

The child's comments on working on his own at home are inconsistent with parent claims:

I: How long does homework take, say on an average night?
MS: Average night? 15 minutes. It's not very long. You don't usually get much . . . If you don't finish math, then you have to do that at home.

The student does not get help from parents very often, and prefers not to:

I: Do you need it very often?
MS: No, not really
MS: I don't really like to.
I: How come?
MS: I don't know. I don't like having someone look over my shoulder while I'm working. . . .
MS: Sometimes when I need help, she goes 'I don't know what you do on this.'

Although the student's grades are mediocre, the parents are apparently satisfied:

I: And your parents are happy with your grades, report cards?
MS: Yes.

On future plans, the student is clear, but limited:

MS: Be a pyrotechnician . . . where you build fireworks. . . .

This case suggests distance between parent and student and little effective influence by parents.

Case 5: Parent as skilful and experienced mediator/intervenor

That is always what our biggest goal is; to make sure that it [school] is a good experience.

Expectations
The student is very capable:

FP: He's a straight 'A' student, he gets very upset when he has a B+.

FP: [On responsibility] Well, he does bring his day planner home, I guess that is step number 1. Some children don't. I mean, he brings his books home that he needs to bring home and I think those are the things that show that he obviously realizes that he has to do something.

I: Does B. talk about the future?
FP: Constantly. Big plans. . . . He talks about either being a teacher or a lawyer.

FP: I think we've brought our kids up just in a way that they realize that our expectations of the school system are as elementary school, high school and post-secondary education. And, best of all, they don't question that. It is just something that is in their plans, it is automatically in their plans.

Mediation/intervention

In this case mediation and intervention are entwined:

> FP: The teacher is very approachable so I'm in there on and off just to discuss his progress or possible problems or whatever I can to facilitate and support him. . . . she has implemented a lot of changes and is always willing to implement changes so we don't have to go to her constantly any more to advocate for him. . . . She is there for him, obviously, she really respects him or she wouldn't be willing to give him the effort that she is putting out to make things smooth for him.
>
> I: Have there been times this year where you felt that you had to stand up for B.'s interests at the school or in the classroom?
>
> FP: You probably need an additional piece of information here. B. has Attention Deficit Disorder. So I'm in there constantly advocating, you know, those changes that are helpful for him in particular.
>
> I: Describe the ways in which you help B. learn?
>
> FP: Um, well by helping him be organized, I think that is the biggest need that B. has, is to remain on task. It takes an awful lot of cueing to remain on task.
>
> FP: [On the ideal relationship between parent and teacher] Awesome communication flow back and forth. I guess that's number 1. And a teacher that is very open to an involved parent and willing to change the style or type of teaching that she does in order to get the needs out to the child. At the end of every day, his teacher will . . . rate him on his overall behaviour. On the amount of smiling faces that he gets indicates how well or not well the day has gone.
>
> FP: Oh, he enjoys school. I think that is always what our biggest goal is, to make sure that it is a good experience. . . . So far, he has enjoyed going to school. He never wakes up and doesn't want to go to school. That is never an issue. So, I'm enthused.

The student

In general the responses are predictable, following the parent commentary.

> I: [On the classroom] Is it a place where it is usually pretty easy to learn and to work?
>
> MS: Yes. We can ask the teacher a lot of stuff and she will answer it . . . I like it when it's quiet, not when it's [noisy], and it's quiet in class.
>
> I: Do you think you would anything differently to make a perfect place for learning?
>
> MS: No. Our teacher does a good job.
>
> I: Do your parents help you with your school work when you get homework?
>
> MS: Yes. If I ask them they will help me. They will say maybe, can you skip that part and then I will come back later if they are busy and they will help you later.
>
> I: What might they say about education?
>
> MS: Keep in school. To get a good job, if you like want to be in sports, . . . like they go get a job first, like at least a degree in something, you know a Masters, like just do something in university.
>
> I: Some kids tell us that they really like working with their parents. How do you feel?
>
> MS: In between. Sometimes I don't and sometimes I do.
>
> MS: [On the planner] Sometimes when someone does a mistake or doesn't do their homework, sometimes she makes the class for one week you have to get initials by your parents done, at the bottom of your page.

This case illustrates a skilled parent working with a student who is receptive to parental values.

Case 16: Parent as reluctant mediator

A lot of time he is downstairs doing his homework and I don't know what he is doing down there.

The parent in this case is satisfied with the child's relationship with the school, but the satisfaction seems to emerge from low expectations, justified by references to stereotypes of teenage behaviour, either causing (or resulting from) reluctance to get involved as mediator or intervenor.

Expectations

The parent thinks the child is bright but does not have high academic expectations for him:

> I: Would you like opportunities to link in with his teacher to help your child in the academic area?
> FP: He can't really do more. He is not straight A but I don't expect him to be.
> FP: He's pretty bright so academically, he's pretty alright except socially, he's too social. She is working on that and I tell him not to talk and be interruptive.
> I: How does your son feel about school this year?
> FP: It's too hard. That's only because grade 6 is a little more serious than grade 5. There's more work and there's more responsibility, you know. . . . He gets a bit under stress with projects and things, you know, because he is one of these type of kids that time management isn't one of his . . . go out and play and leave it to the last moment kind of thing. Typical child. Then pressure, I've got a 15-page project to do in 24 hours and I will be up all night.
> I: Does your son talk about plans for the future, high school after that?
> FP: No. 12-year-olds live for today, not tomorrow.

Mediation

The parent has had occasion to mediate but has let these opportunities go by:

> FP: No, they complain. She is too hard on us. She makes us work too hard. She expects too much.
> I: But he worked out his relationship with his teacher that he really didn't want in the first place?
> FP: Yes. I think they have a pretty good relationship. I think it's mostly his attitude I think she was having problems with, you know which gets pretty . . . you know that age group.
> I: Whenever you have called, you have had a sense they would listen and so on?
> FP: Yes, anytime, I haven't spoke to the teacher at all in the last month so.
>
> I: Have you chatted to his teacher about ways that you might help him to learn time management?
> FP: No, I haven't actually. I don't know what she does in the classroom. I ask him, I say 'why are you leaving it to the last minute' . . . 'Oh I had ball, I had hockey, I had this, I had that'. 'Well, I said, what about Tuesday when you went out and played at whatever?' 'Well I forgot about it.' I don't know if she is going 'don't forget those projects' or . . . yeh I suppose that's part of the learning process, they have to learn to manage their time.

The possibility that the parent might also be part of the learning process here is not considered. Similarly the parent feels the need for more information, but does not act. There are some opportunities open to her, but these are unused:

I: Are there ways that you are involved in the school? Do you visit and call?
FP: Not really. Not unless I am asked to call.
I: So the school does give you those type of opportunities?
FP: Yes. Not a lot. I think I have been invited to the classroom once or twice this year. Not really a whole lot. . . . You go for the parent–teacher interviews and the teacher basically looks her watch and talks about the child and then you are out the door. But they are busy people.
FP: A little more communication with the teacher would be nice, even positive. The only time you ever hear from the school is when he's done something wrong. She has never phoned up and said, 'gee, he gave a really good verbal speech today'. The way I look at it is that they are busy people.
I: Do you feel you have had that opportunity this school year to meet your child's teacher, to chat, not just formally but informally as well?
FP: No, no. And that's probably because I am not around either, you know.

She does on occasion try to help the child with school work, but he needs to make an appointment, and in some areas she feels unprepared to help:

FP: If he has a problem with his work we sit down, if he books a time, we sit down and do it together. If he's doing a project and needs my help, he asks me and we do it together.
FP: It's not like I can help him with his math.

Initiatives from the school to help her help the child would not be welcomed. She seems content to let him cope with schoolwork, and school life, on his own:

I: Do you feel that oh, I could have helped with such and such but you know the teacher didn't seem to make any moves to invite me to help?
FP: I don't think so. I basically have the two little ones so I don't have the opportunity to go and spend an hour at the school a day.
I: Would you like to see him do anything different as far as taking responsibility for his work?
FP: Just work a little harder on his projects that's about it. He studies by himself for his spelling tests. He is fairly responsible as far as doing his homework, I mean I don't . . . a lot of time he is downstairs doing his homework and I don't know what he is doing down there.

Intervention
The parent acknowledges that opportunities to intervene to improve the situation of the child have been passed by. The student is left to sort his feelings and concerns out for himself:

FP: There probably have been times when things have happened at school that I probably should have paid a little more attention to.
I: What stops you from doing anything about it?
FP: Those particular days, I think the baby had a fever of 104 and . . . just coming home in a rotten bad mood and you know something happened in the classroom and you can't get to it until later and so by the time you get to sit down and talk about it, he's all calmed down and it's all straightened out.

Even what many parents would regard as quite serious school occurrences (in B.C. using any form of violence with children is illegal, and grounds for teacher dismissal) are overlooked:

FP: When his teacher hit him. So that was a concern but the situation was handled very professionally. I was pleased with the way it was dealt with.
I: Did you make the initiative to solve that situation or did they contact you? Or was it sort of mutual?
FP: He came home from school and let me know what happened and of course, I asked him if he thought it was serious enough that I should be phoning or . . . and I phoned and they didn't return my call. The principal didn't return my call until he talked to the teacher and then he told me she was just coming down the hall and could tell me what happened. So it was dealt with.

'It was dealt with' without direct parent involvement, which largely summarizes the child's experience.

The student

In this case the student report is almost entirely at variance with the parent report. The student reports significant educational expectations, although no particular career goal. His plans for continuing education were influenced by the parents:

MS: They keep telling me that I should stay in school because it doesn't pay if you don't.
I: [question regarding parent education level] completed grade twelve?
MS: My mom does, but my dad doesn't.
I: So does he say something about that?
S: He says he regrets it. He really wished that he would have finished it, but . . . he's he just didn't want to, so now he regrets it totally . . . because it's hard for him to get a job without his thingy.
MS: I want to finish grade twelve. That's a definite yes, and yes I want to go to university or college. I want to get the . . . I want to do the best I can and keep going.
I: Do you have a particular career goal?
MS: Not really.
I: What comes to your head right now, what do you want to be?
S: Hopefully a sports person . . . doing a sport or something.
I: Is that realistic for you to be a sports professional?
S: Maybe.

He is very positive about his classroom, his teacher, and his school year:

MS: I find it [classroom] really easy to work in because we're usually under control and everything, and everyone's doing their own thing, doing what they're supposed to do. It's really easy.
MS: As long as you don't act up or anything, she's not strict. She's a very nice teacher and I enjoy her being my teacher.
[Asked if anything could be done differently or better?]
MS: No. It's really quite fine the way it is. It's fine. I like it . . . . This is probably one of my better years.

He also reports parent help with school assignments, and his acceptance of responsibility for doing his work (aided at times by the student planner):

MS: Yeah if I'm having a problem or something they'll, I'll just ask them for help. My mom or my dad will say sure whatever, and they'll come and try and help me. They help me out, like they won't tell me, like if it's a math question or whatever, or a spelling answer or something they won't just come out and tell me they'll like help me so I can get it myself.

MS: I never forgot any of my homework. I'd write it down and I'd put it with my homework and I'd be looking for my student planner every night and if I forgot about my homework I'd remember about it. . . . Well now I've just gotten into the habit of doing my homework, like really I don't need the student planner any more. . . . the only time I don't do homework is . . . if I'm busy doing something else.

I: And then how do you, what do you use for an excuse?

MS: I just tell her that, well I just tell her that I was helping someone, or whatever I was doing, and usually she'll say, like excuse me or whatever.

I: How come? How come she doesn't get mad at you?

MS: Because whenever I don't do my homework it's for some important reason.

I: [on the student planner] So, you say they worked great?

MS: They worked awesome.

The disparity between this student's report on his year and that of the parents is quite striking. The ranking of this case in the following section is very much complicated by this disparity.

PREDICTABLES AND ANOMALIES

Ranking the cases

We will now rank-order the 16 cases with respect to our interpretation of parent attitudes and activities. On occasion we took into account the child's perceptions, but in general we were guided by the parent data, as summarized in the portraits (and the 10 vignettes in the Chapter Notes).

Our main questions were:

How do families shape the commitment of children to school?

Do the educational expectations parents hold, and the mediating and intervening activities in which they sometimes engage, play a part in the process of shaping commitment?

Our rankings are shown in Table 3.1 (for convenience this table also shows the comparison with the rankings derived from the survey scores, and the rank order correlation, **which was of course unknown while preparing the ranking shown in Column 1**). A brief account of our reasoning as we prepared the rankings follows.

Case 1 impressed us because of the strength of the parent's conviction that she ought to intervene, to the point of choosing teachers. Similarly, Case 5 is notable for the strength of expectations, and the emphasis on appropriate programming for a child suffering a learning disorder. Case 9 is also a strongly interventionist parent, who chose the school.

The next group (Cases 14, 8, 6, 11, 4, 2, and 12) consists of parents who are active and willing to intervene but have no occasion to do so because of their high regard for teacher and/or school. Distinguishing the ordering here is difficult. For example, although the parent in Case 12 holds high expectations, she seems less connected with the teacher than other parents in this group.

Table 3.1 Comparing rankings of student commitment derived from different data sets

Case	Code No.	Rank from Interv.	Aggregate SC 2			ST rating scale			ST climate SC (H)		
			Rank	Code	Value 1–10; 1=POS	Rank	Code	Value 1–5; 1=POS	Rank	Code	Value 1–5; 1=POS
1	12206	1	6	12306	2.40	6	12306	1.00	7	12306	1.40
5	32202	2	8	32302	2.60	8	32302	1.50	4	32302	1.10
9	44204	3	4	44304	2.20	4	44304	1.00	5	44304	1.20
14	82201	4	5	82301	2.40	5	82301	1.00	6	82301	1.40
8	42201	5	11	42301	5.30	11	42301	2.50	14	42301	2.80
6	33208	6	2	33308	2.00	2	33308	1.00	2	33308	1.00
11	67209	7	7	67309	2.50	7	67309	1.00	8	67309	1.50
4	18202	8	16	18302	6.90	16	18302	4.00	15	18302	2.90
2	14212	9	14	14212	6.00	13	14312	3.00	16	14312	3.00
12	81205	10	10	81305	5.30	10	81305	2.50	13	81305	2.80
15	82204	11	12	82304	5.60	12	82304	3.00	12	82304	2.60
3	16204	12	13	16304	5.90	14	16304	3.50	10	16304	2.40
16	83201	13	1	83301	2.00	1	83301	1.00	1	83301	1.00
7	34209	14	3	34309	2.10	3	34309	1.00	3	34309	1.10
13	81208	15	9	81308	5.00	9	81308	2.50	11	81308	2.50
10	65216	16	15	65316	6.30	15	65316	4.00	9	65316	2.30

The next group consists of parents who are experiencing difficulties of various kinds, with child, teacher, or school. Starting from the bottom up, we identified Case 10 as the most distressing; the teacher reportedly acted in an extremely harmful way. Next to the bottom we placed Case 13; the parent takes an extremely negative view of the usefulness of schooling, which we believed must have an impact upon the child. Ranking next up was Case 7, in which the parent was surprised to be told that the child's grades were poor. In upwards order follow Case 16 in which expectations were very low, Case 3, in which parental expectations and initiative were very low, and Case 15.

For convenience in discussion, Table 3.1 is organized by the ranking derived from the qualitative analysis. The first trio of columns report the results of the coding, by case number. The second trio reports the Aggregate Scale developed by the quantitative analyst, and the third and fourth trios of columns report the data for the Student Rating and Scale H, the components of the aggregated scale. The correlation between the aggregated scale and the components was strong and significant (Spearman .95 and .86, p >.000). However, for the relationship between Aggregate Scale 2 and the ranking from the interview data the correlation is weak and insignificant.

For convenience, the table is split into high and low groups using the rankings from the qualitative data. A careful review of the values in the table for the Aggregate Scale shows the difficulty – excluding two cases (Cases 8 and 4, in bold) the rankings of the eight cases on the high end fall within a very narrow range, 2.0 to 2.6 on a ten-point scale. Within the group of 6 (those ranked high excluding the outliers) the rankings from the two sources are not as different as these minor differences in the numbers make them appear. The same holds true for the lower set of eight. The two outliers are Cases 7 and 16; with these removed the two sets of rankings are quite parallel, taking into account the very modest differences in the actual values. With four outliers removed our predictions are accurate for 12 of the 16 cases.

The last trio of columns report the data for another scale in the analysis, originally intended to be part of Aggregate Scale 1, later discarded. This scale is Teacher/Student Collaboration (Scale E). It is obviously quite parallel to the measures making up the Aggregate Scale, suggesting that in-classroom factors ,such as teacher treatment of students may be part of the explanation for the anomalies, which we will now consider on a case-by-case basis, examining the student interviews in more detail in the expectation that they will help to account for our mis-ranking of the cases.

Examining the anomalies

Cases 7 and 16 show sharp discrepancies in the two rankings. The Case 7 parent interview (vignette) shows low parental expectations, low student achievement, and little concern for improvement. We expected that pattern to translate into low student commitment and dissatisfaction with school, but the student interview shows that the student is very satisfied with school.

The student career expectations are modest: 'I'd like to do tractor work', like his father. This does not require much schooling, although he says 'I want to finish high school', reflecting parent wishes: 'they say you should definitely go to Grade 12 and graduate'.

His all-time favourite teacher is 'Mr B., my teacher this year'. He listens to students, paying attention to their opinions and ideas:

> He really understands them as well. If he doesn't understand he will ask you to explain what you really wanted. Basically people get going on that happening and they just tell him a little bit more.

The teacher is fair: when there are fights 'he is separating them' and 'he'll let each person tell their side'. He is also demanding but not unreasonable:

> like today we had math and there was a whole bunch of questions and most of the people didn't finish the assignment, like he is not saying they are not doing the job, but they were working their hardest and they were doing really good and they just didn't get it done, so they had to take it home as homework.

The scores from the surveys fall at the high end of the positive range. Most revealingly, the student's score on the Student/Teacher Collaboration scale is the highest we show (in Table 1; tied with Case 16).

The Case 16 parent interview (portrait) showed parent satisfaction emerging from low academic and behavioural expectations that were justified by references to stereotypes of teenage behaviour, and parental reluctance to get involved as mediator or intervenor.

The student has fairly significant academic expectations:

> I want to finish grade twelve. That's a definite yes, and yes I want to go to university or college. I want to do the best I can and keep going.

His parents, not particularly well-educated themselves, support these hopes: 'they keep telling me that I should stay in school because it doesn't pay if you don't'. They also provide more support than was apparent in the parent interview:

> If I'm having a problem or something they'll . . . I'll just ask them for help. My mom or my dad will say 'sure whatever', and they'll come and try and help me. They help me out, like they won't tell me . . . like if it's a math question or whatever, or a spelling answer or something, they won't just come out and tell me they'll like help me so I can get it myself.

His present teacher is 'a very nice teacher and I enjoy her being my teacher', but a previous teacher was his all-time favourite:

> She was a split teacher, she taught on Thursday and Friday . . . and her name was Mrs B., she was really nice. I like her a lot. Almost every day after school on Thursdays and Fridays I'd just talk to her and I'd just have a good time on those days. Yeah, she became a good friend to me and she . . . she was nice. She teaches in the school still. She knows me well and I know her well, and . . . we just say hi to each other and stuff now.

As noted previously, this student and the student in Case 7 above have the most positive scores on the Student/Teacher Collaboration scale, suggesting an explanation for the anomalous rankings here – teachers have had a very positive impact on the commitment of these two students to school even when parental support seems weak or limited by circumstances.

Turning now to the cases in which the survey rankings were far lower than those we derived from the parent interviews, we find that Case 4 was the lowest ranked case on Aggregate Scale 2, yet our ranking from the parent interview was at the midpoint. It could easily have been much higher – on being asked whether she felt comfortable calling the teacher at need the mother said, memorably, 'Well, for one thing, I would do it anyways.' Yet on every scale from surveys shown in Table 4, including Student/Teacher Collaboration, the student is ranked 16 or 15.

The problem does not seem to be associated with low expectations, or lack of parental support:

> My mom said it is my choice of what I get to do, she is not going to tell me what to do just like she's not going to tell me who my friends are going to be, right? She just thinks whatever I do is going to be good. I want to be a teacher.

> They always tell me after I get my report card that they think this is a really great school and that I am getting really good marks and that I'm learning everything well.

> Sometimes my mom quizzes me on stuff and it's really neat. Every day after school, my mom asks me what we did in school and what we got on our tests and everything.

However, the student interview reveals a somewhat different side to the 'great school'. Asked about the classroom, the student gives a rather detailed picture:

> FS: Most of the time it's noisy but I always get my work done.
> I: How do you manage to sort of not let the noise bother you?
> FS: Most of the time I just get really involved in my work and I can't hear anything, I just block it out of my head; sometimes if it is really bad I'll ask the teacher if I can go work in the hall. Other classes, uh huh. They are much more quieter than ours.
> I: I wonder why one classroom is noisy and one's not. What do you think makes the difference?
> FS: I don't know. Maybe the way the teacher is, maybe the way they handle it.
> I: Do you have a sense that she could, that Mrs C. could handle it differently?
> FS: Maybe, I guess.

Although this concern is not strongly emphasized, against a general background of student optimism and positive commentary about schools and teachers, it stands out as potentially important.

In Case 8, with respect to academic intentions the student responds: 'Um, I'm not sure. I haven't really thought about it.' Regarding career interests she says:

> FS: Well, I used to want to be like, um, conducting cause I'm always listening to music and stuff but I don't think I'm going to do that cause I might find an easier job, not an easier job but like a job that you don't have to have that many skills like music or anything.

With respect to the classroom, she says:

> FS: Well sometimes it's hard because some of the trouble-makers in the class make like a lot of noise and one of them is in my group so it's kind of hard for me to work,

but if they're somewhere else it's easy for me to work, or if they aren't making a lot of noise.

I: Do you ever feel that things could be done differently or better in your classroom?

FS: Um, sometimes, like if we could just work on the noise level or something.

This conversation describes what we have learned is a very common problem in B.C. schools and classrooms; students who want to learn are often distracted and disrupted by those who do not. Not surprisingly the scores on these cases are far down the Teacher/Student Collaboration scale; Case 4 ranks 15/16; Case 8 ranks 10/16.

Cases 7 and 16 we miss-ranked on the low side because we did not pay sufficient attention to the student's positive comments about the student/ teacher relationship; here in Cases 4 and 8 we miss-ranked on the high side, again because we did not pay sufficient attention to the student's comments about the student/teacher relationship and the classroom environment. In sum, our judgments based on parent expectations, mediation, and intervention accurately predicted student satisfaction and commitment in 12 of 16 cases. In the remainder, unusually positive or negative teacher and classroom circumstances influenced student feelings about school, making them unpredictable based on parental attitudes.

These results provide an interesting illustration of the importance of anomalies. As Sulloway (1996, p. 196) comments in a massive mixed methods study of birth-order effects on the careers of scientists:

> by focusing on the model's mistakes – particularly the individuals who most defy its predictions – we can begin to appreciate the limitations of a family dynamics model *and to highlight the kinds of influences it fails to include.* It is the model's errors, not its success stories, that provide useful insights for further understanding.

The results also illustrate the benefits of mixed methods of data collection and analysis. Not only can we test the reliability of the findings, but we can account for anomalies, turning what might have been simply disappointing results from statistical analyses into insights regarding the formation of student attitudes. Our general triad model, which emphasizes the importance of collaboration between all three parties in producing positive student attitudes, is strongly supported by these findings. Furthermore, the consequences of not allowing 'voice' to the students, a political decision by educators (Erickson and Shultz, 1992), are clearly negative for students and for teachers, who could presumably ensure more order in the classrooms if they were aware of the negative consequences of failing to do so.

ASSESSING THE SIGNIFICANCE OF THE HIDDEN LINK

Our questions, posed at the beginning of the chapter, were:

How do families shape the commitment of children to school?

Do the educational expectations parents hold, and the mediating and intervening activities in which they sometimes engage, play a part in the process of shaping commitment?

What the chapter tells us

Our attempt to describe the salient aspects of the cases and link them to the survey data is in large measure a demonstration of the power of the family to form students' school (and later) careers. Both mediating and intervening activities were common, and often seemed to shape students' views. The four anomalous cases illustrate that parents cannot school-proof their children, however.

What we believe we have demonstrated in the 12 cases in which our hypotheses were sustained is **specific and dynamic within-family forms of 'social capital'**, 'the norms, the social networks, and the relationships between adults and children that are of value for the child's growing up' (J. S. Coleman, 1987a, p. 36). In contemporary societies 'many families at all social levels fail to provide an environment that allows their children to benefit from schools as they currently exist' (*ibid.*). That educative environment is vital to the welfare of the student – in most instances schools cannot make up for its absence.

Our initial model, developed in the previous chapter, suggests that **parent efficacy is a consequence of invitations by school and teacher to participate**. That may be the case for some, but most of the parents described in this chapter obviously derive efficacy from other sources. Hoover-Dempsey and Sandler suggest that parental role-definition, plus experience of success, may generate efficacy, which can then be sustained by school invitations to get involved (1997, p. 28).

The implications for school improvement

Given that parent involvement is essential to children's learning, does not exist in many families (Lareau, 1989; Hoover-Dempsey and Sandler, 1997), but can sometimes be developed and sustained by school actions, we suggest that the most important task facing the school in the immediate future is collaboration with parents in building active communities of learners, of the kind advocated by Chrispeels (1992), Martin (1992), Swap (1992) and many others. These learning communities would effectively revive the positive features of families and communities which James Coleman and colleagues have described (Coleman and Hoffer, 1987).

Walberg and Wallace (1992) have described several action programs for involving parents in their children's learning that have been successful but have also been of small scale and short duration. Until such collaborative learning communities are seen as the norm for all schools, and until they become part of the (almost) universal experience of students, the social problems associated with alienated and under-educated students, with drop-outs, and with unemployed and unemployable youth are unlikely to be solved. Creating such schools constitutes an immense challenge for district and school leadership.

The essential lesson of this chapter, then, is that for parents and students, mediating and intervening activities are a vital part in forging that connection with school and schooling that will predict, not only the educational future of the child, but also much of the working career and the 'citizenship' as well. When school and home are connected, schools **usually sustain and sometimes reinforce** positive attitudes brought by students from the home. Schools rarely create such attitudes, although **some teachers do compensate for home attitudinal disadvantage by forging strong connections with students.**

4

The Good Teacher: Parent Experiences and Preferences

The other woman in the child's life.

(Lightfoot)

Here we examine the important relationship between parents and teachers. Our model predicts (and our introductory analysis in Chapter 1 suggests) that collaboration will hold a prominent place in this definition. Once again, though, we seek to 'let the data speak'; we enter the analysis without specific hypotheses or categories of information. Rather, we pose one simple question:

What do parents regard as the most important qualities of a good teacher, and how do they arrive at the beliefs they hold about teacher quality?

We expect to find some references to collaborative relationships between parents and teachers that contribute to positive parental perception of teachers (and hence of the school).

ASSESSING TEACHER QUALITY

Studies of schools in the USA have found classroom level differences in teaching practices between effective and ineffective schools. Teddlie and colleagues, in the long-running Louisiana School Effectiveness Study, find that the kinds of teacher practices associated with high levels of student achievement occur both more frequently and more reliably in effective schools at both the elementary and junior high school levels (Teddlie, Kirby, and Stringfield, 1989; Virgilio, Teddlie, and Oescher, 1991).

However, much teacher work is carried on with other participants in the educational process. Thus another important source of information on teachers is parental (and student) judgments. These judgments have been shown to be both reliable and valid sources of information; not surprisingly, parents are most concerned about certain aspects of teacher work that are directly relevant to them (Epstein, 1985). Parents consider the good teacher to be one who collaborates with parents; this has a positive effect on the parent perception of the teacher, of school climate and of school quality.

But teacher collaboration affects more than parental judgments. Virtually every major study of school effectiveness has found parent involvement in instruction to be critical to school quality. Such involvement is dependent on teacher willingness to collaborate. Thus we argue that **teacher collaboration with parents is fundamental to both teacher quality and school quality.** No assessment of schools or of teachers can afford to overlook this vital teacher variable.

A portrait of school district practices with respect to parent involvement suggests that they are rather standardized throughout the province of British Columbia (Coleman and LaRocque, 1990). In British Columbia most of the variance with respect to parent involvement occurs between classrooms. Yet our conclusion in the pilot analysis summarized in Chapter 1 was that within quite diverse groups of parents and students, the basic attitudes towards school are very consistent, and the experience of schooling during the year confirms rather than modifies them. Thus, although teacher collaboration at classroom level is likely to be very important in shaping parent perceptions of school quality in B.C., and probably elsewhere, we should not expect wide variations in such teacher behaviour.

PARENTS AND TEACHER COLLABORATION

The statistical analysis reported in Chapter 1 suggested that:

1. parent perceptions of teacher concern about parent involvement are critical to all parent attitudes to teachers and schools, and vary significantly between classrooms;
2. parent efficacy, communications with school, perception of school climate, and rating of school are all partially dependent upon this initial perception.

The parents for interview for the analysis which forms the basis for this chapter were randomly selected from the participants in the data collection for Year 1 – the data set already used in Chapter 1. We first look at general parent attitudes revealed in the data, and second at some of the most and least positive classrooms, in order to clarify by contrast the practices of the 'best' and the 'worst' teachers within the experience of this group of parents.

Although the interview questions mixed school, classroom, teacher, and student as topics, the parent responses emphasize the child's present teacher. But the parents had great difficulty in focusing upon a specific teacher. Many of the parents had several children in school, and their comments kept slipping from child to child and hence from teacher to teacher. Also, the parents were reflecting upon the totality of their experience with teachers. The portrait here often describes a generic teacher, not specifically those individuals involved in our project.

The general findings of the analysis of interviews are presented in three categories: collaboration and parent efficacy; parent–teacher interaction; and teacher–student interaction. We focus in this section on capturing that which respondents considered important.

Collaboration and parent efficacy

All the parents in our sample believe that they can help their children to be successful students. All parents believe that they can help more with a little assistance from the teacher. Though there are obstacles that sometimes prevent them from helping their children at home or helping at the school, such as time and work, parents are willing and do feel able. One parent here speaks for all:

> I told him (the teacher) if there's any time you want us to say something to him, if we can help you, just give me a call. There's no problem. . . .'

The following points are commonly made by parents:

1. Parents want teachers to provide them with curricular information, preferably in written form. Curricular outlines, project outlines, and expectations for classroom work and behaviour would all help parents in understanding their child's experience in the classroom and enable them to help more effectively at home:

> Actually, some of the years through his schooling, the teacher used to send home a bit of a newsletter every month saying, 'We learned such and such in math and reading.' And it was great. Then I knew where he was.

2. Parents would also like teachers to let them know about the academic weaknesses of their child so that they can work on these troublesome areas. Parents are often frustrated when they are not informed about a difficulty that their child is experiencing that they could have helped to resolve through regular assistance at home.

> If you know that they're having a problem you can work on it here as well. More communication is necessary I would say.

3. Whether children are experiencing difficulties at school or not, parents want to know what to help with and how exactly to help (what to do) at home. This is particularly important with respect to teaching methods which parents find nowadays are often different from those they experienced in school – in mathematics, for example.

> I enjoy helping him when I know exactly what he is doing. Lots of times he needs help and I'll help him my way, but it's not the way the teacher teaches them so it confuses him and he says that's not how you do it. He gets frustrated and then I get frustrated . . . and then we end up arguing.

Parents are keen to be **taught** exactly how to help, including not only what their children have learned in class but also how it has been taught to them. They would appreciate training from the school. One parent says:

> They just bring it home and we are supposed to know what we're supposed to do.

4. In general parents would like teachers to respond to their overtures. Parents are keen about helping not only at home, but also in the classroom. They offer to assist with classroom activities and volunteer their time in the

classroom, but these offers are often not followed up by teachers. Nor are parent requests for suggestions and advice about helping at home pursued:

> When I did have the two days off a week I'm sure I could have been used for more things, particularly the first year. I signed up saying that I was available these two days and I was never called.

Parents are particularly offended by teachers who do not return phone calls. In general, parents are disappointed and frustrated if teachers do not respond to their overtures.

In sum, parents are favourably disposed to helping in the classroom and they would welcome the opportunity to observe in their son or daughter's classroom. In many cases they volunteered extensively when their children were in the primary grades, but now often sense a reluctance on the part of teachers to involve them instructionally in the classroom.

> For the first three grades . . . you are included in more things. In the higher, intermediate grades you don't . . . they seem to want less parents to help inside the classroom.

Participation in the classroom at these grade levels usually means only occasional special activities, performances, and field trips. When they are present in the classroom parents are thankful for the opportunity as it enables them to see what is going on with respect to both curriculum and level of performance expectations, and to judge how their child is performing compared to other students.

When their overtures are rejected by the teacher, parents are disappointed. When they ask for extra work for their children to do at home or ask how to help at home, parents are irritated and at the same time mystified by teachers' refusal to assist them. The ultimate rejection occurs when teachers regard parental involvement as interference and communicate this to parents:

> I heard her comment once that parents were there to feed and clothe their children and give them a lot of love at home and she was there to teach them. Parents weren't expert at teaching so they probably wouldn't be much of an assistance to her.

Few teachers or scholars would regard teaching at the elementary level as *primarily* about instructional expertise; the management of teacher–student personal interactions is more salient in teachers' lives, and more important to teacher satisfaction with their careers (McLaughlin and Yee, 1988). It is also more important to students, as we shall see in later chapters. Parents are normally 'expert' with regard to the attitudes and behaviour of their children, and teachers need this information if they are to enjoy satisfactory instructional interactions with students.

Parents are reluctant to initiate collaboration with their child's teacher if they sense at all that the teacher would not welcome assistance:

> I guess there are things I feel that I could perhaps do, but you have always got to leave it up to the discretion of the teacher . . . although I always made the offer they don't necessarily want you in a classroom situation.

Teachers themselves must issue the invitation to parents and make the overtures that will lead to greater teacher–parent collaboration The invitation from teachers is important with respect to both contact and communication from the teacher (classroom) to the home, and involvement by the parent at home. As one parent summarizes the situation:

> Really, without them saying that they need any help there is not too much you can do.

Parent–Teacher interaction

The following major points emerge here:

1. Parents are concerned that there is not enough face-to-face contact between teachers and parents. One or two formal interviews each year are not sufficient.

> If I didn't make the effort to go into the school as I do we would have no personal contact with the teachers at all other than interview days and that would not be sufficient.

When interviews with teachers do occur they are too short and parents feel pressured to get in and out as quickly as possible. For the most part, they listen while the teacher talks about the achievement of their child. They ask questions about achievement, but are rarely asked by the teacher to provide information about their child. Variations on this approach are well received by parents:

> As opposed to often in the past the teacher would give her information on how the child is doing so this conference was one that was more with both of us talking and both of us sharing information. It was very positive.

Teachers rarely provide information in this setting about curriculum and their expectations regarding work. Parents often cannot comment on the state of their relationship with the teacher, because they do not know him or her, as contact is so infrequent. Generally, few opportunities are provided for parents to meet and get to know their child's teacher, particularly for those who work full-time.

2. Parents would like teachers to communicate with them about their child's work on a day-to-day or week-to-week basis They are appreciative of teacher-implemented strategies such as sending work home to be signed, or homework books, that keep them informed about what their children are doing in class. They see these strategies as avenues for parent–teacher communication and are disappointed when teachers do not participate in this way by attaching comments to students' work, for example, or sending notes to parents in the homework book.

3. Parents would also like teachers to call home to give positive feedback. They complain that if they receive a phone call at all it concerns a problem:

> Unless they're having problems with your child they don't call.

Parents want to hear not only what is not going well at school for their child, but also what is going well and where the student's strengths lie. If there is a problem, however, parents do wish to be contacted by teachers immediately so that they are not only aware of the situation at school, but can also intervene at home. After having spoken to the teacher several times during the year about a difficulty with her child this mother remembers:

> And then I got a phone call towards the end of the year and instead of it being a bad phone call it was how much he's improved. And she was really pleased with what he had done. . . . Now I really respected that because instead of just getting the bad phone calls I got the correction.

4. When conferences, meetings and discussions take place that are related to either behavioural or academic difficulties of their children, or any other concerns, parents want teachers to follow up immediately and communicate with them about resolutions. Often problems are not resolved and parents are dissatisfied and frustrated. They would like to know that what has been discussed does actually take place. They are particularly irritated when decisions are made about their children's program at school without their participation or knowledge.

> A lot of times, I imagine because of the time factor, they don't get back to the parents and say, well, you know, we've looked at this problem. A lot of times parents are left wondering.

5. Parents often have concerns about teacher behaviour and practices (in addition to, and sometimes related to, concerns about their child's achievement), and even though they are confident that it is their right to communicate to the teacher about these concerns, they sense a reluctance on the part of teachers to confront these kinds of issues. Parents are disappointed that it is often not possible to offer suggestions to teachers about handling and interacting with their children that would be helpful to these teachers in the classroom.

Overall, parents want to know that they can contact the teacher at any time about anything and that they are welcome in the school and in the classroom. Regular communication that is productive and fruitful is important to them. They appreciate the efforts of teachers who are willing to talk and answer parent questions and make themselves available to parents:

> I thought he was great . . . I remember a statement made by him that any time that I had any questions that I was to feel free to contact him, that any time that I wished to observe the classroom that I was welcome.

The warmth, openness and receptivity of teachers are signs to parents that the teacher is approachable and also suggest to parents that the teacher may be willing to collaborate with them in other ways.

Parents are sometimes uncomfortable with their child's teacher and intimidated by him or her. The invitation to parents to join in the education of their child can alleviate these feelings:

I think the teachers are open to or happy to see me if I arrive. You know, they sort of make time to talk and ask about the kids. I feel that there is time made available if I arrive with a concern.

Teacher–student interaction

Within this topic the main points made by parents are as follows:

1. Parents ask for standards of performance that are high but reasonable. They are impressed when teachers set high expectations in class and communicate these to students and parents alike, but gear them to the abilities and needs of each individual child.
2. Parents are satisfied when their children are given individual attention in class by the teacher and are concerned when this is not taking place. They are pleased when the child's questions are answered and that when teaching the teacher explains things until the child understands.
3. Parents wish their children to be treated respectfully as individuals by teachers and not to be singled out and criticized openly in the classroom. They are sensitive to the efforts of the teacher to get to know their child individually and the ability of the teacher to bring out the best, academically and personally, in that child.

   He shows an interest in them, each as an individual. I've never heard him say anything negative about a child. He's always looking for the best.

   I guess I think she respects him because she takes him seriously in whatever little subject that is very serious to him.

4. Parents are concerned that there are negative classroom consequences for their children as a result of their complaints to the teacher. They often hesitate to bring up issues or concerns because of their fear of retaliation against their child by the teacher. This concern is expressed so frequently that it seems that there must be some basis for it. (We did illustrate this reaction in the previous chapter.)

   Sometimes you wonder if bringing up an issue with the teacher will result in retaliation against your child. I don't know . . . I imagine it does happen.

5. Parents are also concerned about discipline problems in the classroom which are troublesome for their child because they make study difficult in the classroom.

The general picture here is of some frustration, and lack of optimal relationships which must certainly, given the findings in Chapter 3, be somewhat harmful to student commitment.

COMPARING TEACHER COLLABORATION PRACTICES AND RESULTS

Focusing on the interviews from high and low scoring classrooms is intended to reveal more clearly the differences in teacher attitudes and practices that are

CLASSROOMS CODES-PARS	LINE	11/226 +	11/226 −	11/227 +	11/227 −	12/205 +	12/205 −	12/211 +	12/211 −	12/219 +	12/219 −	14/205 +	14/205 −	14/212 +	14/212 −	14/219 +	14/219 −	16/201 +	16/201 −	16/222 +	16/222 −	16/228 +	16/228 −	25/201 +	25/201 −	25/218 +	25/218 −	25/219 +	25/219 −	TOTALS POS	TOTALS NEG
ACQuain w/teach/sch	3	3	1					4		2				7		5		1									1		1	25	4
BARRKN to inv (KNow)	4	1	1	3		4		3			4			7		1	2			2					7		5			14	20
BARR STudent feelings	5	2		3						5	5		4	7		5	4										5			18	18
BARR Work/Time	6										4		2						6	2	2				3		5		10	5	32
CLASSR visits/help	7	1		1				4		2				3			4				2					3	5			13	10
COMFort level of par	8	2	2					7		2	5	3		4		4		2		2	3			2		5				30	7
NEWSletter SCH/T	9							2		2	3	2		4		7		2										2	1	27	4
PADVisory committee	10										1	2			2							3	1							6	11
PANXiety conflict	11			5	2				3		5		3		1						4	3	7				5		5	7	36
PRINcipal	12						1	2			3	2										2	2	4			2			7	12
PTCONFerence	13	2	1			3	4				3	1		2	2							2								18	11
STREPort on sch/cl	14		1					3			2				2	6		3	3				1			7				11	9
STRESPonsibility	15		2	5	5	5		1	4	2	8	8		3		6			7	5								8		50	11
THELP PRes/PAst*	16	1			5	2		1		2			4				6	2									4		5	11	27
THELPKN curr/method	17		6			2		5		2				4		4				2										20	14
TINFOP st performance	18					3		3		1	2	5		2		2		2	3		1		1							21	5
TPINV inv in instr	19													5		3	3													7	6
TPRELPA att fr history	20		2	3		5		8			10	6	2	5	2	5		23		2	7	7	6	8	8		8	9	16	70	78
TPRELK/T know of t	21	3		2				4	4	2	1		3	8	2	7			1	3		1		5	5		4		2	25	31
TPRELTA att to p invol	22	5		6		8		4	5	6		2		8	8	8	2	3		10	5	5		4	4	2	8	3	3	45	40
TSTRELations	23	2	3	3		11	5	11	1		6		3	3	3	4		4	4			5		8		3	2	7		67	40
VIS sch PRes/PAst*	24	1	1										3	3		2		2								3			3	9	12
WELC in sch or cl	25	3	2	3		6		5		4		4	2	5		6		5		3		3		2	2		3			50	4
VOLunteer PRes/PAst*	26	2	4	2			6	2	2	3				3			4				5		6							11	33
VOLAV willing/avail	27		1			2		2								2				1				1						13	1
TOTALS		13	29	30	8	39	33	73	12	30	43	46	17	71	27	70	26	50	23	31	25	29	16	52	12	25	47	30	46		

*past experience not included in pos/neg totals

NOTES: BARR – positive means none perceived; negative means this is a barrier.
PANX – positive means anxiety about school successfully resolved; negative means unresolved.
PAST – means a reference to another year/child, not involved in the project.

Figure 4.1 Coding summary sheet

important to parents. This analysis uses the quantitative analysis reported in Chapter 1 to establish contrasting classrooms. A comparison of mean scale scores by classroom revealed that there were statistically significant differences between the classrooms. The classrooms selected for analysis by this judgmental process were 11, 12, 14, 16 and 25. (We will identify the sources of comments by parents by classroom number.)

Several issues emerged early in the analysis of the subset: first, that past/present contrasts were going to be important; second that positive/negative reports were going to be given on a variety of issues, and that the balance between these was important. In some cases negative coding indicates something that the parents think should happen. For example, the following comment is coded as negative:

> So I think that if the curriculum is known a little bit better, even just sending home letters and, you know, these are the types of questions that we want answered or whatever, I think that would make things a lot easier.

The responses present a contrasting set of themes and categories of information, not predictable from the questions we asked. Figure 4.1 presents an emergent pattern of themes and issues.

General findings from the hi-lo analysis

The opinions expressed about teachers were almost always flavoured strongly by the circumstances of the particular child concerned, although as we have noted that reference was not always to the child involved in the project. The triad relationship that is the basis of our general conceptualization (Chapter 1) functions very strongly here: even when parents speak of the instructional problems or successes of one of their children the reference is almost always coloured by some comment about the relevant teacher. For parents, relationships with teachers are mediated through children, but also instructional relationships with their children are mediated through teachers.

There are some commonalities. These can first be reported by reference to each coding category, reading across the chart and using the totals in the final columns of the coding summary sheet in Figure 4.1. The categories can be clustered for discussion. Then a cross-parent discussion will examine classroom level commonalities, using the totals at the bottom of the chart.

Commonalities by category
   Acquaintanceship/comfort with the school/teacher (LINES 3, 7, 8, 25, 26): all reported some reasonable level of knowledge (3), few visits to the classroom (7), high comfort levels (8), feeling welcome (25) in school or classroom, and decreased frequency of volunteering compared to the past (26). (Negatives here refer to little knowledge, few visits, lack of comfort or welcome.)

   Barriers to involvement in coproduction (LINES 4, 5, 6): three kinds are reported – lack of knowledge of curriculum and methods; student feelings (desire for independence, sense of personal responsibility); and lack of time because of work or other commitments. (Negatives here mean that the issue is seen as a barrier.)

The first barrier is more common than not in this sample, although some here do not find it a problem (there are a number of teachers or ex-teachers in the sample). The second of these is to some extent unanticipated, although in choosing these grade levels for the project we anticipated finding a very different pattern of relationships between students, parents, and schools for students than those reported in the literature for children of primary grades.

This comment is representative:

> It's probably nice for the teachers to have help once in a while, but I think the kids are probably wanting a little more independence from mom and dad too so. There's probably still kids that could use the extra help, somebody extra to read to them. It's probably the age where the kids, it's kind of a natural thing. (14219)

Parents certainly feel this difference between grade levels. It seems to be a combination of teacher attitude and perceived student attitude:

> When I used to go with M. all the time between the grades of kindergarten and grade 3 there were lots of moms that came and went so the kids were used to seeing moms. Very few dads of course because they were working. But they were used to having the moms come and go so there was no big deal. (16201)

On the other hand, there are sharply contrasting views, held by a parent in the same classroom as the first one quoted:

> Well, I think it's sort of not just the place that they go, it's the place that their family is involved with. Their brothers and sisters are there and then Mummy is always coming in. It just makes the atmosphere more relaxed for them. Plus we know then that we are concerned about what goes on at the school – it isn't just simply that they go and do by themselves. (14212)

This particular parent opinion is certainly in tune with the general notion of co-production.

Those parents who have visited the classroom or school (11226, 11227, 12205, 14212) feel more comfortable suggesting that student independence is an anticipated rather than a real problem. Nevertheless it indicates one important task for any teacher concerned about the good opinion of parents – to reassure parents about the possibility of a productive instructional relationship with their children at these grade levels.

School-wide activities for parents (LINE 9, 10, 11, 12, 13): all reported some reasonable level of knowledge from the newsletters; some distance from the activities of the Parent Advisory Committee, which is seen as irrelevant to instructional issues by some parents; considerable difficulty in resolving conflicts (which are overwhelmingly not resolved in the eyes of parents, by a margin of 36/7); little contact with the principal, except in the conflict resolution context, in which it is usually unsatisfactory; and some dissatisfaction with the parent–teacher conferences.

This can be illustrated:

> Like, the parent–teacher interviews are a joke. Fifteen minutes is not long enough especially when they're already running ten minutes late and you know, there's too much pressure to get through. And that's mostly when you get a chance to talk and it would be nice to be able to actually make an appointment and go in and talk to them for a half an hour on a completely different day. Not when they've scheduled everybody. (12218)

> At the parent–teacher conferences, you go in and you're trying to talk to a teacher and there are thirty other parents in the classroom. We haven't had this problem yet but if there was a major behavioural problem, I would not want to discuss my child in front of other . . . you don't have the privacy required. (12205)

Student reports, responsibility, student relations with teachers (LINES 14, 15, 24): there was not much information coming home from students, although a high level of satisfaction with student acceptance of responsibility was reported. These two features are compatible (and probably also relate to the Barrier – student feelings – discussed above). Relations with teachers vary widely, with some strong positives, and some negative. The negatives are often associated with past events, in which student–teacher relations were poor.

> We have nothing but fights with various teachers of H.'s. I'm afraid I have a little bit of a chip on my shoulder as far as teachers go. And I will admit that I have never had any problems with any of the teachers over at (the project school), they have all really been good about it. But I tend to walk in expecting a confrontation. (12205)

This suggests an important task for teachers that is probably not usually considered – they must establish a positive relationship with each member of a group of parents of whom some have not enjoyed such relationships with previous teachers.

Reports on collaboration (LINES 19, 26, 27): the very low levels of collaboration at present contrast with some past experience. Most report having worked as a volunteer in the past (negative column) and most report some present willingness, given teacher invitation.

> I guess there are things I feel that I could perhaps do. But you have always got to leave it up to the discretion of the teacher. Two years ago when D. was in grade 5, his teacher was a very welcoming person. I said to her at the beginning of the year 'If you ever need any help in the class'. 'Wonderful, what day can you come?' And I went in every day all year and that was super. And then that hasn't happened since. Because although I always made the offer they don't necessarily want you in a classroom situation. And that's fine. You have to recognize that. I certainly enjoy going into the classroom and I think the children enjoy it. (14212)

Reports on attitudes from history (LINES 16, 20): parents have generally not enjoyed help from teachers in the past. Some report very positive experiences; others report very negative ones:

> Last year or the last couple of years I've had to go over and have a specific explanation of how something had to be done so we could do it here. Now that's as far as the cooperation has ever had to go. They explained where G. was having the problems,

how to work around the problem. How to get him doing it correctly so that every-body could understand it on the same wavelength. I don't know if the guy could do any more. This happened with D.'s teacher too. D.'s teacher this year has been excellent that way, sat down and brainstormed about how we could get this kid to actually do what we wanted him to do. So in that regard there's a tremendous amount of cooperation from the school. (11227)

The teachers don't tell you how you can help your child and in fact you get the feeling that he is supposed to be doing it himself, I shouldn't help him. (14212)

Paralleling this is the rather negative view of teachers derived from past experience.

Reports on current attitudes (LINES 18, 21, 22): while some report very positive experiences with respect to teacher attitudes to parent involve-ment, others report very negative ones. There is a tendency for the posi-tives and negatives in line 22 to be matched with those in line 21, knowing the teacher.

On being asked about relations with the teacher:

Parent (M): I'd say, fairly distant really, at least for us. We see them face-to-face maybe two or three times a year.
Parent (F): But there is a communication there.
Parent (M): Oh, it's there but it's sort of once removed. Most of the time it is through K. – secondhand. (14205)

Interviewer: How do you think your child's teacher would respond to that question? What would it look like from her perspective?
Parent (F): Well, because we haven't spoken to K.'s teacher yet this year she must have the same feeling. I just hope that if there is a problem she would contact us. (14205)

Interviewer: Do you feel that your child's teacher sees you as a partner/team member in your child's education?
(P): I really don't know. (In previous years) I've never felt that way. I guess basically because there's no encouragement to help the kids from the school, basically from the teachers. Like, the schools are always looking for participation, not necessarily in the educational department, but you know, like, they like you to come in and help in the library and do all that sort of stuff, but as far as helping the individual child, they really don't seem to encourage that. (25218)

When teachers do indicate a concern for parent involvement by reaching out, it is very much appreciated, and seen as expressing real concern for student welfare:

Well, I think that the teacher should phone the parents – make a sort of a voice contact periodically. But I realize that is a lot of work for teachers too. But it is certainly nice to know. For example, this year Mrs M. did contact me about D. earlier on and it was just so nice to know that she was concerned about him other than him just being a number on a report card. And, 'Oh, I have to do this parent interview'. (14212)

Generally, however, parents perceive that teachers at this grade level are not particularly welcoming. On being asked how teachers would respond regard-ing the relationship between parents and teachers, one parent responded:

They'd say, I don't have time for that. (14212)

Commonalities by classroom
When we look at groupings of results using the totals at the bottom of the chart, three main points emerge:

1. there is much diversity of view between parents in the same classroom, and this is related to their previous experience;
2. the linkage between parent attitudes and knowledge of teacher is very strong and positive, and can overcome negative experience from the past (compare parent 12219 with 14212); and
3. failure to 'permit' parent involvement can confirm negative stereotypes from the past, creating if not parent hostility at least very generalized negative feelings. These characteristics help to explain the overall status, in which classroom 14 and 16 are positively perceived, and classrooms 25, 11 and 12 are quite negatively perceived.

The general pattern can be summarized thus:

1. In classrooms 11 and 12 there are sharply divergent views. In 11, family 11227 has had negative experiences in the past (lines 16, 20) but perceives the present teacher to welcome parent involvement (line 22) despite having little knowledge (line 21), and is generally positive; family 11226 perceives the teacher not to welcome parent involvement, and is generally negative based at least in part on past experience.

In classroom 12, there is even sharper diversity of opinion; family 12211 is overwhelmingly positive, family 12205 is neutral, and family 12219 is largely negative. In each case, both an attitude from history and the parent perception of teacher–student relationships seems important in shaping current attitudes.

2. The pattern of attitudes in one of the more positive classrooms, 14, is clear – the parents feel generally well-acquainted and welcome in the school; they do not perceive student feelings to be a barrier, they see teacher–student relationships in a positive light, they receive good information about student performance, their experiences in the past have resulted in positive attitudes to teachers, and they know the teacher fairly well. Even here though, there is considerable ambivalence regarding the teacher's attitude to parent involvement. In this instance, it seems that positive attitudes from the past are overcoming present uncertainties.

Classroom 16 is also quite positively perceived; here the strengths are generally positive attitudes from history, and feeling welcome in the school. There is little or no contact with the teacher. Most important though is the universal perception that student–teacher relationships are excellent.

> I think he's just the greatest teacher, like I, as far as grade 7, I wish that every kid could see him because he really all of a sudden broadens them, he makes them feel like they're individuals. When he talks to me about her he makes her very much an individual. He always makes the kids feel real good. He makes everybody feel real individual. (16222)

This is the clearest illustration of the importance of the triadic conception: teacher–parent relationships are mediated by students. It is also true that parent–student instructional relationships are mediated by teachers, who have the curricular and methodological knowledge that parents need.

> (I): Do you feel comfortable at meetings with the teacher?
> (P): Of course not. I felt comfortable as far as comfortable went but I'm not well educated myself so then what do you ask, what do you need to know? It takes a long time to figure that out. Now that I'm not working I would like to see a lot more involvement with C. and with C. at the school. Now that I have the time I would like to see a lot more communication. If you know that they're having a problem you can work on it here as well. You've got the time that you can spend working on it but if you don't know? (16222)

3. In the case of the generally negative classroom, 25, in which the balance in line 29 is overwhelmingly negative for all three parents reporting, there are three main contributing factors: barriers to involvement involving both knowledge and time/work; parent anxieties/conflicts which have not been resolved; and some negative perception of teacher–student relations. Additionally current negative reports with respect to knowing the teacher and the perceived teacher attitude to parent involvement are matched with very negative histories of parent–teacher relationships. Thus the balance is composed of a complex of personal constraints on involvement, school-level difficulties, student problems, and parent–teacher present and past relationships. It is worth noting that this school, School B in the site descriptions (see Appendix), serves a diverse population, with some poor families. Although the quantitative analysis did not find a general connection between family education level (in British Columbia the best proxy for relative advantage/disadvantage; Coleman and LaRocque, 1990), at the level of individual families we are convinced that education level can influence parent–teacher relationships.

These parents are all veterans of the school wars – they have seen their children through many grade levels, experienced good teachers and bad, been both heavily involved and withdrawn. Not surprisingly present attitudes are extensively shaped by these experiences. Most reported that they did not really know much about their child's current teacher; they had not had an opportunity to meet, or had only a very brief and hurried meeting. Student reports of classroom and school events were much less important than we had expected – parents were forced to rely upon their own knowledge of the school or classroom, in the absence of much data from students. Thus current knowledge is scarce; the importance of attitudes from history is reinforced in such circumstances.

THE BELIEFS AND ATTITUDES OF PARENTS

All parents believe that they can help their children to learn more and more effectively, and that they could help more with a little assistance from the teacher. Overall, parents:

(a) want to know that they can contact the teacher at any time about anything and that they are welcome in the school and in the classroom;

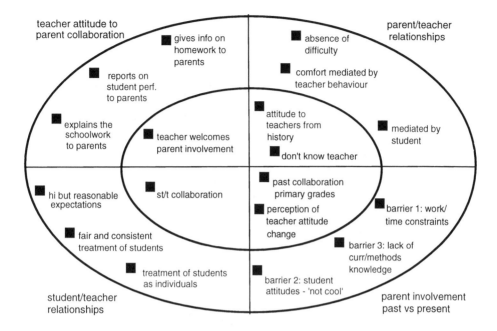

Figure 4.2 Teacher behaviour centrally important to parents

(b) wish their children to be treated respectfully as individuals by teachers;

(c) are sensitive to the efforts of the teacher to get to know their child individually and the ability of the teacher to bring out the best, academically and personally, in that child.

We summarize what we learned here in Figure 4.2. There are four topics of equal importance: parent–teacher relationships; family history of involvement; teacher–student relationships; and the attitudes of teachers to parent involvement. Within these topics there are major (inner) and minor (outer) themes. For example, at the core of student–teacher relationships desired by parents is the idea of collaboration, rather than the superior–subordinate relationship recalled by parents from their own schooldays. At the core of the teacher–parent relationship is the notion of teacher welcoming parents as collaborators.

For parents, relationships with teachers are occasionally mediated through children, but more importantly **instructional relationships between parent and child are almost always influenced by teachers.** We asked 'Do you feel that your child's teacher sees you as a partner/team member in your child's education?' The most memorable response was:

They'd say, I don't have time for that.

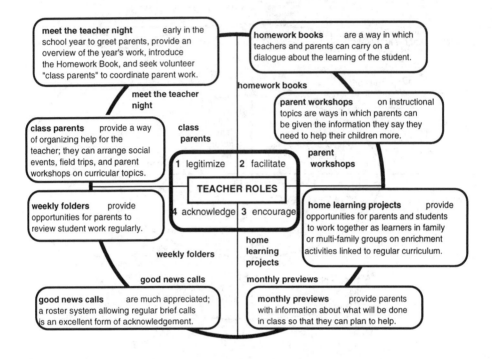

Figure 4.3   The Coproduction Classroom

Meeting the expectations of parents

These parents have all worked with teachers in the past for whom they had great respect. That respect was often a function of what parents saw as a welcoming and collaborative attitude towards working with parents on the common task, the learning of the child. Parent perceptions of desirable teacher behaviour are both well-developed, and readily articulated. Such teacher practices in total would result in what we call the Coproduction Classroom, summarized in Figure 4.3.

ASSESSING THE IMPACT OF THE GOOD TEACHER ON THE BELIEFS AND ATTITUDES OF PARENTS

Our single question here was

What do parents regard as the most important qualities of a good teacher, and how do they arrive at the beliefs they hold about teacher quality?

What the chapter tells us

The response derived from our data can be expressed as a series of suggestions for teachers, suggestions that will allow them to maximize their positive impact on parents, and as a consequence upon the children in their classrooms.

Teachers must (1) **realize** that parent efficacy with respect to instructional involvement (collaboration) is **dependent upon teacher invitation**; (2) **legitimize collaboration** through an assertion to parents of their rights and responsibilities with respect to collaboration; (3) **facilitate collaboration** by arranging for parent–teacher conversations of various kinds, and by providing parents with the knowledge of curriculum and methodology they need; (4) **encourage collaboration** by providing activities that parents and their children can do together; that is accepting the role of instructional mediator between parents and their children; and (5) **acknowledge the results of collaboration** by providing adequate and timely information about student performance. For us these constitute vital teacher roles in the Coproduction Classroom.

The implications for school improvement

The most interesting issue raised by this analysis is: why are the fairly basic expectations of parents so rarely met by teachers? Are teachers unaware of parent preferences, or are they unwilling to collaborate to the limited extent desired?

One missing element is worth mentioning: principals were much less important than the school effectiveness literature, or even some previous work in British Columbia (Coleman, 1984) would suggest. These parents barely mentioned the principal at all; when they did it was in the context of conflict resolution, which did not happen to their satisfaction.

Together these points suggest one major implication for school improvement: as we have suggested already, and as other chapters will further demonstrate, the **parents in the school community constitute the most important resource the school has for school improvement. Hence, the most important task of the school principal who is concerned about quality is to activate parents as instructional supporters of their children. This work must be done through classroom teachers.**

The charts above suggest some mechanisms, although it must be emphasized that **mechanisms are less important than attitudes.** The teacher who understands and accepts the importance of parental support, and also takes responsibility for strengthening parent efficacy, is vital to school improvement. There is of course an immediate benefit for such teachers in the improvement of the attitudes of the children in the classroom, as later chapters will show.

Although the data here are Canadian, there are strong parallels with the work of Epstein (1985, 1986) and more generally with Rosenholtz's work on teachers' workplaces (1989), suggesting that teacher roles with respect to parent involvement and collaboration are rather generalizable, and not very positive at present. The 'best' classrooms in our sample are characterized by strong positive relationships with students but not generally with parents. We believe the collaborative approach to relationships with parents is rare everywhere (Rosenholtz, 1989).

This failure of collaboration is bad for teachers, for schools, and for students. The upper elementary years are particularly important since it is here that the influence of the home, and the relationship between home and school, can break down. Quite modest changes in teacher practices, and relationships with parents, have the potential to alter student attitudes to school and schooling. In the next chapter we examine the 'levers of change' for parent and student attitudes in detail. Not the least of the benefits for teachers is the possibility of much more productive in-school behaviour by students.

5

The Levers of Change: The Impact of Teachers on Parents and Students

One swallow does not make a summer.

(English country saying)

Instructional collaboration is that form of parent involvement with schools and teachers which is focused upon instructional issues; collaboration is the process at the heart of the co-production of learning – joint efforts by families and schools to ensure student success. Some collaborative techniques and practices of good teachers were described in the last chapter.

But attitudes are much more important than techniques: the collaborative relationship between teachers and students, students and parents, and teachers and parents is based upon mutual respect, shared goals, and agreed-upon operational roles. At various times and for various purposes, each triad participant is both teacher and learner, initiator and responder; each shares in the collective responsibility for producing the desired outcome – the successful student.

This chapter will identify and describe the teacher attitudes and practices associated with collaboration – the set of instructional relationships between parents, teachers, and students which contributes to positive parent and student perception of teachers and school.

IDENTIFYING THE LEVERS OF CHANGE

Our approach to parental involvement has been to treat it as a necessary element in school improvement and effectiveness, rather than as an issue emerging from family studies, or multicultural interests. For example, we consider the good teacher (Chapter 4) to be one whose interactions with parents are such that the parent perception of school climate and school quality is positively affected. Here we hope to clarify the main ways in which teacher practices shape parent and student perceptions of quality. It seems likely that teacher practice change with respect to collaboration is an important lever for reshaping parent and student perceptions, and hence for school improvement.

The survey data analyzed here are drawn from Year 1 and Year 2. (See tables in Chapter Notes.) The Year 2 data includes some private school parents and students. One sub-group was enrolled in three public schools serving a working/middle class suburb. The second sub-group was enrolled in a private school set in an affluent suburb. This allows us to compare the perceptions of parents who have chosen to pay fees amounting to $(Canadian)6,000 per child per annum to those of parents whose children attend neighbourhood schools. We thought that some interesting contrasts might emerge.

Two detailed questions are posed in this chapter:

What parental and student perceptions of schools, classrooms, and teachers shape the overall rating given to schools by these participants, and how generalizable and stable are these perceptions?

Do these perceptions vary over time and between classrooms?

Since our general intent is to discover levers of change, we have focused here on those parent and student perceptions which appear to be causally related to the rating of the school, and on the teacher attitudes and practices associated with them.

THE ATTITUDES OF PARENTS AND STUDENTS

Our first concern was to try to establish an understanding of the pattern of relationships over time within the attitude sets of parents and students. The relationships between the various attitude scales for Time 1 and Time 2 (Year 1), and Time 3 and Time 4 (Year 2) data were analyzed using stepwise multiple regression. This technique identifies the relative strength of each variable as a predictor of changes in others. The outcome measures were, for parents, perception of school climate and rating of school, and for students, rating for Year 1, and climate and rating for Year 2. This statistical technique **describes possible causal relationships,** and hence we speak of the impact of 'predictors' (the independent variables) upon variance in outcomes (the dependent variables). An appropriate analogy is the lever – the predictor 'levers' change (variance) in the outcome.

In what follows we identify causal chains – working backwards from the outcomes. There are limitations – statistically significant effects are often practically unimportant. Hence the 'levers' we describe may be **useful** but they are by no means **reliable** tools. Some readers may find that scanning the charts focusing upon the 'leverage', the effect of each attitude variable upon the next in line, gives them all the information they need. However, we also describe them verbally.

Key items in the parent variable 'school climate' included the following:

24. Students are excited about learning in this school.
28. The academic emphasis in our school is challenging to students.
30. Students are proud of our school.

Key items in the (new) student variable 'school climate' included the following:

64. Teachers in this school treat the students with respect.
66. Teachers treat students fairly in this school.
69. If I had a choice, I would choose to go to this school

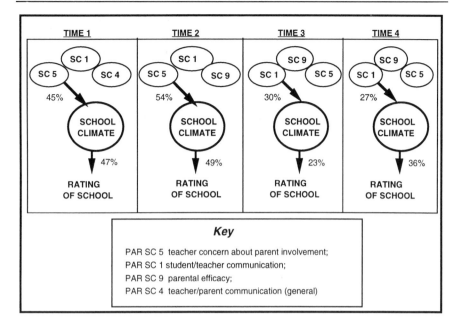

Figure 5.1 Parent attitude data, Times 1, 2, 3, 4, showing the power of predictors to influence outcomes

The parent data

With respect to parent data, stepwise regression shows very little change over time in the relationships between the outcomes and the predictors. Consistent patterns emerge for all rounds of data collection (see Figure 5.1). School climate (Scale 8) accounts for 47%, 49%, 23%, and 36% of the variance in parent rating of school for Times 1, 2, 3 and 4. (That is, for Time 1, if in a classroom the perception of school climate changed from lowest to highest amongst our sample, the accompanying rating of school could improve by 47%). For this kind of statistical work, that is a very large change.

Perception of school climate is always the most important predictor. In turn, school climate perception is usually influenced by Scale 1, perception of student/teacher collaboration, Scale 9, perception of parent efficacy, and Scale 5, perception of teacher concern about parent involvement.

For Time 1 Scales 5 (perception of teacher concern about parent involvement), 1 (perception of student/teacher collaboration), and 4 (perception of teacher/parent communication about general classroom matters) account for 56% of the variance in the school climate measure. Scale 5 contributes most strongly, accounting for 45% of the variance overall. For Time 2, Scales 5, 1, and 9 are linked to school climate, but as in Time 1, Scale 5 contributes most strongly, accounting for 54% of the variance in school climate. Altogether Scales 5, 1 and 9 account for 61% of the variance in school climate.

Results for Time 3 and Time 4 are particularly consistent although the relationships here are not as strong as in Time 1 and Time 2. Scale 1, Scale 9, and Scale 5 account for 41% of the variance in school climate in Time 3 and for 36% of the variance in Time 4. Scale 1 contributes most strongly: it accounts for 30% of the variance in school climate for Time 3 and 27% of the variance for Time 4.

For these parents overall **perception of school climate shapes the rating given to schools.** Parental attitudes and perceptions regarding school climate in Time 1 and Time 2 (the study's first year; all public school parents) are shaped by their perception of the teacher's concern about parent involvement and their perception of collaboration between their child and the teacher.

For parents in Time 3 and Time 4 (the study's second year; public and private school parents), attitudes and perceptions regarding school climate are shaped first by their perception of the extent to which collaboration between students and teacher occurs in the classroom and then second by their perception of their ability to help their child with schoolwork. Their perception of the teacher's concern about parent involvement is also significant, but is less important for this group of parents.

The student data

The results of the analyses of student survey data seem less consistent. For Time 1, Scales E (perception of student/teacher collaboration), C (perception of school/home communication), F (perception of parent valuing school), and D (perception of personal efficacy) together account for 26% of the variance in student rating of the school. For Time 2, Scales B (student values school), E, and G (perception of peer group values), together account for 22% of the variance; Scale B alone accounts for 16% of the variance overall.

But Time 3 and Time 4 are more consistent, both with the parent results and with each other. The new Scale H (perception of school climate) introduced for the second year helps to make the relationships more comprehensible. It accounts for 54% and 35% respectively of the variance in student rating of the school. Perception of school climate is affected by Scale B and Scale E. For Time 3 these two scales account for 51% of the variance in Scale H, and for Time 4, 39% of the variance.

For the students in Time 3 and Time 4 the perception of school climate largely shapes the rating given to schools. In turn, student attitudes and perceptions regarding school climate are shaped most strongly by their general valuation of schooling and their perception of the extent to which collaboration occurs in the classroom between themselves and their teacher. To a somewhat lesser extent, their perception of their own efficacy at school and the attitudes of their peers are also significant. For Time 2, 3, and 4 the student's valuation of school, together with the student perception of collaboration with the teacher, are the key predictors. These results are summarized in Figure 5.2.

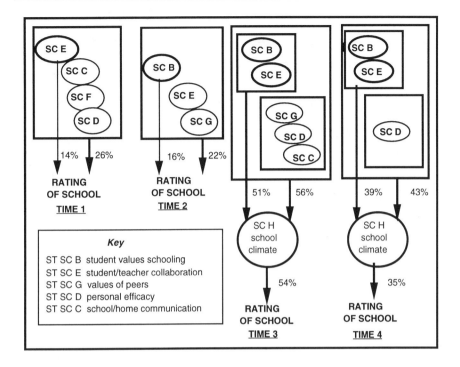

Figure 5.2 Student attitude data, Times 1, 2, 3, 4, showing the power of predictors to influence outcomes

COMPARISONS OF ATTITUDE SETS BY SITE

For Time 1 and Time 2 quantitative data were collected at public schools in two different sites. There are no important differences between the sites. For Time 3 and Time 4 data were also collected at two different sites, but one of these consisted of a private school. The public school and private school data from Time 3 and Time 4 were analyzed separately, to see whether the two groups of parents had different expectations and attitudes, reflecting the sharp socioeconomic differences between them.

The parent data

Among these four sets of data – Time 3 and Time 4 for both public and private school parents – analysis reveals some differences. These results are summarized in Figure 5.3.

For public school parents in Time 3 the assessment of school climate is affected primarily by the extent to which parents perceive there to be collaboration between students and teacher in the classroom. For private school parents in Time 3, on the other hand, the rating of school is influenced by the

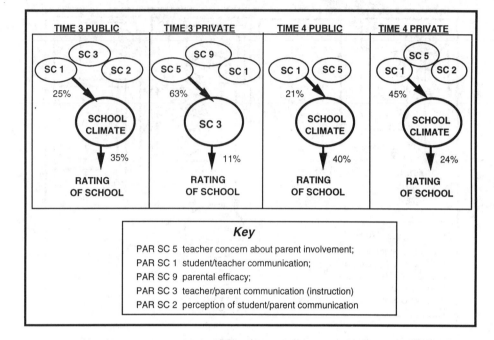

Figure 5.3 Parent attitude data, public and private schools, Times 3, 4, showing the power of predictors to influence outcomes

extent to which they perceive that the teacher communicates to them about instruction. This variable (Scale 3 – perception of teacher/parent communication regarding instruction) is affected greatly by parent assessment of the teacher's concern about parent involvement, and to a lesser degree by parent perception of their own ability to help their child with schoolwork and the degree to which they perceive there to be collaboration between students and teacher in the classroom.

The student data

For private and public school students some differences also emerge. For Time 4 public school students, school climate is linked to student rating of school. Here Scale H accounts for 36% of the variance in student rating of school. However, the scales that are associated with school climate here are Scales C and D; they account for 39% of the variance in the school climate measure.

For both public and private school students for Time 3 and Time 4, perception of school climate shapes the rating given to schools. For public and private school students in Time 3 and private school students in Time 4 students' attitudes and perceptions regarding school climate are shaped most strongly by

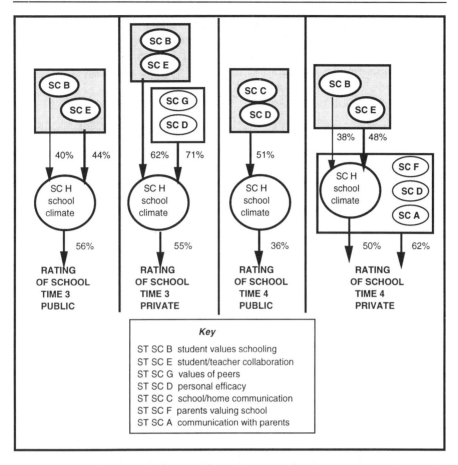

Figure 5.4 Student attitude data, public and private schools, Times 3, 4, showing the power of predictors to influence outcomes

their own valuation of schooling and their perception of the extent to which collaboration between themselves and their teacher occurs in the classroom.

For Time 4 public school students the assessment of school climate is affected primarily by students' perception of the extent to which their teacher communicates with the home and their perception of the importance of schooling. Over the eight months between fall and spring (the times of data collection) a shift in attitudes apparently occurred, in which in-school effects (teacher collaboration) became less important than effects linked in some way with the home (perception of school–home communication; student valuing of schooling).

These patterns provide a response to our first question, which was:

What parental and student perceptions of schools, classrooms, and teachers shape the overall rating given to schools by these participants, and how generalizable and stable are these perceptions?

This socially and economically diverse sample of parents and students, dwelling in quite different parts of the province, had consistent values with respect to their participation in the co-production of learning. Their fulfilment or disappointment had a strong effect upon the judgments arrived at about the school attended, for both parents and students.

Teacher behaviour strongly influences the attitudes of these parents and students. For parents, the most important variables accounting for variance in school climate perception are Scale 5 (teacher concern about parent involvement); Scale 1 (student/teacher communication); and Scale 4 (teacher/parent communication, general). The only important variable unassociated with teacher behaviour is Scale 9 (parent efficacy). There is some suggestion in Chapters 3 and 4 that such efficacy can be to some extent dependent upon teacher activity.

For students, the most important variables are a combination of home and school variables: Scale B (student values schooling) and Scale E (student/teacher collaboration) are the major predictors of student perception of school climate and hence of student rating of school.

These responses to the first question lead us to expect that analyses by classroom would confirm that **teacher behaviour was instrumental in shaping both parent and student attitudes.**

COMPARISONS OF ATTITUDES BY CLASSROOM

Responding to the second question, 'Do these perceptions vary over time between classrooms?', requires an examination of the data from each round, by classroom. Between-classroom variations are of particular importance since our initial phase included the piloting of some modest interventions that we believed were differentially implemented in classrooms (see Note 3 in Chapter Notes).

We used statistical tests to determine whether any significant differences existed between classrooms over time that could be attributed to our attempts to change teacher practices. For the first year group of classrooms, for parents, we found few differences between classrooms in the fall measures, but significant differences in the spring, for those variables closely related to school. (Results are given in Table 5.3 in the Chapter Notes.)

The changes over the year suggest that for parents their experience with a particular teacher affects various attitudes towards school; these are unsurprisingly those which reflect most directly teacher practices of communication with the home. **Teacher behaviour with respect to the home is potentially a powerful lever for change.**

For students in the fall, the significant differences between classroom groups describe different levels of collaboration between student and parent. For the spring, classroom by classroom differences on Scale E (student/teacher collaboration) and student rating of school, not significant in the fall, became significant. This suggests that **the experience of the student with respect to** collaboration with the teacher during the school year differed by classroom, and had an impact on student rating of the school.

For the second year group of parents, there were again few differences perceived between classrooms in the fall, but for the spring those scales concerning **teacher communication practices differed by classroom.**

For the second year group of students in the spring, the scores on many scales and on student rating of school showed significant classroom level differences. These results suggest that **teacher practices as perceived by students were differentiated by classroom, and helped students form judgments of their own efficacy, and of school quality.**

Given that at least some of the scales do in fact differentiate between classrooms, particularly towards the end of the school year, we can examine the specific differences for each classroom that emerge over the year.

Comparing classrooms over time

Parent and student general perceptions can become more or less positive over a school year (see Chapter Notes, Note 4, Table 5.4). We also ran statistical tests to see whether there were clear trends for this group of classrooms. All the significant results showed negative shifts.

Our second research question was:

Do these perceptions vary over time and between classrooms?

The statistical tests suggest that the unique qualities of teacher practice in each of these classrooms became more noticeable to parents and students over the school year; but they certainly did not become better classrooms in the eyes of parents and students.

USING THE LEVERS OF CHANGE

We began the chapter with two questions:

What parental and student perceptions of schools, classrooms, and teachers shape the overall rating given to schools by these participants, and how generalizable and stable are these perceptions?

Do these perceptions vary over time and between classrooms?

What the chapter tells us

We are confident that we have identified the levers of change, the parent and student perceptions which count, in these longitudinal analyses. For parents, they are Scale 5 (teacher concern about parent involvement); Scale 1 (student/teacher communication); and Scale 4 (teacher/parent communication, general). For students, they are Scale B (student values schooling) and Scale E (student/teacher collaboration). Values on such scales tend to decline during the school year.

The modest changes in teacher practices regarding parent involvement that were recommended as part of the Coproduction Project were apparently not consistently and powerfully implemented in any classroom, in ways that were obvious to parents and students. But such changes are necessary to offset what seems to be quite general disappointment amongst parents and students about their school experience over the year.

The implications for school improvement

This chapter reminds us that if teachers wish to improve their practice with respect to collaboration, they will have to make **many of the kinds of changes** suggested in Chapter 4, and make them consistently and obviously over **a whole school year.** Few, small and temporary changes are not helpful. This suggests that a school-wide program of practice change is needed, sponsored and supported by the school administration, with frequent reminders about the program and feedback with respect to attitude changes amongst parents and students.

Others have made similar suggestions. Louis and Smith (1992) argue that teacher engagement, that is changes in attitudes and practices with students, is a necessary precursor to student engagement. To change teacher practices requires very significant changes in school leadership, culture and structure (they refer to secondary schools). At the elementary level, similar conditions seem to apply. **Both breadth of change and persistence in the modified practice are essential;** we return to this topic in later chapters. For the moment, we conclude that it takes a lot of swallows to make a summer, when the summer is student and parent perceptions of improvements in school climate and quality.

6

Varieties of Teacher Collaboration

I don't know how we could connect.

(Working parent)

This chapter focuses on teacher attitudes and behaviours associated with home/school collaboration. We are here concerned about possible gaps between teacher hopes and preferences and the actual impact of their practices upon the students and parents in their classrooms. As we saw in the previous chapter, teacher practice changes are often not visible to parents and students, perhaps because they are short-lived. Teachers have good intentions with respect to collaboration, also, as we see in this chapter. But these too may not be obvious to the potential collaborators. Or, more pessimistically, it may be that teachers do not make the effort to reach the 'hard-to-reach' parents.

ASSESSING TEACHER COLLABORATION

For us, parent involvement is largely but not exclusively parent engagement in learning activities in the home. Such engagement was fully described in Chapter 3. It includes both actual learning tasks, such as helping with homework, and the 'curriculum of the home' – the 'patterns of habit formation and attitude development that prepare a child for academic learning and (that sustain) the child through the years of schooling' (Redding, 1992, p. 1).

Many parents, though well-intentioned, are not empowered by their own backgrounds and school experiences to act in ways that would benefit student achievement (Lareau, 1989). Parents often feel 'progressively less competent in relation to school curriculum as children grow older' (Cyster, Clift, and Battle, 1979). Teachers frequently fail to give parents the curricular information they need, as we saw in the previous chapter.

The collaborative approach envisions teachers recruiting parental support with the intention of developing a partnership based on mutual respect, reciprocity of responsibility, and an exchange of knowledge and skills for the purpose of promoting positive attitudes to school.

To examine the extent to which this is occurring, the questions we posed were:

Do teachers see themselves as acting in a collaborative way with parents?

Do their actions (as seen by parents and students) reflect these collaborative attitudes?

HOW WE SOUGHT ANSWERS TO THE QUESTIONS ABOUT COLLABORATION

Our data set here consisted of seven schools from two school districts. The findings reported draw on survey data for 162 parent–student dyads, and interview data for 12 teachers and 35 parent–student dyads, at Times 1 and 2.

The qualitative data were used to develop teacher profiles. This was done in two stages. First, using self-report data, individual profiles were constructed that reported teacher:

(a) attitudes and practices regarding parent involvement;
(b) attitudes towards students, both in general and with regard to student ability to accept responsibility for learning; and
(c) professional efficacy.

The teacher profiles also report general contextual information to give the reader a sense of the school and community environment in which the teacher was working.

Secondly, and without referring back to the profiles just described, another set of teacher profiles was created. These reported *parent perceptions* of:

1. the teacher's attitude toward parents and parent involvement;
2. teacher parent involvement strategies;
3. teacher regard for students; and
4. student regard for school and teacher;

and *student perceptions* of:

(a) the classroom learning environment;
(b) whether he or she 'counted for something' in the classroom; and
(c) student regard for school and teacher.

Then teacher, parent, and student data were combined to form a complete profile for each participating teacher. On the basis of these profiles, teachers were labelled collaborative or non-collaborative.

Using data from all three referent groups to generate individual teacher profiles is consistent with the study's emphasis on the importance of triadic relationships (between and amongst teachers, parents, and students) as a measure of effective classrooms and, by extension, effective schools.

The approach alleviates the possible negative effects of self-report data – we are all biased witnesses when testifying about ourselves and our actions. Cross-validating the data has two effects: one, it either supports or calls into the question the teacher self-report data; and two, parent and student data often provide information regarding teacher practices that the teacher had not reported. These practices are perhaps **important to the potential collaborators but not to the teachers**.

On the basis of the procedure described above, six of the twelve participating teachers were labelled collaborative and six non-collaborative. The non-collaborative label suggests that their practices in this regard were weak, inconsistent, and/or primarily reactive. These teachers did not reach out to parents. In some cases, the non-collaborative label also indicates a discrepancy between word (expressed positive attitudes toward involvement) and deed. In a final step, quantitative data were used to check the results obtained from the qualitative analysis, to provide another form of validation.

ANALYZING TEACHER PRACTICES

Here we examine behaviours and attitudes generally representative of teachers. The discussion draws on Blase's (1987) work on the effective principal. This framework was used because during the analysis it became clear that members of each referent group (teachers, parents, and students) spoke of teacher attitudes and behaviours that reflected Blase's distinction between task-relevant and consideration-related factors.

Blase describes task-relevant competencies that focus on planning, defining, organizing, and evaluating work. Within this domain, the effective leader demonstrates strength in the following areas: accessibility, consistency, knowledge-expertise, decisiveness, goals and directions, follow through, ability to manage time, and problem-solving. Consideration-related factors, on the other hand, focus on meeting the social and emotional needs of others (Blase, 1987).

Task-relevant competencies

With regard to goals and directions, students reveal an interesting distinction between collaborative and non-collaborative teachers – the extent to which students working with the former describe their classrooms as places to work and learn. Statements like the following are typical: the teacher 'teaches you a lot'; the classrooms are 'workable'; and when students enter these classrooms, they 'start working right away'. Students working with collaborative teachers consistently refer to their classrooms as places where they work hard and where learning occurs.

Students associated with non-collaborative teachers do not volunteer this kind of information. The collaborative teacher has created a climate that conveys a clear goal-oriented message to students.

Teacher knowledge, both declarative and procedural (knowing how to facilitate collaborative partnerships at the grade 6 and 7 level) is often referred to. This process is contingent, of course, on the teacher's willingness and ability to provide parents with the information they need to work effectively with students in the home. It is contingent, as well, on the extent to which teachers encourage students to view parents as partners in learning.

This is exactly what the collaborative teachers in our study do. For one teacher, this is a matter of professional responsibility. 'One of my jobs,' she comments, 'is to let the parents know' what is happening with their children and to let them know 'that they can take part.' Although each collaborative teacher approaches this responsibility differently, amongst them we see examples of teachers who provide parents with weekly curricular updates and examples of work completed during that time; keep parents informed of homework assignments, project due dates, and test dates through the use of homework books; and provide parents with *specific* information on how to help their child with learning tasks assigned for home completion.

Parents who are associated with uncollaborative teachers mention such things as: 'I wouldn't mind a bit more information coming home' or 'I don't know what is going on in the classroom. I wish there was really more . . . notifying parents as to what is expected.' One important difference between collaborative and non-collaborative teachers, then, is the extent to which they share knowledge and are receptive to receiving it from other members of the triad.

If parents and students cannot access that knowledge, goals become more difficult to realize. Blase (1987) defines 'accessibility' as 'availability and visibility'. Accessible principals are professionals who 'arrive at work early and stay late', 'work hard and long hours', 'circulate a lot', are 'involved in everything', and are 'everywhere'. Principals and teachers will differ in what and how they are 'involved in everything', but this characteristic of the effective principal is a characteristic, as well, of collaborative teachers.

One collaborative teacher, for instance, is very much involved in extra-curricular activities. One parent perceives this teacher's involvement beyond the classroom as having a positive 'spill over' effect on her daughter's school work. This mother describes the student as having a 'more positive attitude . . . this year'. She attributes this to the teacher's involvement in extra-curricular sports activities, which provide the focal point of her daughter's school life. With one exception, non-collaborative teachers seldom mention, nor do parents or students report, teacher involvement beyond the classroom or the regular school day.

Time is not a deterrent to collaborative teachers. They find time-efficient ways to keep parents informed. Two project teachers, for instance, adopted a folder system, which saw student work sent home on a designated day each week. These teachers assigned students the responsibility for creating the folders and for accumulating the materials to be sent home. They safeguarded their own time to prepare and/or respond to comments in the section of the work folder designed for that purpose.

Collaborative teachers also *make* time for both students and parents. One teacher reports that 'we've got to, as teachers, fit our timetables around (parents) to make it more convenient for them.' Parents indicate that this teacher is true to her word. She scheduled 7.30 am meetings with one family in order to accommodate both a father's work schedule and his interest in meeting with her.

A second teacher distributed her home phone number to parents during the first week of school and specified the hours during which she could be reached: 6.00 to 8.00 pm. This time is used to contact parents and to receive incoming calls. One father reported feeling uncomfortable phoning the teacher at home but, remembering the teacher's invitation to do so, he took advantage of this opportunity to discuss a problem his daughter was experiencing.

Parents associated with non-collaborative teachers report serious time problems. One mother, for instance, described the relationship between teachers and parents as poor and attributed this to lack of communication. Because she works outside the home, she, like many working parents, feels that she has little opportunity to communicate with the teacher. She does not fault the teacher, who, she believes, 'probably thinks that I am free to call her and like it's up to me to go to her and make the move.' She continues: 'I'm sure we could talk on the phone. She could phone me at work, (but) I don't expect her to do that . . . . I am never home until six or six-thirty and I mean she's finished at school . . . she has had her day . . . . I don't know how we could connect.'

Parents working with collaborative teachers do not have this problem. They know how and when to connect because the collaborative teacher has recognized the importance of the teacher taking the first step in establishing positive home–school partnerships.

Collaborative teachers are consistent. One aspect is the extent to which teachers hold students accountable for homework completion. One collaborative teacher, for instance, comments: it 'doesn't take (students) very long to realize that the 85 excuses really aren't going to work' – homework must be done. Collaborative teachers are consistent not only in their expectation that students do the work assigned but also in their reaction when expectations are not met. As one teacher noted, 'there's no death penalty' when students fail to complete a homework assignment but they know they will be held accountable: student and teacher discuss a realistic completion date for the outstanding work.

Non-collaborative teachers speak of the importance of students following through on their responsibilities, but they seldom give concrete examples of how that responsibility is developed. A teacher comment characterizes the collaborative teachers' sentiment on this topic. Students 'have to be taught the skills. It isn't fair to say: "You are now thirteen and you have to (be responsible)" . . . . First, they have to be taught or shown that this is possible. Secondly, they have to be given a chance to practise these skills.'

Consideration-related factors

Based on comments from all three referent groups, there is consensus that collaborative teachers hold students and parents in high regard. Parents and students working with collaborative teachers generally report that students in these classrooms enjoy school, like their teacher, and feel respected. Parents whose children are assigned to collaborative teachers typically comment: that their children are more engaged academically than they have been in the past; that they are enjoying their schoolwork more than in previous years; that their children feel 'really good' about school; and that school is 'like a second home.' The following comment is the norm: the teacher has 'a really good relationship

	Comparative profile of the Collaborative vs. the Non-collaborative teacher	
TASK-RELATED COMPETENCIES	COLLABORATIVE	NON-COLLABORATIVE
goals/direction	Students: classroom places to work and learn; teacher 'teaches you a lot'; students 'start working right away'.	
knowledge/ expertise	Teacher: 'one of my jobs to let the parents know' what is happening, and 'that they can take part'.	Parents: 'I wouldn't mind a bit more information coming home'; 'I don't know what is going on in the classroom'.
accessibility	Parent: teacher involvement in extra-curricular activities has a 'spill-over' effect – student has 'a more positive attitude this year'.	no teacher involvement beyond classroom or school day.
ability to manage time	Teacher: 'we've got to fit our timetables around (parents) to make it more convenient for them'.	Parent: relationship with teacher poor, lack of communication: 'I am never home until 6 or 6.30 and she has had her day . . . I don't know how we could connect'.
consistency/follow through	Teacher: holding students accountable for home-work: 'it doesn't take students long to realize that the 85 excuses really aren't going to work'.	
CONSIDERATION-RELATED FACTORS	Parents: hold teachers in high regard – students enjoy school, like the teacher, feel respected; they are more engaged academically. The teacher 'doesn't talk down to them – talks to them as an equal'.	Parent: teacher has guidelines of what constitutes 'a perfect student' – he is telling me that my kid doesn't meet that criteria (sic).'
	Parents: 'no doubt' that parents are viewed as partners; teacher knows parents ar capable of assisting in the home; the teacher provides information that helps them do so.	Parent: relationship is 'distant': 'we just don't see each other, though we are working towards a common goal'.

Figure 6.1   Profile of collaborative and non-collaborative teachers

with his students. . . . I really feel it. . . . He doesn't talk down to them. He talks to them as an equal.' Students share this perception.

Parents of children assigned to non-collaborative teachers offer information that reveals important differences between the two types of teacher. One father reports that the teacher has 'guidelines' of what constitutes 'a perfect student' and what he is telling me is that 'my kid doesn't meet that criteria. . . . My son knows it, too.' Other parents report that their children are 'not really all that happy.' There are several reports, as well, of unfair disciplinary practices.

Consideration-related factors reflected in parent–teacher relationships are just as revealing. Parents associated with non-collaborative teachers often express the feeling that the relationship between parent and teacher is 'distant'. This often has to do with lack of communication or the sense that the teacher wishes to keep the parent at bay. One father, for instance, mentions that: 'We just don't see each other, even though we're working toward a common goal.' The most extreme comment comes from a mother: 'I wouldn't know her if I fell over her on the street.' To this mother, the relationship between parents and teachers is a 'big joke . . . I don't think it's there.'

Even when there is contact between non-collaborative teachers and parents it does not necessarily create a spirit of partnership. One mother reported that although she and the teacher were working together more towards the end of the year than they were at the beginning, she continued to 'get the sense . . . that he figures he can handle it himself better.'

In sum, parents associated with collaborative teachers report with great consistency that: there is 'no doubt' that parents are viewed as partners in their child's education; the teacher appreciates the advocacy role parents play on behalf of their children; the teacher appreciates, as well, that families are interested in and capable of assisting in the home; and the teacher provides specific information that permits them to do so.

In summarizing his findings, Blase (1987, p. 606) reports that effective leadership was linked to the development of productive social and cultural structures in schools. Collaborative teachers do likewise at the classroom level. They create an environment in the classroom that balances the importance of academics with the importance of positive teacher–student social relationships, increasing the likelihood of student satisfaction with school and academic success (Metz, 1993). They extend the mutually respectful dyadic relationship they create with students and form a similar type of relationship with parents, resulting in the triadic relationship we believe is optimal.

Figure 6.1 summarizes these profiles of the teachers into more and less collaborative attitudes and practices. We now assess these profiles against the quantitative data.

A SECOND ANALYSIS OF TEACHER PRACTICES

The quantitative data were analyzed after the profiles had been developed. Because the teacher sample was small, quantitative analysis was limited to parent and student data. The main purpose was to check classroom level differences in scale scores, within the group in the fall measures, and between fall and spring. (Table 6.1 in the Chapter Notes lists scales for which statistically reliable differences were found.)

At Time 1 (fall measures) only two scales yielded statistically reliable differences: Parent Scale 8 (school climate) and Student Scale C (home–school communication). Parents associated with relatively non-collaborative class-rooms tended to perceive school climate less favourably than those with students in classrooms labelled collaborative.

There are two possible explanations for this. One, schools with a less favourable school climate recruit less collaborative teachers at the outset and/or do little to nurture home–school collaboration amongst staff members. This top-down explanation suggests that what happens at the level of the school impacts classroom life. We do know that schools have such effects from the work of Teddlie and Stringfield (1993) and Rosenholtz (1989).

Another explanation reflects a bottom-up perspective and suggests that parent familiarity with a particular classroom shapes judgments about overall school climate. All our previous work (especially the analyses presented in the previous chapter) suggests that this is the more likely explanation; students and parents generalize upwards from their experience with teachers in classrooms to their views of the school itself.

On the student side, only one Time 1 scale (student perceptions of home–school communications, Scale C) distinguishes amongst some classrooms in ways that the teacher profiles would predict. This is not surprising. Because the fall surveys were administered early in the school year (October), teachers, students, and parents had not had much opportunity to become sufficiently acquainted with one another to permit discriminating judgments. By Time 2 (spring, May/June data collection) we would expect both students and parents to make more discriminations amongst classrooms.

Indeed, we do find more differences in Time 2 (spring) data. Two student scales discriminate amongst classrooms at Time 2. Student perception of home–school communication (Scale C) and student perception of student-teacher collaboration (Scale E) discriminate as the profiles would predict – that is, teachers who were identified as more collaborative from the interviews were also seen in the surveys as more collaborative by students. Although statistically reliable differences are not always found, the mean scale scores show that students generally perceive that more home–school communication occurs with collaborative teachers than with their non-collaborative counterparts.

Focusing now on parent scales for Time 2, five parent scales discriminate amongst classrooms. The statistically reliable differences that emerged again supported the collaborative/non-collaborative distinctions derived from the qualitative data. For example, with respect to Scale 6 (parent perception of parent–school communication), the mean scale scores indicate that parents feel free to and/or do contact collaborative teachers more than they do non-collaborative teachers.

These results justify the use of multiple measures: if quantitative data only were used at Time 1, and even at Time 2, important distinctions between and amongst classrooms would go unnoticed. On the other hand, apparently important differences in perceptions in the qualitative data do not always predict the results of quantitative analysis.

THE SIGNIFICANCE OF COLLABORATIVE PRACTICE FOR PARENTS AND TEACHERS

The questions we posed were:

Do teachers see themselves as acting in a collaborative way with parents?

Do their actions (as seen by parents and students) reflect these collaborative attitudes?

What the chapter tells us

Summarizing the work of many, Chrispeels (1992, pp. 9, 10) reports the following characteristics of effective schools. They demonstrate:

- instructional leadership by principal and staff;
- clear school mission;
- opportunity to learn and student time on task;
- high expectations;
- frequent monitoring of student progress;
- a positive, safe, orderly learning environment;
- positive home–school relations.

The qualitative data in this study reveal that collaborative teachers create a classroom setting that reflects many of these characteristics. They convey to students and parents alike the message that in their classrooms students work hard and 'learn lots' (opportunity to learn). They do this in an environment that is perceived to be conducive to learning and in which students are kept informed of what is expected of them (high expectations) and how well they have achieved those goals (frequent monitoring of student progress). The collaborative teacher extends learning opportunities beyond the school house (student time on task) by keeping parents informed of what youngsters are learning in class, how well they are doing, and how parents can support learning goals and activities in the home (positive home–school relations). All this is done in a way that conveys to students and parents that they are engaged in a mutually respectful, mutually beneficial relationship that is working toward a common goal – student learning and success.

Other teachers convey, usually wordlessly, the message received by one parent: 'he figures he can handle it himself better.'

The implications for school improvement

Collaborative teachers, then, nurture the kind of 'proximal variables' that Wang and her colleagues (Wang, Haertel, and Walberg, 1993) describe as having a strong effect on student learning. They describe these as student characteristics (metacognitive, cognitive, motivational, and affective variables); classroom practices (management, instruction, and quality of teacher–

student relationship); and home and community educational contexts. For them 'The home environment includes not only the educational characteristics of the home but also parent activities and attitudes that support student learning' (p. 278). It is the 'curriculum of the home' referred to earlier.

The second of the two proximal variables identified by Wang and pertinent to this study is the relationship between teacher and student. Both academic interactions and teacher and student social interactions are important (Wang, Haertel and Walberg, 1993, p. 277). Collaborative teachers demonstrate an ability to focus on and maintain a balance between both aspects of the teacher–student relationship. They do so with positive effect upon students' and parents' attitudes.

Collaborative and non-collaborative teachers differ in the extent to which power to influence the triadic relationship is left to the student. The former group of teachers takes on the responsibility to establish links between the two adult members of the triad. Students in these classrooms are not the sole link between home and school. Collaborative teachers act on a belief that when parents are brought into the relationship, it makes education **'easier . . . for the kid, the parent, and the teacher, because there's three of you involved now instead of just two.'**

7

Seeing the Teacher as Partner

Special thanks to . . . all the teachers who really did make a difference: Mrs Webb, Ms Risutto, Ms Scherer, Mr Mann, Mrs Edgar, Mr Rowett, Richard Mitten, Ron Krikac, Diana Spradling, Mario Pena, Leon Bryant, Larry Pedicord, Edith Skinner, Elizabeth Smith, Robert Williams, Judy Leibowitz, James Kozminsky, and also Peggy, whose last name kept changing, so simply Peggy.

(Kelsey Grammer, *So Far*)

Here we again examine the theme of teacher collaboration, with a different data set, and emphasizing the perspectives of the students, together with parents. (As we have learned from previous analyses, attempting to understand student perspectives without taking into account parent influences is unproductive.) We have seen, in Chapter 5, that teacher practices with respect to parent involvement are not easily changed. Yet in Chapter 6 we saw that parents and students can distinguish between more and less collaborative teachers with some precision (by the spring, although not in the fall).

Since the student perspective is not often given, some background information will help the reader to understand the questions we posed for this analysis.

TEACHER/STUDENT COLLABORATION AND STUDENT COMMITMENT

We believe, on the basis of the studies reported in the previous chapters, that teacher/student collaboration is vital to student commitment, **especially when the collaboration is supported by the home.** Others from different perspectives have made similar suggestions.

In one of the early sub-studies which supported the Coproduction Project, Raddysh (1992) focused upon the drop-out issue. She identified twenty students, ten of whom graduated and ten of whom did not. The two groups were closely matched, one on one, in other respects – elementary school attended, family circumstances, academic record in elementary school, age, and gender. Raddysh interviewed the students regarding their elementary school experience, and developed a series of contrasts between the individuals making up the two groups. Her findings strongly supported a (slightly amended) participation/identification model (Finn, 1989) of the drop-out process. The graduates, when in elementary school, became actively engaged in school activities, in and out of the classroom. They were strongly supported by their parents in this engagement, and in planning their later academic and work careers. As Raddysh summarizes her work:

> I believe the family support the graduates talked of is critical in differentiating the two groups. . . . The family's values permeate the interactions about learning and school that occur in the home each day, even before the child starts school. The graduates in this group shared the feeling that their families had been extremely supportive of school. Their parents expected them to do well and supported their endeavors
>
> (1992, p. 121)

This case-study work in British Columbia essentially parallels the longitudinal (19 year) studies reported by Garnier, Stein and Jacobs (1997) in the USA. The student/teacher collaboration essential to school success for the students in the groups Raddysh studied was based upon the virtually daily preparation for schooling which occurred in the family, and was described in Chapter 3.

Such collaboration may require changes in power relationships in classrooms and schools. Sarason (1990) argues that this issue must be addressed if schools are to be restructured. Shedd and Bacharach note the need for consistency: 'If schools are to teach creativity and problem-solving and cooperation and involvement, they must practice them, not just in the classroom but at all levels of the system' (1991, pp. 193, 194). Sykes (1990) notes that power shifts are already occurring in classrooms. The 'power equalizing' theme recurs in many different perspectives on school restructuring (Elmore, 1990). Collaboration, of course, occurs between peers, not between 'masters', as teachers were (are?) called in the UK, and (presumably) student 'servants'.

Related to issues of power are the effects of school life on students. Much of the research on student/teacher relationships has emphasized the boredom of school life. The theme emerges again and again (for example, Sedlak *et al.*, 1986; Goodlad, 1984). John Goodlad, on the basis of a massive study of schools in the USA, summarizes the typical classroom thus (our paraphrase):

> the dominant pattern of classroom organizations is a group to which the teacher most frequently relates as a whole. Much of what goes on is conditioned by the need to maintain orderly relationships among from 20 to 30 persons in relatively small space. Each student essentially works and achieves alone within a group setting. The teacher is the central figure in determining activities as well as tone of the classroom. The teacher is virtually autonomous with respect to classroom decisions.
>
> The domination of the teacher is obvious in the conduct of instruction. Most of the time the teacher is engaged in either frontal teaching, monitoring students' seatwork, or conducting quizzes. Rarely are students actively engaged in learning directly from one another or in initiating processes of interaction with teachers. When students work in smaller groups, they usually are doing the same things side by side, and these things tend to be determined by the teacher. There is a paucity of praise and correction of students' performance, as well as of teacher guidance in how to do better next time. Students generally engage in a rather narrow range of classroom activities – listening to teachers, writing answers to questions and taking tests and quizzes.

The portrait of the classroom Goodlad provides generalizes beyond the USA. One of the sub-reports of the recent Royal Commission on Education in British

Columbia, Canada, *The Learners of British Columbia*, written by Marx, Grieve and Rossner, finds that few of the students they interviewed think of school as occupying a central and meaningful place in their lives. Some students indicated that 'a particular teacher did cause them to be actively involved'. Such teachers were seen as models of learning for learning's sake. But they are rare in the experience of students.

The writers recommend that the following basic propositions guide classroom activity:

1. The learner is an active participant in the schooling process and has the responsibility for his or her own education.
2. Learning is hard work. While learning can be enjoyable, to imply that learning should be effortless is to do a disservice to the learner.
3. Individual differences are best met through the provision of options to the learner.
4. Schools should be viewed as agencies that assist learners to attain an education. Learners should use schools as they achieve an education, not take full direction from them.

(Marx, Grieve and Rossner, 1988, p. v)

With respect to teaching practices to facilitate such propositions, Marx, Grieve and Rossner recommend what we would consider to be a collaborative model of student–teacher relationships:

teaching methods must require that students be active, that they must talk and work together, . . . that they must ask questions just as much as they answer them. They must provide resources and help for others just as much as they use resources and help provided by others, and they need to work in cooperative environments just as much as they need to work in competitive environments.

(1988, p. viii)

This report also emphasizes the relationship between choice and motivation for students. Like other workers, for example teachers, students find that being able to exercise control over the conditions and processes of their work enhances their ability to complete it successfully. Much of the recent scholarly work with reference to students suggests that student can and should take responsibility for their own learning (see, e.g., Good and Brophy, 1987, p. 499). We can expect responsibility to be a crucial element in collaboration; it is addressed in the next chapter.

Our work so far leads us to expect that student perceptions of student/teacher collaboration will turn out to be vitally important to triad relationships. We expect that collaboration will involve 'mutuality', that is, some balance in the perceptions of collaboration amongst the partners, with each sharing the responsibility for initiating some forms of collaboration. We also expect that the collaboration in the classroom between teachers and students should be perceptible to parents, and that between parents and students should be perceptible to teachers. The 'visibility' of collaboration is a vital intermediate step in shaping attitudes to school (amongst parents), or to home (amongst teachers).

For students, the notion of collaboration might include such things as accepting responsibility for their own learning, active participation in the classroom, and positive relationships with teachers. For parents, collaboration might include sharing of information, including curricular and pedagogical information (e.g. how to help students learn), helping students to learn, and opportunities to observe and share in classroom activities. Our previous findings (see Chapter 5), suggest that teachers who succeed in creating collaborative relationships will be positively perceived by students and parents.

Our questions then are:

Are triad relationships seen as collaborative?

Are these perceptions mutual?

Do these perceptions seem to be connected with positive student attitudes?

HOW WE ASSESS STUDENT AND PARENT VIEWS ON TEACHER COLLABORATION

A single cohort of grade 6 and 7 students are the subjects of this report. They were enrolled in a variety of suburban schools and constitute the second-year population of the larger study (the same group was used in Chapter 5; a different group was used in Chapter 6).

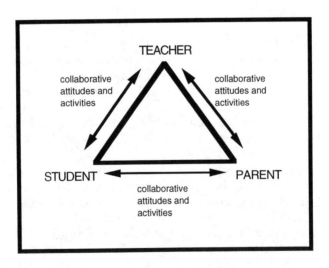

Figure 7.1   Mutual perceptions of collaborative attitudes and activities

In Step 1 we created composite portraits of four classrooms, two from each site. These portraits reported on collaboration from the perspective of each party. Figure 7.1 illustrates the six sets of opinions needed for this. In Step 2 we drew a set of comparisons, between classrooms and between the two sites. Finally in Step 3 we compared the reports of collaboration given in interviews with the survey data (from a much larger group of respondents) available for each of the four classrooms, to see whether the reports given in the interviews are representative of the opinions of other parents and students. (A detailed discussion of procedures is provided in the Chapter Notes.)

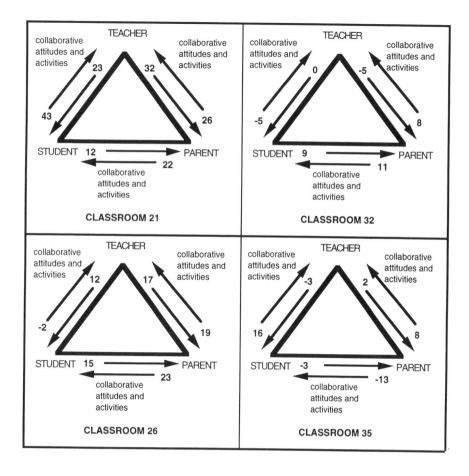

Figure 7.2 Comparing collaborative attitudes and activities in classrooms, by combining reports by and for all participants

THE PORTRAITS OF COLLABORATION

The analyses of the interviews are summarized in Figure 7.2, which reports results by classroom. The numbers represent the frequency of mention of collaborative activities. Thus in classroom 21, the teacher made 23 references to collaboration with students; students made 43 references to collaboration with teacher (the references are balanced between positive and negative, so that they are net results, and negative totals are possible).

Figure 7.2 allows us to examine the first two questions:

1. Are triad relationships seen as collaborative?
Do the classrooms (and sites) seem different in the patterns and extent of collaboration?

2. Are these perceptions mutual?
For example, in the parent/student reports, do the parents report about the same amount of collaborative activity as the students in each of the triads?

We will examine each of the dyads in turn (parent/student, teacher/parent, student/teacher).

Collaboration between parents and students

There is collaboration, but the extent varies widely between classrooms. There is some mutuality; students and parents are roughly in agreement about both the extent of their collaboration on instructional activities, and the fact that parents initiate more. Teachers report some parent/student and student/parent collaboration, but are far less aware of this activity than the immediate participants. The teacher in Classroom 35 reports many barriers to collaboration. Classrooms 21 and 35 seem somewhat different; indeed Site 2 (21 and 26) seems more collaborative generally than Site 3 (32 and 35). We will return to this issue.

Collaboration between teachers and parents

Teacher and parent reports are somewhat at variance here. Parents almost all perceive a good deal of parent/teacher collaboration, but little in the reverse direction That is to say, there is little mutuality. Student reports of parent/teacher collaboration are very limited indeed. Either it occurs at times and locations unknown to the students, or it is not important to them. There are also differences between classrooms, with Classroom 21 reporting much collaborative activity, and Classrooms 32 and 35 reporting little on balance. Parents in Classroom 32 are very inclined to see barriers.

Collaboration between students and teachers

Again there is not a high degree of mutuality here. Students and teachers report somewhat different levels of collaboration in almost every triad; there is a tendency for students to report more student-initiated collaboration. Parents are extremely alert to the collaboration between students and teachers, both on the positive and negative sides. In most triads they report more instances of both than do teachers. In some cases their reports are at variance with those of the student in the triad, suggesting different levels of expectation or preference. There are sharp differences between triads, between classrooms, and between sites.

These summaries of the patterns in four classrooms suggest a very mixed pattern of collaboration, with rather low levels of mutuality. There are obvious differences between classrooms and between sites. The perceptions of respondents will help to explain these differences.

NARROWING THE FOCUS: TWO CLASSROOMS

We will focus on the two classrooms that differ most sharply, 21 and 32. By examining the views of the members of the two triads in these classrooms, we may be able to begin to understand the features of classrooms which affect perceptions of collaboration. We will first compare the two teachers' attitudes to various aspects of collaboration between parents and students, teachers and parents, and teachers and students. Then we will trace these same aspects through comments of other triad members.

Collaboration between parents and students

Four topics emerge as important here: helping parents learn what they need to know to help their children; perceived barriers to parent/student collaboration; supporting and encouraging home instructional activity; and encouraging parent presence in the classrooms.

First, with respect to helping parents to help their children:

t32
(Q. Have you helped parents to learn things that make it possible for them to assist their child with school work?)
In a few isolated cases but not very often.

Except for encouraging them to work with the student at home. When the child is having difficulty in a subject I encourage that parent to work with them.

t21
I have demonstrated to parents things – how I go through the procedure. Maybe a research report – step-by-step directions are given to the students; my intro to every subject has a little explanation. Only through them coming in and talking to me.

In Classroom 32 parents perceive a lack of teacher attention to curriculum planning and overviews, an essential tool for parents wishing to help their children:

pb32 (two parents and two children, a and b, were interviewed for each classroom)
At the beginning of the year we got a very broad and vague overview scribbled out.

When we inquired at Easter about the projects for the term we were told they would be developed over spring break.

This may be because Teacher 32 perceives significant barriers that prevent parents from helping their children to learn:

t32

(Q. What prevents parents from doing more to help their child to learn?)
Perhaps their own inability to explain. I am thinking about math. They may be more familiar with a higher level of method of solving the problem than the child is capable of understanding. I had one instance the other day where one of the girls worked with her father for an hour and she said she just could not understand the fractions.

This contrasts with parent and student attitudes in that classroom:

pa32

(Regarding a problem the child was having with mathematics:)
We know what it was; we spent 20 minutes one evening and he is now back getting A's again.

sa32

(Q. Do your parents help you learn?)
S: They help me learn by . . . instead of just the normal classroom techniques, they give me some tips to do some things and they have other ways that work a bit better than the normal classroom ways.

sb32

(Q. Do you ask your parents for help with homework from time to time?)
S: Yep.

Teacher 21 also perceives barriers, but of quite different kinds:

t21

There are a lot of parents still unable to meet in that type of situation in the classroom; not that they don't want to be here, they just can't.

Third, with respect to parent presence in classrooms, the two teachers show contrasting attitudes. Teacher 32 seems ambivalent:

t32

(Q. Could parents help in the school more than they do?)
I think they could. It would have to be a consensus between teacher and parent about their role.

It is a difficult question – I would like to say that it would be wonderful to have them all the time.

(Q. Do you welcome parents in your classroom?)
Very little.

(Q. How would you describe the relationship between parents and teachers?)
Striving effort to bridge the gap. There is a feeling within the school they [parents] run the show or would like to; resentment would be one word in isolated cases.

On the other hand, Teacher 21 feels supported:

t21

(Q. Could parents help in the school more than they do?)
Help with me has been wonderful although there are a few students who I am concerned with their parents.

This teacher describes a variety of instances of parent classroom involvement, for example:

t21
I had a parent in the other day and she was interested in what I do; she likes snakes – she brought a corn snake. She set up a little exercise for the students to do at the end of it.

Asked about student reaction to parent participation in the classroom, the two teachers again show very different attitudes:

t32
I am not sure that it would benefit a particular child to have a particular parent there.

t21
I see a feeling of 'I am glad my mum is there'.

Student perceptions do not reflect teacher attitudes in Classroom 32; in response to the question 'Do students accept the presence of parents in the class?' the responses are:

sa32
S: Yes, they do.

sb32
(Q. Do students in your classroom accept the parents when they come in? They don't feel disturbed by their presence?)
No.

There is similar student response in Classroom 21.

sb21
(Q. What is it that Mr S. or the kids do to make parents feel welcome?)
Well, we're having fun and we're learning new things on Canada.

(Q. And that would make parents feel welcome to come in?)
Yeah.

sa21
(Q. Do you think parents are welcome in your classroom?)
Yeah, definitely.

The contrasts between the two classrooms in this dimension, collaboration between parents and students, are sharp; the quotations help to account for the different levels of collaboration reported. Much here seems to depend upon teacher willingness to demonstrate to the students that **the teacher accepts and encourages parent participation in student learning.**

Collaboration between teachers and parents

The collaboration between teachers and parents can be expected to reflect the attitudes already reported. Parents in Classroom 32 perceive teacher-made barriers; there is reluctance to seek assistance, either from the 'class mums' who are asked to volunteer to help each year in this school or more generally from parents:

pa32
The homeroom mothers – very few requests this year.

pb32
(Q. Are there ways in which you and the teacher work together in your child's education?)
It would not appear so. Nothing has been asked of us.

sb32
(Q. Does your teacher sometimes call home for help?)
Not that I know of.

sa32
Uhm . . . only if we're going on a class party, like we're going on today. If we're going on a field trip.

By contrast Teacher 21 actively seeks out parent assistance:

t21
We start off with me taking time out to phone them to invite them in; they feel extremely surprised. The response is positive but they aren't used to it.

The following comments refer to a multi-class/age activity concerning an event in Canadian history, 'driving the last spike' in the link between East and West provided by the Canadian Pacific Railway.

t21
We had a Canada Day celebration – driving the last spike. Each multi-grade class designed a piece of a map of Canada.

I tried to involve 6–10 parents.

Parents got to see how students worked as a group.

It gave parents from the classrooms involved an opportunity to see what we were doing in school.

This activity was memorable for parents and for students:

pa21
(T21) and I together were going from table to table helping them.

sb21
(Q. Have there ever been parents helping out in your classroom during the day?)
Yeah, when we work on our multi-age projects.

(I: Is that what this was here?)
Yeah . . . our parents help . . . parents come in and help us kids.

(Q. Have other parents come in to show different things or to help with projects like that?)
Yeah, sometimes.

Again by contrast, Teacher 32 made a decision that limited parent involvement even at home:

pb32
The decision to get all project work done in school; it was because he wanted it to all be the child's work, but it doesn't help to build relationship with parents.

With respect to other instructional activities also, Teacher 21 seems deliberately to adopt processes with collaborative elements; he speaks of holding students accountable and ensuring that parents understand the work, the basis for grading, and their helping role:

t21
After every quiz or written work parents are to read and sign it giving feedback and helping the student with math if they have had difficulty.

Collaboration between students and teachers

There are three main elements here: one, the sense of student responsibility for learning; two, teacher effects upon students (often dependent upon the amount of individual help teachers provide); and three, student–student effects, which are dependent upon the classroom climate created by the teacher.

Teacher 21 teaches responsibility; this allows students to work independently; Teacher 32 has reservations about student acceptance of responsibility.

t21
If I give an example of good work the majority of the class really work to make sure it is to that standard to the best of their ability.

They have got into that organizational habit of making sure of what's for homework; they write it down in the student planner.

I allow in math certain students to move ahead under certain guidelines; they use a teacher guide to self-mark their work.

t32
(Q. Do you believe that children can take responsibility for their own education?)
There are a number who could but 10 or 11-year-olds over half will have a lot of difficulty organizing on their own. Less than half are capable of doing it entirely on their own. They are still children and they don't understand the full responsibilities and necessities.

(Q. Do children in your class have opportunities to choose what or how they will learn?)
In certain cases. Most often not . . . what they learn is not up to them.

Student reactions tend to match teacher expectations:

pb21
(Q. Do you feel he takes responsibility for his own education?)
From the beginning of the year that has changed . . . now I just kind of glance at it – he's got everything written down – and we don't sign it every day. I still check every day – 'do you have homework?' – but now he's very responsible.

He is taking major control of his education.

sa32
(Q. Who decides things on how you study or what you study?)
Any range of teachers that I have.

The teachers also seem different with respect to teacher–student effects, particularly the help provided to individual students:

pb21
He needs the extra help. But he has improved tremendously.
(I: Oh, has he?)
P(F): Yeah, his independence and his confidence level are much better.
(I: Why do you think that is?)
(Teacher 21).
(I: The teacher?)
A hundred per cent . . . yeah . . . he has really worked with him.

sa21
(Q. How does he (T21) make it different or special?)
Well, lots of times we do lots of activities that usually other classes don't get to do, so that's really the difference that we have.

sb21
(Q. What do they like about him?)
That he's nice . . . and he helps me.

In the other classroom, parents report differently:

pb32
He got a B at Christmas – he hadn't understood one concept in math. The teacher hadn't taken him aside and helped him once. We know what it was; we spent 20 minutes one evening and he is now back getting A's again.

With regard to student–student effects, Classroom 32 clearly contains some problems:

pa32
There is an athletic group of boys in class and a lot of teasing going on. Our boy was out of sync with level of maturity . . . the long-term attitudes haven't been dealt with. These are class dynamics that other parents have noticed; it is not just us that has had the difficulty; our son has been the recipient . . . I wrote a letter to (T32) and said that the children were being relentless.

(Q. How does your child feel about school this year?)
Uncomfortable. He goes out there every day and tries again. He loves his English lessons and his band. As far as class is concerned social factors have had a large part to play.

sa32
(Q. Has your attitude changed at all during the school year?)
Yes. At the beginning of the school year I was looking at it as 'oh, great, all those teasing boys are in my class', but now I'm looking to it as 'oh, who cares about them'.

(Q. Any changes in your attitude towards the school or the classroom during this school year?)
Uhm . . . except I really hate those boys.

Some boys discourage you. They say 'oh you're so bad' so you don't really feel like you're actually doing good.

There are clear differences between these two classrooms. One is strongly collaborative in tone, the other is not. We are describing two very different teacher orientations to triad collaboration. The contrasts here also suggest the ways in which teacher attitudes and practices 'leak' from one dyad into the others, for example from teacher–student relations in Classroom 32 to student–student relations. The extent to which teacher practices are known to parents is also obvious here. 'If schools are to teach creativity and problem-solving and cooperation and involvement, they must practice them' (Shedd and Bacharach, 1990, pp. 193, 194); our Teacher 21 is in this respect an exemplary teacher, but Teacher 32 has yet to learn how to model these values for students.

COMPARING TWO DIFFERENT ANALYSES

We first look at the general pattern of scale scores. (The scale labels are given in Figure 7.3.) When we compare the results reported here (Table 7.1) for the four classrooms with the results of quantitative analyses reported elsewhere (e.g. Chapters 5, 6), we see again that scale scores worsen (i.e. rise), and parent and student ratings of school decline over the school year.

With respect to Classrooms 21 and 32, the following patterns emerge: for the parent scales, 1 through 7 are those most likely to be affected by teacher practices; for Classroom 21, four of these seven improve, and three worsen. For Classroom 32, all seven worsen, with those reflecting teacher–home communication (SC 3, 4, 5) very sharply different at the end of the year. For the student scales, A through G are the most sensitive to teacher activities; for Classroom 21, 6 of the seven improve; note the positive shift in Scale A, student–parent communication about school. For Classroom 32, there are few changes; note, however, the sharp decline in Scale C, home–school communication.

For the four classrooms, Classroom 21 is more positively perceived than most on almost all scales. On Scale 5, teacher concern about parent involvement (as perceived by parents), this classroom is very strongly perceived

LIST OF SCALES	
Parent attitude to/perceptions of	**Student attitude to/perceptions of**
Sc 1. student/teacher communication	Scale A. communications with parents
Sc 2. student/parent communication	Scale B. student values school
Sc 3. teacher/parent communication (instruction)	Scale C. school/home communication
Sc 4. teacher/parent communication (general)	Scale D. personal efficacy
Sc 5. teacher concern about parent involvement	Scale E. student/teacher collaboration
Sc. 6. parent/school communication	Scale F. parent valuing school
Sc 7. parent values schooling	Scale G. peer group values
Sc 8. school climate	Scale H. school climate
Sc 9. parent efficacy	

Figure 7.3 List of scales used

Table 7.1 Mean scale scores for Time 3 (fall) and 4 (spring), by classroom. (low = positive for scale scores; high = positive for ratings)

	TIME 3					TIME 4			
SCALES	CL21	CL26	CL32	CL35	SCALES	CL21	CL26	CL32	CL35
SC 1	2.18	2.49	2.32	2.21	SC 1	1.95	2.46	2.71	1.96
SC 2	2.11	1.93	1.82	1.98	SC 2	1.88	2.04	2.00	1.75
SC 3	2.40	2.90	2.61	2.71	SC 3	2.34	3.16	3.34	2.64
SC 4	1.93	2.70	2.59	2.49	SC 4	2.08	2.64	3.20	2.33
SC 5	1.65	1.90	2.01	2.00	SC 5	1.51	1.89	2.40	1.87
SC 6	1.65	2.09	1.90	1.95	SC 6	1.82	1.96	2.17	1.71
SC 7	1.64	1.78	1.45	1.41	SC 7	1.66	1.69	1.50	1.39
SC 8	2.11	2.06	1.83	1.82	SC 8	2.20	1.96	2.00	1.71
SC 9	2.15	2.16	2.09	2.00	SC 9	2.04	2.20	2.07	2.13
PRATE	7.08	7.56	7.75	7.50	**PRATE**	6.25	7.44	7.26	7.50
SC A	1.68	1.80	1.75	2.09	SC A	1.33	1.93	1.79	2.01
SC B	1.78	1.93	1.50	1.75	SC B	1.60	1.62	1.68	1.80
SC C	1.97	2.89	2.58	3.02	SC C	2.08	2.94	3.57	2.95
SC D	1.52	1.82	1.72	1.67	SC D	1.47	1.64	1.58	1.64
SC E	2.00	2.92	2.88	2.10	SC E	1.83	2.45	2.82	1.94
SC F	1.86	2.20	1.88	1.80	SC F	1.80	1.79	1.84	1.76
SC G	2.21	2.67	2.00	1.84	SC G	2.15	2.14	1.98	2.07
SC H	1.86	2.41	2.23	2.32	SC H	2.08	2.02	2.25	2.20
STRATE	7.33	7.00	6.75	7.00	**STRATE**	6.58	6.56	7.67	6.91

indeed. On most student scales, the absolute values for Classroom 21 are better than those for any other classroom. In particular, Classroom 21 stands out with regard to Scales C and E, home–school communication and student–teacher collaboration, the most important of the student scales with respect to predicting attitudes to school according to the causal model we developed (in the pilot study described in Chapter 1) to guide these analyses.

However, the ratings of school are not linked with these classroom scores. For both parents and students, the ratings tend to fall between Times 3 and 4 (fall to spring) for all classrooms. Classroom 21, although clearly a very successful classroom, does not help to maintain the rating of the school, amongst either parents or students. In Classroom 32, however, the school rating improves noticeably amongst students, though not amongst parents. Certainly the collaborative classroom generates much more positive student attitudes than the non-collaborative one, but these do not generalize beyond the classroom to the school level, contrary to our suggestion in the previous chapter.

STUDENTS AND TEACHER COLLABORATION

Our questions for this chapter were:

Are triad relationships seen as collaborative?

Are these perceptions mutual?

Do these perceptions seem to be connected with positive student attitudes?

What the chapter tells us

Teacher attitudes and practices can have a substantial impact upon the perception of collaboration – the sense of partnership that can be generated amongst parents and the sense of teacher/student collaboration that can be generated amongst students. Even subtle differences between teachers' practices are perceptible to parents and students and some practices are strongly preferred.

The teacher attitudes to parents that predict collaboration can be summarized rather simply from the interview data: a valuing of parental assistance; a realization that students and parents do in fact collaborate at home; and an acceptance that student classroom attitudes reflect parent attitudes to classroom and teacher. These are not surprising, given the information presented in previous chapters. But these attitudes do differentiate between teachers.

The teacher attitudes to students that predict collaboration can also be summarized from the interview data: parents in Classroom 21 noted the teacher impact upon student responsibility: 'his independence and his confidence level are much better'. The student comments 'he's nice . . . and he helps me'. This comment does not reflect the master/servant relationship of some traditional classrooms; it does reflect the findings of the massive review of the predictors of school learning already cited in the previous chapter. Both academic interactions and social interactions are important to students (and contribute to student achievement; Wang, Haertel and Walberg, 1993, p. 277).

The implications for school improvement

Collaborative teachers maintain a balance between both aspects of the teacher–student relationship; their impact upon students does not take place in an affectively neutral classroom:

> 'Wasn't everyone you know saved by that one English teacher who gave you a glimpse of a better life' asks a mother who grew up in a New England mill town . . . 'Mine would invite me over for espresso after school and give me books to read'.
> (Atlas, 1997, p. 35)

If schools are to enhance the lives of students, such interventions, occurring at critical moments, can shape student engagement or commitment to schooling and drop-out decisions, and many other later decisions. However, in an era of 'engaged' parents (Atlas, 1997) teachers must see themselves as collaborators with both students and parents. A commitment to such 'teacher engagement' is more likely on a school-wide basis (Louis and Smith, 1992), although of course our data have shown that individual teachers can and do make a difference. In subsequent chapters we will return to this theme.

8

The Responsible Student: Influences on the Development of Responsibility

He is taking major control of his education.

(Parent)

This chapter examines student acceptance of responsibility for learning as one area in which parents might make a difference. Acceptance of responsibility by students, we believe, helps to account for student 'engagement' or 'bonding' with school (Finn, 1989) and for student achievement.

STUDENT RESPONSIBILITY

The child is best served when the institutions responsible for the socialization and the education of the young work collaboratively (Hoover-Dempsey, Bassler, and Brissie, 1987). But collaboration requires acceptance of responsibility by all parties, and student acceptance of responsibility for learning cannot be assumed.

We presented some of the arguments for a 'power equalizing' approach to promoting student responsibility in the previous chapter. Others who accept these values argue that student responsibility is supported by 'teaching for understanding':

> the core principles of this new vision of instruction include (1) a conception of knowledge as constructed by the learner and therefore situated in the context of prior knowledge, skills, values, and beliefs; (2) a conception of teacher as guide, as co-constructor of students' knowledge; and (3) a conception of the classroom as a community of learners, in which shared goals and standards, an atmosphere of mutual trust, and norms for behavior support students in taking the risks and making the sustained efforts entailed in serious learning
>
> (Talbert and McLaughlin, 1993, p. 169)

But such in-school influences are only part of the story. Family attitudes to schooling, and particularly the extent to which the family values schools and schooling, might strongly influence student attitudes towards accepting responsibility. Our previous analyses have demonstrated considerable family influence on other student attitudes.

Furthermore, as we showed in Chapter 3, student relationships with teachers **are themselves often shaped by parent attitudes.** Indeed in every chapter so far we have shown that the influences within the student/teacher/parent triad are strongly interconnected. We anticipate that student responsibility will be shaped by both teachers and parents, but neither influence will be independent.

For this chapter we use survey data to allow testing of the relationships between various kinds of attitudes. Then we look at case studies of relationships within triads. We seek to identify:

1. **the student attitudes associated with student feelings of responsibility towards school work; and**

2. **the home (parent attitudes and practices) and classroom (teacher attitudes and practices) influences which shape changes in student acceptance of responsibility over the school year.**

TRACING CONNECTIONS IN THE SURVEY DATA

The issue of student responsibility emerged from previous analyses, and we had not anticipated its importance in constructing our survey and interview instruments. We did, however, include items that related to the topic, and these items were used in constructing a new scale, student responsibility (see Figure 8.1).

This analysis used the Year 1 and 2 populations of the Coproduction Project (see Chapter Notes). We calculated scale scores for the participants as in previous chapters, and then developed tables of simple correlations between the scores. A number of relevant inferences can be drawn from the relationships between scale scores. (See Chapter Notes for the details. Note that the strong relationships with Scale B are irrelevant – many of the questions used as a measure of responsibility are drawn from that scale.)

STUDENT SURVEY ITEMS FOR THE SCALE 'STUDENT RESPONSIBILITY'

.30* 21. It is important to me that I graduate from high school.

.39* 25. I feel comfortable makings suggestions to my teacher about activities we could do in the classroom.

.43* 27. I don't stay home from school unless I'm really sick.

.50* 28. It's important to me that my teacher knows that I am doing my best in school.

.51* 32. It's important to me that my parent(s) know that I am doing my best in school.

.57* 33. It bothers me if I am late handing in assignments.

.46* 41. I stay away from school whenever I can. (REVERSED)

* item-total correlation, showing the importance of the item to the scale.

Figure 8.1 Responsibility survey items

The strong and consistent statistical relationships in the fall and spring suggest that

1. student perceptions of level of responsibility changes during the school year, because the fall (SR3) and spring (SR4) responsibility scales are correlated but not strongly;
2. student talk with parents about school may be an important influence on sense of responsibility, because Scale A (communication with parents) is more strongly associated with responsibility in spring than in the fall;
3. student personal efficacy is also much more strongly associated with responsibility in the spring than in the fall.

Furthermore, since the mean scores (shown in Table 1 in the Chapter Notes) decline, it is probable that for most individual students scale scores decline between the fall and spring.

It is easier to understand the possible significance of these relationships if we recall the ideas within the scales which we attempted to capture in some of the survey questions (Figure 8.2).

Additionally, the set of relationships between scales suggested by these correlations, when arrayed in a chart, become more easily interpretable (Figure 8.3).

'Associations' here means typically occurring together, so that more positive scores on student responsibility occur together with more positive scores on Scale B, Scale D, and Scale E. Some attitudes also vary together – for example, personal efficacy and communications with parents.

One way of interpreting this set of relationships, then, is to think of them as a kind of supportive network, within which the student develops (or doesn't) a sense of personal responsibility. If the supports are in place, the student becomes more responsible in the course of the school year. Home and school influences both affect the student. During the school year the in-school element influencing sense of responsibility is the degree of collaboration with the

---

Scale A: communications with parents

.58* 13. I feel comfortable asking my parents for help with my homework.

.59* 17. I feel comfortable talking to my parents about school work.

Scale D: perception of personal efficacy

.65* 48. When I make up my mind to do well in school I usually succeed.

.67* 50. I feel that I have the ability to do well in school if I want to.

Scale E: perception of student/teacher collaboration

.56* 25. I feel comfortable making suggestions to my teacher about activities we could do in the classroom.

.54* 30. My teacher is interested in hearing my opinions even when I disagree with her/him.

Figure 8.2 Centrally important items from scales A, B, D and E
(*measures of correlation between item and the whole scale)

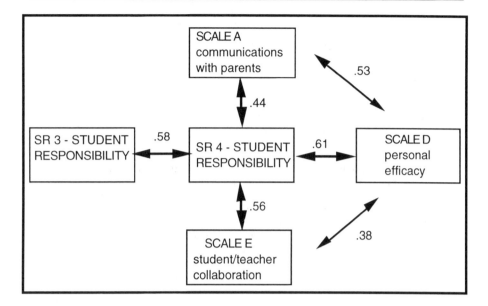

Figure 8.3 Relationships between scales, Time 4

teacher perceived by the student. The home factors of most importance are communications with parents, linked with sense of personal efficacy. The qualitative data analysis may shed more light on the details of these relationships.

INFLUENCES SHAPING STUDENT RESPONSIBILITY

For the case studies a subset of students was selected on the basis of two criteria – first that the responsibility scale score had changed by at least half a point during the school year; second that student, parent, and teacher interviews were all available for analysis. We here examine the attitudes and opinions of a group of students for whom perception of personal responsibility for learning had increased or declined during their school year.

The results will be presented as brief reports on selected triads. Parent, student, and teacher perceptions of interactions around the general theme of responsibility will be presented in turn. Each of the four triads shows a distinctive pattern of events and activities. (Note that teachers were asked about general classroom activities, rather than specifically about individual children.)

(Triad labels are arbitrary; P = parent, M and F = mother, father; I = interviewer; T = teacher.)

Triad K: An optimal portrait

In this triad there is a sense of difficulties overcome, and improvement in the student, partly as a result of out-of-school interests which have generated a new interest in and valuing of school.

Parent perceptions of student responsibility
The parents feel confident that their son has improved in acceptance of responsibility over the previous year.

> P(F): I think he's pretty much on track with his homework which wasn't the case for the last couple of years and so something he's doing is right.
> P(M): Because he realizes that he's growing up; we stress that school is his work.
> P(F): He's usually on time – sometimes he's a bit of a dawdler but usually he's on time – and he goes every day and he participates in everything and he doesn't make trouble at school and so I guess that means he probably likes it.
> P(M): Yeah – we're having far less negative reports and I guess that has got to be positive.
> P(M): I can't remember a time when we've had to sit him down like we did last year and say to him 'okay, I., you've got to have this done'.
> P(F): And he is doing his work in a nice, orderly fashion instead of getting two weeks behind and then suddenly doing two weeks work in three nights.
> P(M): So obviously he's taking some responsibility for his work because he has made a decision and he has got to get that work in on time.

They believe that outside interests with career potential have contributed to this change of attitude:

> P(F): I thought that he would have stuff outside and then school would be forgotten but it has really helped everything that he has done because he knows that if he doesn't get his school work done then he can't go to (inaudible) or he can't go flying that day or whatever.
> P(F): And so it has helped him have discipline in everything. . . . he knows what he needs if he wants to continue doing what he really enjoys. So I think if he hadn't of joined Air Cadets and you had asked that question (re academic future) I would of said 'Grade Ten' because his ability sometimes is not that great.
> P(F): Like I didn't think it would work with I. to have activities outside of school because [he] was having so much trouble with school but now I've really changed my mind and I think it's really important for the kids to have activities outside because his activities outside have helped him focus better on school.
> P(F): Also I. has been really involved in Air Cadets and he knows that if he wants to go further in Air Cadets as an adult – like join the Air Force or something – that he'll need Grade Twelve.

Additionally some events in the school have contributed:

> P(F): I think the other thing that has made him really feel that he wants to do better is there's a guy at school who is in a wheelchair and since I. really seems to like helping people the teacher has asked him if he can help him whenever he needs help – to push the wheelchair if they're going somewhere or to make sure that he has got his books or that type of thing – and I think that I. feels like he's doing an important job.
> P(F): I don't know what they're doing over there but they've certainly sparked his interest in a lot of different things.

Parent perceptions of help to student

The parents have also contributed to the attitude shift:

> P(M): I think the question is whether I. sees us as a team member.
> P(F): I think he does . . . he knows that he can come to us for help . . . he never asks for something and then doesn't get help.

Parent perceptions of relations with teacher

The teacher too has been communicating regarding the student's progress; she is skilled at dealing with students as individuals and provides help on an individual basis. Perhaps consequentially the relationship between students and teacher is characterized by mutual respect:

> P(F): Teacher had phoned me and said that I. had a project that was late and she said that it's the first one that he has been late on this year.
> P(F): I find it amazing when I go in there and it's just about time to quit and she has got all of the kids sitting at their desks and she is at the front and each child manages to say how they felt about the day – and there's nobody shouting and there's nobody pushing in – and then she goes around and does all of the diaries and everything. So there's certainly a real feeling of cooperation and of respect.
> P(F): She even manages to draw out the kids that are quieter . . . the girls tend to be quieter because they are teenagers and they tend to be a bit shy and so all of them get to say.
> P(F): Sometimes he'll go in at quarter to eight in the morning if he's having problems with his math and he knows that she's there at seven thirty and so he will take his book in and he will work with her for a while – and she doesn't mind putting aside her marking or whatever it was she had planned to do to work with him.
> P(F): I've noticed in the classroom that it's definitely a mutual respect in that I. really likes her and respects her opinion – it's the reciprocal – in fact the kids really respect her.
> P(F): She just shows a real interest in all of the kids . . . not just in I.

The teacher also accommodates parents' desires to collaborate in the classroom:

> P(F): She will schedule . . . if you really want to help in the classroom and you show a real interest in a particular project . . . like I was really interested in helping with this Japan project and she scheduled me for an hour every day – the same hour so that if another parent wanted to come in they could come in during another hour. She is very organized and she has got it all really worked out.

Additionally the introduction of student-led conferencing (a system of reporting to parents in which the student reports on his or her progress to the parents, in the presence of the teacher, and then goals are set jointly for dealing with weaknesses) has given parents a stronger sense of participation:

> (I): Do you think his teacher sees you as a partner or team member in his education this year?
> P(F): I think so because this year must be the first year they've put in that program where the child tells you what they've been learning at school and they have to fill out a progress sheet and bring it home.

Student perceptions of acceptance of responsibility
The student has clear notions about responsibility:

> (I): Whose job is it to make sure that you learn?
> (S): More mine.
> (I): Why is that?
> (S): Because it shouldn't be your parents' responsibility to ask you if you're through with your homework and all of that.
> (I): You say 'more mine' which leads me to believe that you think it's kind of partly somebody else's job too?
> (S): Well, it's some of your parents' job to help you out but it's more your responsibility.

Student perceptions of parent willingness to help

He is also confident of help when needed:

> (I): Could you describe for me the ways in which your parents help you learn?
> (S): Well, if I'm ever stuck on homework I can just bring it to my dad and he'll show me how to do it.
> (I): Do you and your parents work well together?
> (S): Yeah.
> (I): No disagreements?
> (S): Not really.
> (I): No fighting?
> (S): No.
> (I): Nobody gets frustrated occasionally?
> (S): Well, sometimes me.

The classroom setting, and the teacher, are supportive. The teacher calls parents if there is a problem:

> (I) What about your classroom – what is it like as a place to learn?
> (S): It's pretty good because the teacher helps me out as much as she can and there's not really anybody talking that much and so you can pay attention to your work and you can just keep working.
> (I): So she has called home how many times?
> (S): She calls home when I'm not keeping up and she phones and tells when I am just so that they know.
> (I): Does she call home ever for other reasons?
> (S): Sometimes for homework.
> (I): Has she done that in your case?
> (S): Yeah.
> (I): I assumed that when she called home for homework it was because it wasn't done?
> (S): Yeah just to make sure that I keep up a little bit better.

Teacher perceptions of student responsibility

The teacher perceptions of the classroom are at odds with those of the student and the parents. With respect to parent volunteers in the classroom, she was surprised by the response:

(T): Surprising – I have never had parents volunteer to come into the room before; I had three or four volunteers and they showed up. Maybe it was the fact that they were invited. I don't know.
(T): The kids were a little leery at first; in the end I don't think any of them even noticed.
(T): Yes. I would do it again, I know so.

She is troubled by the difficulties she encounters regularly with student behaviour:

(T): I have one who has been suspended. I have three or four boys . . . who lose it three or four times a day.
(T): Taking responsibility? Some of them are at the point where they don't even care.

Teacher perceptions of parent relations

She has been trying a technique recommended in the project, the 'good news phone call', and trying to encourage student responsibility by giving students curricular choices:

(T): I make the good news phone calls – 'he is keeping up on the homework and he got it done'.
(T): At the beginning of the year I was making the choices for them – they have different activities. Initially I showed them how; now I give them a list and say 'choose'.

Summary

Activities at home, including outside interests, are supportive of high expectations for the student. Furthermore, despite the gloomy view of the teacher, which we assume results from the very high expectations she holds for herself and for the students, it is clear from the perceptions of the parents and the student that the classroom is a productive workplace, in which students are encouraged to accept responsibility for their own learning, and the teacher's relationships with parents are supportive of that goal. This case provides clear evidence of the folly of relying on the testimony of one observer in assessing an instructional relationship – **even when that observer is the teacher.**

Triad I: Strained relations

Parent perceptions of student responsibility

The parents acknowledge that the student is not accepting responsibility:

(PF): He had six weeks work to do in one weekend, after Christmas . . . . He told us he lost it . . . he said I did it and I can't find it.
(PM): But we didn't believe him.
(PF): We have to police A. If you expect him to come in and put the books out and start doing his homework, he wouldn't.
(I): What would you like to see him do differently?
(PM): I'd like to see him be more enthusiastic about doing his work. He still has a tendency to put things off.

Parent perceptions of help to student
Although his parents are supportive and help him, this is sometimes difficult:

> If there's anything on, like science fair, we always go and support him.
> (PF): We go to everything.
> (I): Do you feel comfortable helping him?
> (PM): Oh yeah. He enjoys it.
> (PF): Well it's nice to see your child learning.
> (I): Is there anything that prevents you from doing more to help him learn?
> (PM): When he gets really upset . . . . that's again when he gets way behind.

Parent relations with teacher
As a consequence of these problems the parents find the student-led conference, or any contacts with the teacher, difficult:

> (I): When you've met with the teacher, what kinds of things have you typically discussed?
> (PM): Oh, just the negative things that A. has been doing. She . . . will mention some things that he's done a good job [on], but she spends way more time on the negative.

Indeed there is conflict with the teacher regarding helping the student, arising out of the student responsibility issue:

> (PF): She wouldn't have done that unless I asked and he needs that help. She reckons that it's not her responsibility and she says that to me quite often: it's not my job – he has to learn this by himself.
> (PF): Her attitude was 'he's responsible for himself'. We're his mom and dad and so we're responsible for him.
> (I): What words come to mind when I mention the relationship between parents and teachers?
> (PM): A strain I'd say because I'm thinking of A. We've had it only with this one teacher. Before it's been very comfortable.

Student perceptions of acceptance of responsibility
Despite the obvious difficulties with accepting responsibility seen by the parents, the student says he believes that learning is his responsibility.

> I: Whose job is it to make sure that you learn?
> (S): Well, it's mine.

Student perceptions of parent willingness to help
The student perceptions confirm those of the parents – that he requires external pressure to do his homework, and that his parents help him, and that neither parents nor the student get on well with the teacher:

> (I): So you have a homework book, do you? You fill it out every day?
> (S): Yeah, then I get the teacher to sign it.
> (I): And then your mom signs it? (assent)
> (S): They don't just say – well you don't have to do your homework – they make me do it. They tell me you do your homework and then after you can go out to play.
> (I): Any changes during the school year – say with your parents helping you – more or less?

(S): No, they always just help me lots.
(I): What is it about her that makes her not their favourite teacher?
(S): I don't know. I don't like her too much.

Teacher perceptions of student responsibility
The teacher believes strongly in individual student responsibility:

> (T): I think a lot of the responsibility is on the student as to how much are they going to participate in, and be involved in, and how are they meeting their own needs.

She has implemented changes in the classroom to encourage responsibility by giving curriculum choice:

> (I): What about choice of things that they are going to learn, or are learning in the classroom – any changes in that?
> (T): Yes, actually – on the last project that we did, the theme was to do a story mural and the framework was quite loose. We had them working on salmon for eight weeks and they'd gathered all this information in a variety of different ways and now they had to put together a mural that depicted some part of this whole unit. So I let the framework be quite loose so that they had more choice and there was certainly variety, in what was done.

She, like many teachers, is uneasy about 'reaching' all the students:

> (I): What about the business of reaching all the students; any changes during the school year?
> (T): No, I think you're right – it's still a big concern. I think partially because I had forty students within a month and a half, one that speaks no English, and one that speaks very little English, it added to the dilemma of trying to reach every student. I felt like it was almost an impossible task when that happened.

With respect to parent collaboration, she believed the student-led conferences had been very successful in improving collaboration:

> (I): What about the relationship between parents and teachers? Any changes this year?
> (T): I think that probably because of the conferences, parents and teachers have more communication. There's less of a gap. There's more talking that's going on. The door was opened with the initial parent meeting back in September/October, but I think when we did our first interviews and conferences, that was the beginning point. But by the time the second one came around, there was a lot of freedom as to what people were saying.

Summary
This triad suggests that when parents and teachers have conflicting views about student responsibility, and how it is nurtured, collaboration falls off. The teacher here expects the student to be responsible; she does not consistently teach responsibility (compare the next triad). In such cases, even with strong home support, the student will not develop any strong sense of personal responsibility, and will continue to rely on others rather than accepting responsibility for his own learning.

Triad O: On the right track

Parent perceptions of student responsibility

The parent believes there have been major improvements in acceptance of responsibility, largely attributable to the efforts of the teacher:

> (I): Do you feel that he takes responsibility for his own education?
> P(F): From the beginning of the year that has changed – now he's very responsible. He has got his books home and everything. He is taking major control of his education.
> (I): Why do you think that is?
> P(F): (B.).
> (I): The teacher?
> P(F): A hundred per cent – yeah. He has really worked with him – if you get their confidence up and the kids think that they can do it then they try harder.
> P(F): And it was B.'s way of catching too what they didn't comprehend. J. thought he understood certain concepts but was making just little errors – like with long division.
> P(F): Like he was way behind and he worked very hard – and B. did work with him a lot.

The parent sees great improvement:

> (I): Any change in his attitude over the year or over the previous years?
> P(F): Yeah, he's very confident in himself – he's not hesitating and holding back like before. I don't hear 'I can't do it' – in fact I haven't heard that in a long time.
> P(F): He has come way up and he knows that he is right up there with the other kids. This is the first time in his life that he has felt just like one of the kids.

Parent perceptions of help to student

The parent and the student work well together; the parent continues to support, especially by checking student work:

> (I): Does he ask for help at home sometimes?
> P(F): All of the time – every time.
> P(F): With J. especially because we need to keep up on him – he needs the extra help. But he has improved tremendously . . . we just go over what he has to do – he knows what he has to do and everything but even if sometimes I just sit at the table and drink a coffee and read the newspaper . . . while he's doing it – and then 'is this right?' 'Is that right?' . . . that's an excellent way of keeping up without having to go into the class all of the time. And then when they go to bed for the evening my husband and I usually grab their books and go over them and read them.
> (I): Take a look . . .?
> P(F): Yeah – it really gives you a good view of what they're doing.
> P(F): We had their day book and we made sure we signed it every day so that he couldn't slop-off on homework and on things like that.
> P(F): I still check every day – 'do you have homework?'

Parent perceptions of relations with teacher

Asked about how parents can promote a positive relationship with teachers and the school, the parent comments:

P(F): Show more of an interest. I mean I know lots of parents who never go into the school . . .

P(F): Helping in classrooms anytime I am asked – sports days – and track and field – they know they can call me any time.

Some of this in-school activity involves active classroom collaboration with the teacher:

P(F): B. and I together were going from table to table helping them.

(I): Any changes in the way that you and J.'s teacher have worked together over the year?

P(F): I don't think so . . . we've kept in close contact all of the way through.

P(F): Any little problems that start to arise whether they be learning problems or behavioural problems we jump on right away and so they never become big problems.

(I): Could you describe the ideal relationship between parents and teachers?

P(F): Right now I think I have the ideal relationship – an open door policy where you can go in and discuss any problems quickly and efficiently without tying up the teacher's time and your own time.

Student perceptions of acceptance of responsibility

Despite the perceptions of the parent, the student does not claim personal responsibility for learning:

(I): Whose job is it to make sure that you learn?

(S): My teacher's.

(I): And what can your teacher do to make sure that you learn?

(S): He can help us.

Student perceptions of parent willingness to help

(I): Could your parents help you learn . . . more than they do?

(S): No – they help me.

(I): Do you ask your parents for help with school work from time to time?

(S): Yeah.

(I): Do you and your parents work well together?

(S): Yeah.

Student perception of relations with teacher

The student likes the school, as do the parents:

(I): What do you think? Do you think it is a good place to learn?

(S): Yeah. There are good teachers who teach . . . and people come in and help you do work.

(I): What do they (parents) like about it?

(S): They like that I have a good teacher this year.

(I): What do they like about him?

(S): That he's nice – and he helps me.

Teacher perceptions of student responsibility

The teacher finds the students very responsible; but that is because he establishes and enforces expectations, including models of good work.

(I): Do you feel that children can take responsibility for their own education?
(T): They have from the beginning to the end; they have got into that organizational habit of making sure of what's for homework. They write it down in the student planner. They are really willing to make it very exact in the way that I would like to see it done . . . if I give an example of good work the majority of the class really work to make sure it is to that standard to the best of their ability.

Teacher perceptions of relationships with parents
The teacher goes to considerable trouble to involve parents in classroom activities, to help and so that they can see what the students are learning:

(I): Do you welcome parents in your classroom?
(T): We start off with me taking time out to phone them to invite them in; they feel extremely surprised; the response is positive but they aren't used to it. . . . From that point when there is an activity coming up they are invited by letter or phone calls. From day 1 there were always parents in the classroom helping with reading exercises. (We) get lots of stuff from parents willing to help. I needed a house nearby that was able to cook something – I had one who was moving – she unpacked and made pancakes for the students. I had a parent in the other day and she was interested in what I do; she likes snakes – she brought a corn snake. She set up a little exercise for the students to do at the end of it.

The teacher described in some detail a classroom activity which culminated in a display of work for parents:

(T): The event brought a lot of parents to come in to see what was happening. Canada Day celebration – driving the last spike. Each multi-grade class designed a piece of a map of Canada. . . . Parents got to see how students worked as a group . . . (It) gave parents from the classrooms involved an opportunity to see what we were doing in school.
(I): Could parents help in the school more than they do?
(T): Help with me has been wonderful.

General student reaction to all this parent activity in the classroom is contrary to the expectations of some teachers and parents:

(T): I see a feeling of 'I am glad my mum is there'.

The teacher does a great deal to facilitate parent help for students:

(T): I make parents aware that they understand what is going on in the classroom. After every quiz or written work parents are to read and sign it, giving feedback and helping the student with math if they have had difficulty.
(I): Have you helped parents to learn things that make it possible for them to assist their child with school work?
(T): I have demonstrated to parents things; how I go through the procedure . . . maybe a research report step-by-step directions are given to the student. My introduction to every subject has a little explanation.

Summary
This triad is the clearest case in our data of collaboration between home and school to bring about improved student learning, and specifically learning to accept responsibility for academic work. The teacher explicitly states

expectations, and teaches responsibility. The parents support him in this at home and in school. The impact on the student is more perceptible through the comments of the parents than from those of the student; however, that is a common phenomenon in these analyses – students tend to be reticent.

Triad R: Signs of trouble

Scanning the frequency counts of various codes here gives an immediate impression of problems; the parent notes academic difficulties, dislike of school, and poor motivation of the student. She seems to have no help in dealing with these problems.

Parent perceptions of student responsibility

> (FP): He's very irresponsible. I guess he gets his assignments done at school, because he has to stay after school.
> (I): What would you like to see him do differently so that you could say, yes he does take responsibility?
> (FP): I would like him to fill in his day planner, each day, for each subject; tick off the things that they've done. If he could get that going and get himself organized.

By comparison to the other children in the family, this child has difficulties:

> (I): How does he feel about school?
> (FP): He hates it.

The parent has great difficulty understanding what is happening with the child at school:

> (FP): We're reading the *Best of James Herriott Memoirs*, and this is a kid who gets a D in reading in school, and yet he's eating up a book like this. He's reading it, we are reading it together. That doesn't make sense. I think the system is in trouble and he might be a statistic that drops out.
> (I): Because the school's not doing . . .?
> (FP): He's had some years of negative [experience].
> (I): So his experience this year is not any different than in previous years?
> (FP): I'd like to think it's better, but I don't know. He's not been positive about school.
> (FP): And yet, I don't want to go in and have to browbeat my kid all the time either. But at the same time you want to know how you can help the teacher, help him help.
> (I): What about homework, or things that are assigned specifically?
> (FP): He's doing his homework at home, under much protest. It depends what it is.
> (I): Do you think, it's because he doesn't know *how* to go about it?
> (FP): The whole thing overwhelms him. He loves books, he just loves to read, but he doesn't know how – I don't know – he can't do the essays or the questions on the books . . . . He loves history. He watches it on TV, but applying it is another thing . . . . I don't know. I think we'll have an extreme struggle. And the teacher says he's a bright child and I don't know if he is, or if he's just snowing everybody.

Parent perceptions of help to student

The parent seems to be trying hard to understand and to help but without much success:

(I): Is there anything that you could do to help that you don't do now? That you might do if the partnership was stronger? Have any of his teachers, this year or previous years, helped you to learn things that enabled you to assist him with his school [work]?

(FP): No. Specifically to help him? No.

(I): In general?

(FP): No, I don't think so – I can't think of anything. None of them have suggested anything. I mean the only thing I have done is, the suggestion from that seminar [a district-sponsored workshop for parents] to read to them. She really felt that if you read to them, it'll help.

The parent is quite blunt about the difficulties she has in working with the student:

(I): What prevents you from doing more to help K. learn?

(FP): Time, conflict, personality conflict between the two of us . . . his attitude towards schoolwork.

(I): Do you enjoy working with him?

(FP): Not particularly. I enjoy reading with him because he enjoys that as well, but I don't enjoy other. I have to go back and learn how to do math all over again. I really think they should have classes for parents.

(I): Does K- enjoy working with you, or getting help from you when he needs it?

(FP): It depends what it is and how keen he is.

Parent perceptions of relations with teacher

The parent believes that her relationship with the teacher is complicated by the student's attitude to school:

(FP): As a parent, you have different relationships with that teacher because they look at you and think your kid is a problem and although they try to stay positive it's hard.
. . . In general with teachers – you have a more positive relationship with teachers when you have children who achieve, who are easy in the classroom.

(I): Any changes in the school year or do you feel the same as you did?

(FP): Uhm, I was hoping for higher expectations [held by] of the teacher.

(I): Do you feel that his teacher sees you as a partner?

(FP): I think and hope that he feels that we are very supportive. We don't really have too much of a problem with him at all as far as relationships go, he's very quick to phone if there is a problem, or we'll phone him. If we phone and leave a note, we'll try to get together . . . he's very open.

(I): What words come to mind when I say 'the relationship between parents and teachers'?

(FP): Most times I would call the relationship quite positive.

Student perceptions of acceptance of responsibility

There is no uncertainty in the student's mind about responsibility for learning:

(I): Whose job is it to make sure that you learn?

(S): Probably my teacher's and my parents'.

In the classroom he does not get many opportunities to choose things to study, a technique some teachers use to encourage responsibility:

(I): In your classroom, who decides things about what you're studying and what you're learning?

(S): The teacher, always. Well, most of the time.
(I): What about the times when you get to choose things or decide?
(S): That'd probably be independent projects. We decide what countries and we choose what we want to do and stuff. A country he chooses, but you can choose three sub-topics.
(I): Any changes during the school year? Are you making more decisions about what you learn, or is it about the same?
(S): About the same. We've done three reports now. We're going through the third right now, and nothing much has changed.

The student has no clear career plans:

(S): My parents say a teacher is the best job you can get because you get three months off every year.
(I): You don't want to be a teacher?
(S): No, I want something more exciting.
(I): Have you thought about what you're going to do after you leave school?
(S): I'll probably try to get into a good college and go on to college.
(I): What do you want to study?
(S): No idea.

Student perceptions of getting help from parents
The student seeks and gets help from parents:

(I): What things do you ask for help with?
(S): If I'm confused, like with my math sometimes. And with current events and stuff like that.
(I): Could you describe the ways in which your parents help you learn?
(S): They just help me with my homework and stuff.
(I): Do you and your parents work well together?
(S): Most of the times.

Teacher perceptions of student responsibility
The teacher has had some difficulties with individual students, and adopted a variety of techniques for dealing with them:

(I): Do you feel that children can take responsibility for their own education?
(T): I think of one or two key individuals. It has been a real grind to get them to complete work. Around Christmas time I decided this one student case was no longer my problem. I placed it on the shoulders of the student. It didn't always involve consequences but always a reminder. Speaking with the parents of the children who avoid responsibility has served some[times] to make the situation better.
(T): I have made homework books mandatory. Four of my students have required to sign from the parents and that has resulted in more successfully completed homework. At the beginning of the year I make homework book mandatory for all my students. That is one initiative that the school has been thinking about.

(I): Do children in your class have opportunities to choose what or how they will learn?
(T): There has been quite a bit of that. I have utilized that mainly in social studies and reading. Choosing activities based on their reading material – a variety of choices. Science I haven't found it as easy. Giving them socials project and presentation work for kids lacking motivation – it really brings them around.

Teacher perceptions of parent relations
In general the teacher does not have parents in the classroom but does use other strategies to improve relations with parents:

(T): The use of strict contracts and guidelines has helped to bring the parents into a more involved state.

(I): How would you describe the relationship between parents/teachers?

(T): Teachers are more accessible to parents through the conferencing program and that has been communicated in the feedback that has been available [from parents]. The parents no longer view the teacher as the sole means of evaluation of their child. The child perception is important and that has impacted on the parent perception of teachers and their role.

(T): [Student-led conferencing] was extremely successful and the feedback I got from my parents was very positive; there was feedback from the first one about students not being prepared but in March they were all more comfortable with the process.

(T): My belief [is] that parents feel more welcome because of the conferences. Playing a more active role.

Summary

This case is the clearest one in our data set of wasted talent. There has been a breakdown in student–teacher and teacher–parent relationships. The teacher sees his relationship with children only in terms of eliciting work, and with the parents only in terms of compelling the children to work. The triad is in sharp contrast to Triad O, **in which the teacher taught students how to behave responsibly.** The parent prediction that the child will drop out of school seems likely to come true, in the absence of any career interests to be served by the school.

HOW TEACHERS AND PARENTS DEVELOP STUDENT RESPONSIBILITY

We set out to examine:

1. **the student attitudes associated with student feelings of responsibility towards school work, and**
2. **the home and classroom influences which shape changes in student acceptance of responsibility over the school year.**

What the chapter tells us

When the development of student responsibility occurs it is a function of the attitudes and practices of all three triad members. The vital elements are: (a) for teachers, beliefs about parental involvement, student capabilities, and the importance of deliberate teaching of responsibility in classrooms; (b) for students, communication with parents about school, confidence in the ability to do the work, valuing school for its importance to the future, and collaboration with teachers; (c) for parents, valuing school, an 'invitational' teacher attitude, and communication with students about school.

To build and sustain student acceptance of responsibility for learning requires much stronger collaboration between triad members than is typically found in the schools in which we worked, which we believe are a representative sample of schools in British Columbia.

For families, the stimulus for such collaboration is based upon the perception that parents can help, that teachers want help, and that school is vital to the future of the student. The last is of particular importance: virtually all the students who seem disconnected from school have no sense that it can serve their purposes. Marx, Grieve and Rossner recommend that 'Schools should be viewed as agencies that assist learners to attain an education. Learners should use schools as they achieve an education, not take full direction from them' (1988, p. v.). The families of successful students see schools as a service for their use, not an agent of the State which takes their children in for several hours a day, and about which they have nothing to say.

The implications for school improvement

Schools must be seen by parents and students as being of central importance, and providing a vital service. Parents need to be intolerant of bad teaching and poor learning; they would be more so if the reality of the connection between schooling and the child's future were clearer to them. Some of the parents described in Chapter 3 do demand, successfully, good service from the schools. They are after all paying (through taxes) about $5,000 (Canadian) per year for the service.

At the same time, it is unlikely that schools anywhere can be improved without the presence of substantial numbers of teachers who accept the view that the work of teaching has a dimension that goes beyond simple curricular activity. What students need to learn goes far beyond mathematics and science. Yet teachers often seem to expect student attitudes and behaviour that they have neither taught nor modelled. The topic of student responsibility reveals quite different role perceptions amongst teachers; by comparison students and parents seem quite similar in their views.

9

The Good Teacher: A Student Perspective

The teacher is real nice and she teaches, she doesn't play around and play games, she teaches.

(Student)

Relationships between students and teachers, mediated through families, contribute to positive student perception of the school. Some teachers 'reach' students through personalized help. In Chapter 8, a student comments: 'he's nice, and he helps me'. These may be distinct and separate teacher activities – co-curricular and curricular. This dualism is often reported; so for this chapter we developed a new scale, a measure of 'teacher caring', to try to capture this co-curricular element.

We look first at student perceptions of teachers to develop a grounded conception of the teacher attitudes and practices which are valued by students. We use this information to draw a profile of the good teacher/classroom from the student perspective. Then we test the profile of the good teacher by using it to look at classrooms; that is, we add together the information from all the students in each classroom to see whether or not there is a consistent student view of their classroom.

We think it worth trying to generalize in this way because previous analyses of student data cause us to see the teacher as mediator of student collaboration within the classroom. In Chapter 6 we saw that more and less collaborative teachers produced quite different responses amongst individual students (and parents). But in that chapter we saw that teacher activities with individuals also tended to shape general perceptions. Indeed, our survey research has shown that student perceptions of school climate and school quality are shaped by students' general valuation of schooling, a home factor, and their perception of collaboration in the classroom between student and teacher, a school factor.

The findings reported in previous chapters helped to frame the questions for this chapter:

What teacher attitudes/actions are important in shaping student perceptions of the classroom and the teacher?

Do students perceive major differences between teachers, and do these differences contribute to differences in student commitment?

Are student attitudes to teachers clustered by classroom, so that all or many of the students in a classroom share perceptions?

TRYING TO UNDERSTAND STUDENT EXPERIENCES

Little is known about student experience in school; Erickson and Shultz suggest that:

> The absence of student experience from current educational discourse seems to be a consequence of systematic silencing of the student voice. Most fundamentally, student experience goes unheard and unseen for what appears to be ideological reasons. . . . Much of classroom life is a monologue followed by a test. In the absence of interchange, of genuine conversation in the ways we usually teach, students are prevented from developing voice – a critical awareness of their own ends, means, and capacities in learning.
>
> (1992, p. 481)

Our analysis of student opinions and attitudes so far supports the view that they have yet to develop a confident and assertive voice. This seems to be connected to weak personal relationships with teachers. We know that dropouts are usually students who have failed to connect with teachers.

This problem has been recognized by educators, in particular with respect to middle schools – those serving children in the 10–14 age groups. Middle school 'advisory programs', common in the USA (Galassi, Gulledge, and Cox, 1997), are predicated on the assumption that 'every student needs to have a relationship with at least one adult in the school which is characterized by warmth, concern, openness, and understanding' (George and Alexander, 1993, p. 201). In our terms, that is a 'caring' relationship; it can and should sustain student engagement, as a preventative to dropping out of school.

Student engagement

Some recent empirical work describes 'engagement' and its importance thus:

> The most immediate and persisting issue for students and teachers is not low achievement, but student disengagement. . . . Engaged students make a psychological investment in learning. They try hard to learn what the school offers. . . . For teachers, the challenge is how to get students to do academic work and to take it seriously enough to learn; for students, the challenge is how to cope with teachers' demands so as to avoid boredom, to maintain self-respect, and at the same time, to succeed in school. . . . Students cannot be expected to achieve unless they concentrate, work, and invest themselves in the mastery of school tasks. That is the sense in which student engagement is critical to educational success; to enhance achievement one must first learn how to engage students.
>
> (Newmann, 1992, pp. 2, 3)

For the classroom teacher, the problem is of winning assent from students (Metz, 1993).

In British Columbia, a Royal Commission sub-report on students has found that:

> Students tend to make implicit or explicit distinctions between doing school work and learning. Work is something expected, assigned and required by someone else, usually a teacher. Learning in this sense has a basically utilitarian meaning and students will use the term 'learning' to refer specifically to school work. But learning

has another, more personally meaningful connotation for many youngsters. It is pursuing those things that really interest them, often passionately, and the expectations and requirements are willingly self-imposed or peer generated.

With this distinction in mind the children we interviewed seemed to sort themselves roughly into four categories. There are those who learn primarily in school; those who learn primarily out of school; those, the majority, who do work to get through school; and those who don't associate school with either work or learning. Those who learn primarily in school or, in other words, who view school as a place of learning in a meaningful sense comprise a very small part (about 5%) of our sample. They were, in most cases, attending private schools.

The majority of students saw the work of schooling as like 'death and taxes', inevitable and unavoidable. To them it is, not unrealistically, the thing you have to do to get a job or pursue post-secondary education or training. Students, teachers, and parents generally agree that it is desirable to do well at school work.

(Marx, Grieve, and Rossner, 1988, p. 55)

Few are engaged then; rather more disengage dramatically, that is drop out of school.

Student disengagement: the drop-out problem

In Canada, very substantial drop-out rates (around 30% of the age cohort) in secondary schools has led to some discussion of student experience, but frustratingly there has been a rapid shift away from the student experience and towards a discussion of educational policies and school programs.

Chester Finn (1989) has suggested that dropping out is not a problem in the USA; students make choices as to what they want, and the primary source of these choices is the family context. Thus, dropping out is not a school problem, to be addressed by social policy, but a personal and family choice. In Canada, Levin has argued similarly: students make choices and these should be respected: 'for many students, leaving school is a perfectly rational thing to do' (1993, p. 262).

However, the majority of 'drop-outs' are in fact *excluded* from the formal schooling process by a sorting process described originally by Talcott Parsons in 'The school as a social system' (1959) and more recently by Oakes (1985), Hallinger and Murphy (1986), and others. Barrington and Hendricks (1989) use school records from elementary schools to predict drop-outs and graduates by the third grade with 70% accuracy, and by the ninth grade with 90% accuracy.

This tacit role of the public schools of sorting students into those with educational futures and those without is analogous to the long-standing 'cooling-out' role of the junior colleges in the USA. These institutions persuade some students not to pursue higher education, but to enter the workforce in socially useful roles but with minimal qualifications (Clark, 1960; McCormick, 1990).

Drop-outs and effective schools?

The 'effective schools' literature on high schools in the USA and the UK is full of instances of schools which do very much better than the norm at providing useful educational opportunities for a broad range of students, including those who would be excluded in ordinary schools (Lightfoot, 1983; Metz, 1993; Rutter *et al.*, 1979; Sedlak *et al.*, 1986). Wehlage and colleagues define good high schools in affective or emotional terms, not in terms of test scores; **such schools reach students on the basis of relationships, not through the promise of academic success** (1989, p. 45). In Canada this point emerges from a contemporary portrait of student engagement and its obverse amongst working-class youngsters (Dryden, 1995).

Finn suggests that 'participatory behaviour' leads to 'bonding': 'without a consistent pattern of participation in school activities . . . it is unlikely that the youngster will ever come to identify with school' (1989, p. 131). Participatory behaviour in a child's school career is shaped, in school, by relationships with teachers. But the student is prepared (or not) for such engagement and such relationships **by home elements**, as we have noted already, particularly in Chapters 3, 6 and 7.

The teacher role in promoting engagement is the subject of this chapter: student perceptions of teachers will provide some clues about attitudes and actions which engage students, and those which have the reverse effect (although we emphasize positive teacher behaviour).

ANALYZING THE INTERVIEW DATA ON STUDENT ATTITUDES

First the student interviews were analyzed to identify teacher attitudes and practices which were positively perceived by students. We used these attitudes and practices to create 'profiles' of positive classroom experiences, of the supportive family experiences reported by students which might have prepared the students for the positive in-school experience, and of the elements in the school setting which seemed to contribute to student attitudes, directly or indirectly.

We also examined the unusual cases, positive or negative outliers, since these could help us to arrive at a composite portrait of a full range of student attitudes towards their teachers, and the teacher behaviour that helps to generate these attitudes.

Finally, we used the Year 5 survey data for an analysis of predictors of student perceptions of school climate and rating of school; this allowed us to test the profiles drawn from the interviews.

THE PROFILES AND THE OUTLIERS

When we aggregate the student interview data for Times 2 and 10 (57 and 25 cases respectively) we arrive at profiles of the classrooms in our study which encompass the majority of our qualitative data. (The outliers will be described later.) The positive profiles consist of those codes which are mentioned often. This profile contains four elements. (The interview schedule changed slightly over the years; there are some contrasts between the two years for that reason.)

The standard profiles

Family environment

These students are well prepared for classroom learning by the home environment. They consistently report eight elements in that environment:

(a) they and their parents work well together on school work (67%);
(b) parents help them often with school work (88%);
(c) parents consistently ask them about their school experience (67%);
(d) they often talk about school (72%), and
(e) also ask their parents for help (74%);
(f) they have thought about career plans (82%);
(g) their formal education is an important aspect of these career plans (67%); and
(h) they have discussed these career plans with their parents (63%).

The flavour of student comments is given in the representative responses which follow. (Interviewer questions and the codes assigned are provided to clarify our procedure.) These commentaries are particularly interesting for the insight they provide into the skill and diligence some parents show in providing instructional support.

Code: St–pts work well together
S13313T2
I'll call on him [father] and he'll ask what the problem is and I'll say some sort of fraction problem or something like that. What he'll do is first he'll, if it's a problem that you have to solve that's in sort of like a paragraph, first he'll read it out and we'll figure out first if it has to be divided, subtracted, or what you know. And we figure that out and then we have to figure out what it said to do. . . . He'll just like he'll point it out and we'll go through it together and **if I still don't understand we'll go through another one together until I absolutely understand it. And then I'll work on my own again.** And that's about it.

S22311T2
I: Do you and your parents work well together?
S: Yeah.
I: No frustrations or fights or . . . ?
S: Sometimes . . . the odd time.
I: What might happen the odd time?
S: **My mom will go on explaining and explaining when I already understand.**

Code: Pt helps st
S11313T2
I: Can you describe the ways in which your parents help you learn?
S: Well like if I come home one day and I'm confused about math . . . then they sit down and explain it to me until I understand . . . they help me with anything . . . **sometimes I feel that my parents help more than the teachers.**

Overall, given the diversity of schools, classrooms, families, and students in which and with whom we worked, these profiles are very consistent portraits of family environments supporting student learning and the schooling process.

Classroom environment

There is much less consistency, within and between the classrooms in our sample, with respect to classroom environment. The students report five elements:

(a) they feel positive about teacher practices regarding classroom work (76%) and regarding
(b) parent involvement (48%);
(c) they like the classroom, seeing it as a good place to learn (62%);
(d) they also like the teacher (46%), and
(e) feel responsible for their own learning (41%).

Many of the students made suggestions about classroom improvement to the interviewer (30 cases) but they were reluctant to approach the teacher, or had used their parents as intermediaries in doing so. The difficulties become apparent in these illustrative comments, which are responses to the question: 'Do you ever feel that things could be done differently or better in your classroom'?

> *Code*: St makes suggestions
> S15312T2
> S: Yes.
> I: Have you ever spoken to your teacher about it?
> S: My dad spoke to my teacher.
> I: How come you had your dad speak to your teacher?
> S: I didn't want to speak to my teacher about that. Afraid she'd yell at me or something.
>
> S21313T2
> I: Have you ever spoken to him about these things – your ideas for improvement?
> S: No.
> I: Why not?
> S: I don't know . . . I'm kind of scared to tell him.
> I: Are you?
> S: Well, not really scared but I just don't want to.
> I: Hesitant?
> S: Yeah.
> I: Why?
> S: Sometimes I think they might be really dumb ideas and he might not like them. And then he would . . . he always makes fun of people sometimes just for fun.
> I: And you would be scared that he would do that?
> S: Well, yeah . . . well, just embarrass me a bit.
> I: And you don't want that to happen?
> S: Not really.

Such comments illustrate precisely the conclusion quoted above about the silencing of students: 'In the absence of interchange, of genuine conversation in the ways we usually teach, students are prevented from developing voice' (Erickson and Shultz, 1992, p. 481).

We were surprised that students did not mention working together in classrooms. Cooperative learning, roughly modelled upon the work described by Slavin and colleagues (1985) has been strongly emphasized in British Columbia for nearly a decade by Ministry officials and teacher training institutions.

School environment
The students report that they:

(a) like school and find it a good place to learn (71%);
(b) feel important in the school (41%); and
(c) feel responsible for learning in the school (41%).

Parent–school relationship
The students report that their parents:

(a) attend events at the school (57%);
(b) visit/feel welcome in the classroom (83%);
(c) like the teacher/classroom/school (100%); and
(d) the teacher initiates communication and actions (100%).

In general these profiles are as expected. The consistency of the first element (the supportiveness of the home environment) is the most striking thing about them.

The exceptional cases

The unusual cases of student–teacher relationships are more interesting. We present these by describing: (a) the uncommon codes (occurring fewer than 7 times in 82 interviews); (b) student descriptions of their favourite teacher; (c) two student cases; and (d) very good classrooms.

Uncommon codes
The codes concerning student behaviour that occurred infrequently (T2 and 10 counts summed) included:

'student helps others in the classroom' (4);
'student comfortable with teacher' (6); and
'student understands teacher practices' (4).

The codes concerning teacher behaviour that occurred infrequently included:

'teacher knows student needs' (2);
'teacher empathizes with students' (2);
'teacher open to questions' (3);
'teacher respects students' (1);
'teacher encourages students' (2).

What was **not talked about** constituted the major surprise here: the absence of strong affective links between teachers and students was striking. Our previous analyses had identified some teachers as strong motivators (for example, the collaborative teachers in Chapters 6 and 7, or the teachers whose classrooms developed student responsibility, Chapter 8). Yet this large group of students from diverse classrooms barely mention affective connections between teachers and students.

Favourite teacher

The responses students gave when asked to describe their favourite teacher were much less revealing than we had hoped. Many students could not answer at all. Those who did responded thus:

S34309T10, t st favour,
I: Tell me about your all-time favourite teacher.
MS: I'd say Mr B., my teacher this year. If you hurt your knee and that and he'll let you down there and get some ice on it, like even though he doesn't think you have, he'll just let you go down just in case it is. Anybody getting hurt or anything. So if anybody is fighting he is separating them.

S66317T10, t st favour,
I: Tell me about your favourite teacher. It could be any grade.
FS: Well, last year I had a nice teacher, Mrs R. and this year Mrs O. is really nice too.
I: So which was the best?
FS: Mrs O.
I: And then why? Can you figure why it is that you like her a bit more?
FS: She is nice to me and she hardly ever gets mad.

S67303T10, t st favour,
I: Now just thinking about you in particular, you in that classroom, just seeing yourself and that teacher, why do you feel he is special for you?
MS: Um, I'm not really sure, like, well, he always, like if I need help or anything, he's always there, like for math or science or LA or anything, I just sort of put my hand up, and that goes for everyone else, but it's something that's kind of special.
I: So would there be anything you'd ever be afraid to ask him?
MS: Uh, about school work?
I: Uh huh.
MS: No. Like, if I'm like having trouble and I just really don't get this I wouldn't be afraid to ask him. A lot of kids do.

S92307T10, t st favour so far, 1,
I: Okay. Tell me about your favourite teacher ever.
FS: My favourite teacher ever would probably either my last year teacher or Mr K.
I: Why?
FS: Well, even though he doesn't buckle down or anything, he is still nice and he understands like, um, he kind of understands how we feel, stuff like that.

Note that virtually all the reasons given concern student perceptions of the human qualities of the teacher, as opposed to instructional techniques or effective teaching:

'If anybody is fighting he is separating them';
'She is nice to me and she hardly ever gets mad';
'Like if I need help or anything, he's always there';
'He kind of understands how we feel'.

The positive individual case that follows illustrates what we expected to find as the norm; in fact it is the exception. The negative case is unique in our data.

Individual student cases

The comments illustrate part of the range of circumstances which together produce the positive perception.

On relationship with teacher

S15314T2, t expects st to help others, 1,

I: What other ways has your teacher conveyed the message to you?

S: She really encourages us to help the person beside you if they are having a problem and she will notice about what she does is she will sit back for a half hour and she will watch you working and she will mark you on how you help people and how you work by yourself, and you are not screaming and yelling and making noise and stuff like that.

S15314T2, t knows st needs, 2,

I: Do you feel comfortable asking those questions?

S: Yes because usually she will, like if I need some help or something she will understand, she knows all our basic needs, like Fred over here needs help with math and then reading or whatever, she will help us with all of them.

S15314T2, t knows st needs, 2,

I: How does that demonstrate respect?

S: Well she knows that you have certain needs, some people that don't understand work will have maybe a couple minutes extra time to do their work or get extra help after school which will result in extra time to do their work.

S15314T2, t empathizes w st, 1,

I: How does it feel being there [three-way conference] with your mum and dad and the teacher?

S: Sometimes it is a little scary because you don't know what is going to come next, but usually the teacher will be very friendly and she won't be not mean or anything but she will like, our teacher is very nice because she thinks like you, like she will know what you feel like and stuff. So usually she knows what we are going through when we have to go in.

S15314T2, Tchr prac classroom work, 4,

Like the schedule our class use what our teacher does she gives us a list of what we have to do on that date and for the first half hour of that day she will discuss all our work like our math and go over stuff and then we have to have it done before recess or by the end of the year [day?] whatever, so which is very good, we can work at our own pace. I like doing that.

S15314T2, Tchr prac PI, 7,

On these monthly interims she will write comments and we have to bring the little slip in that have our parents' signature and our parents can put down comments and if they want an interview with the teacher which we have to come to so we can answer questions and find out what is going on too.

S15314T2, St comfortable w tchr, 1,

S: Yes, they [parents] have asked me if I like our teacher and how she teaches . . . and stuff like that. I like her and I like how we do our work and stuff.

S15314T2, St makes suggestions, 1,

I: If something were to happen in the classroom and you felt there was a need to change would you feel comfortable going to the teacher and talking to her?

S: Usually, but usually there isn't that much of a deal because there isn't very much stuff that happens that needs to be dealt with, because usually the teacher will talk to the class about how certain people have been noisy so I think that everybody should get to work and be quiet and stuff like that, she won't pinpoint people and stuff like that.

I: How are your parents responding to that folder idea? [Coproduction Project innovation – student work folders containing current work are sent home at intervals for parent inspection and sign-off.]
S: They like it because as I said they can see my work and help me with it or whatever. It is good for them because they can ask me if there is a quiz coming up they can take the work from that and just go over it with me and help me study and stuff like that. Our teacher and another teacher started it in our school and now I think there are like six or seven in our school that have it.

S15314T2, t st favour so far, 1,
S: Yes, she is my favourite teacher so far.

S15314T2, triad works well, 1,
S: Well I know that we all get along fine and everything, of the parents, the teacher and I. We all get along fine and usually there are no problems at all.
I: That is a very nice situation to be in isn't it?
S: Yes.

The final comment about the triad summarizes what our data show about student–teacher relationships – when they are good they are often mediated by parents, in the sense that **parents are an important part of the positive student–teacher relationship.**

The negative case is S13313; the comments describe events that produced the student reaction.

On relationship with teacher
S13313T2, st fears t,
I: Yeah. OK. Any other kinds of things that you talk about [with parents]?
S: Well, for example, we have a class clown. His name is D. and what he'll do is he'll goof around and the teacher will get really mad and stuff and this one time I thought it was really out of line when he got sent out of the classroom for being goofy and he was making these funny faces through the little window beside the door and everybody was laughing at him. And he can make these real funny faces, you know. So Mr C. goes out there, slams the door shut, and we hear this thud on the wall, just a real slight thud, I come back and, me and him are socials partners, so I come back there and his face is beet red like he's going to kill somebody. And I said 'What's the matter'? 'How would you like it if the teacher threw you up against the wall?' So I'm going, yeah. I've got to be really afraid of this teacher, you know.

S13313T2, st fears t,
He's really a physical kind of teacher and stuff. He's really bad with this one kid his name was Sam. It was at the beginning of the year and he left this school, because one day he got really mad because he got a lot of paragraphs and ripped them up in Mr C.'s face and threw them on the ground. Was going to leave the classroom but Mr C. grabbed him by the neck and yanked him like this and threw him to the ground and so he got like really mad and left the school because he didn't want to, he was afraid of Mr C. ever since then that he's maybe going to have a broken wrist or something.

S13313T2, t not friendly, 1,
S: It bothers me so much and with all this I haven't seen him smile. I don't think I've seen him smile yet once. I think I've only seen him smile once was when on his birthday, me, Tanya and Doug put on a surprise birthday party for him.

S13313T2, st likes t prac not, 1,
A place to learn? Well, it depends on the teacher. With our teacher sometimes he can make some things kind of fun and other things really boring. Other teachers, they can make them really exciting like, just about every afternoon our next-door class, which is the grade 3/4s, Mrs L. Over there like in the afternoon we can hear all sorts of movies like on science and you can almost hear like all sorts of these art projects and stuff, you know, like for like socials or science. And we're just sitting here reading out of this book and writing down answers for questions. I'm going, like how come they get all the fun? You know?

Student perceptions of the teacher are almost always coloured by how the teacher treats other students, as well as by the personal treatment the student receives. That some of the students organized a birthday party for this teacher seems quite astonishing in the circumstances, yet suggests how much the students would prefer a very different relationship.

Unusual classrooms
We find that 6 of the 20 classrooms illustrate what students prefer.

S15314T2, t knows st needs, 2,
I: Do you feel comfortable asking those questions?
S: Yes because usually she will, like if I need some help or something she will understand, she knows all our basic needs, like Fred over here needs help with math and then reading or whatever, she will help us with all of them.

S34309T10, clrm gd place to learn, 1,
I: I was wondering what your classroom was like?
MS: Our classroom is perfect to work in, it's not too loud and too quiet and it's just like perfect and I get most of my work done.

S61307T10, clrm gd place to learn, 1,
FS: I think in the class we learn a lot.
I: How come?
FS: Well first the teacher is real nice and she teaches, she doesn't play around and play games, she teaches.

S66317T10, tchr nice, 1,
MS: Because the teachers, most of the teachers take the time and listen to you but some of them don't.
I: What about your teacher?
MS: She does.
I: You feel like she listens to your ideas and takes time to hear you?
MS: Yes.

S67319T10, tchr helps st, 1,
MS: Mr B. is a really good teacher.
I: What is the thing that makes him a good teacher for you?
MS: If we ever need help he is there to help us, he wants us to learn. He doesn't want us going away not knowing everything. He wants us to put everything we can in the school year.

S87303T10, tchr helps st, 1,
I: What has she done to help you learn more?
FS: She explains math way better, takes time to help me understand. If I don't understand verbs easily in French she will take time, like after recess to quickly help me.

The exceptional cases suggest that there are two separate dimensions to being a good teacher, co-curricular and curricular. These were identified in the epigraph – being 'nice', by which students mean being kind and understanding, and 'teaching', especially helping them with work.

Summary of profiles and exceptional cases

In sum, the general student profiles suggest that the students are well prepared for classroom learning by the home environment; feel generally positive with respect to classroom environment, including teacher practices regarding classroom work, and see the classroom as a good place to learn, usually alone. Students do not see the teacher in personal or collaborative terms.

From the exceptional cases, we find that preferred teachers are 'nice to me and hardly ever get mad'. They listen to students: 'he listens to lots of people's ideas'. They know student needs: 'she will understand, she knows all our basic needs'. They empathize with students: 'our teacher is very nice because she thinks like you, like she will know what you feel like and stuff'. They are serious about teaching, have high expectations and help students learn: 'he is there to help us, he wants us to learn. He doesn't want us going away not knowing everything'. 'The teacher is real nice and she teaches, she doesn't play around and play games, she teaches'.

There is little that is surprising about this summary portrait of the good teacher. However, the fact that only 6 of our 20 classrooms had teachers who were described in these terms is surprising.

To this point we have responded to the first of the three questions that framed this chapter:

What teacher attitudes/actions are important in shaping student perceptions of the classroom and the teacher?

The duality at the heart of these student perceptions – good practices/technical skills together with good personal relationships with students make up the good teacher – is certainly no surprise (see, for example, the immense summary of research on the correlates of student achievement by Wang, Haertel and Walterg, 1993). However, the first element derives largely from the general profiles, the second from the outlier data. Many of our students experience and appreciate the technical skills of teachers, but **only a few experience more personal qualities and relationships with teachers.**

We now try to assess how well the portrait generalizes as widely shared perceptions of good teachers and good classrooms.

THE SURVEY DATA

We can test the results of the qualitative analysis by using the survey data to develop a set of predictors (using multiple regression) of student perceptions of school climate and rating of school. The details of the analysis are given

Scale K.   Perception of teacher caring/respect for individual student.
   T10 (5 ITEMS) Alpha .87

.67 74.   My teacher cares about how well I do in class.

.70 76.   My teacher makes sure I get a chance to participate in things in class.

.75 78.   My teacher treats me with respect in the classroom.

.75 80.   My teacher makes sure that everyone gets a chance to participate in things in class.

.67 81.   My teacher treats all students fairly in class.

OPTIONS FOR RESPONDENTS ON SURVEYS:

AGREE STRONGLY	AGREE	NOT SURE	DISAGREE	DISAGREE STRONGLY
1	2	3	4	5

Figure 9.1   Scale K – student perception of teacher caring about individual students, with Likert-type response codes from the survey instrument

in the Chapter Notes; here only the significant results are described (see Figure 9.1).

However, Scale K is new, so the items of which it is comprised should be shown (Figure 9.1 also shows responses which students could choose on the survey). These items are closely interconnected, shown by the item-scale correlations in the left column. Note that they represent an instructionally-oriented version of the notion of 'caring'.

Scale B (student values school) is primarily a measure of home influence, as demonstrated in Table 9.3 in the Chapter Notes. When put together with Scale K (perception of teacher caring), our new and very strong measure of school influence on student attitudes, Scale B accounts for 60% of the variance in the student's perception of school climate (Scale H), our measure of student commitment to school.

In turn, Scale H is by far the most important predictor of student Rating of School, accounting for about 40% of the variance in that measure. Figure 9.2 illustrates this pattern.

The importance of Scale K, our new measure of 'Teacher Caring', strongly supports our portrait of the good teacher drawn from the student interviews. We can now respond to the second question posed at the beginning of the chapter:

Do students generally perceive major differences between teachers, and do these differences contribute to differences in student commitment?

Our response is very positive for both parts of the question, **when we focus upon Scale K,** our measure of teacher caring. However, if we focus upon classroom practices, the general profiles presented earlier suggest that there are few differences between teachers.

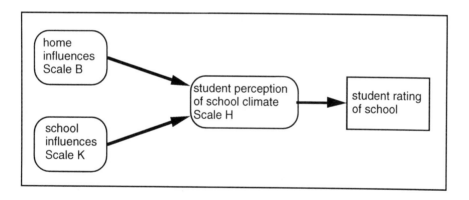

Figure 9.2 Major attitudinal influence upon student rating of school

The third question was:

Are student attitudes to teachers clustered by classroom, so that all or many of the students in the room share perceptions?

The procedure we used is described in the Chapter Notes. We can conclude from the analysis that:

(a) some students have strongly positive opinions about teacher caring for student welfare;

(b) such opinions **are widely distributed amongst our sample of classrooms;** and

(c) only 6 of 36 classrooms contain many students having positive views.

However, **the 6 classrooms in which students in general regard their teacher very positively are not those which emerged from the case studies.**
The six teachers in our sample whose work is so positively perceived by students are undoubtedly extraordinary practitioners, **who combine technical skills with caring about the well-being of students in the classroom. They have a very significant impact upon the commitment of their students.** But it is also true that many individual students in other classrooms respond positively to their teachers. For these individual students, commitment is also strengthened.

It should be recalled that all these 36 teachers committed themselves to participating in the project, and to attempting to improve parental involvement. (Although the actual implementation of change was limited, as we see in the next chapter.) One can only speculate about the results which might be obtained from a random set of 36 middle-school classrooms.

What the chapter tells us

The student interviews generated profiles which suggest, in general, that the students are well prepared for classroom learning by the home environment, and see the classroom as a good place to learn. For most students the class-room is a good but not collaborative workplace. From the exceptional cases, we find that preferred teachers listen to students; know student needs; empath-ize with students; are serious about teaching, with high expectations; and help students individually. There is little that is surprising about this summary portrait of the good teacher.

From the analyses of the survey data, we find that strong positive percep-tions are quite widely distributed amongst classrooms, and are very good predictors of student commitment. However, positive perceptions are not often held by many students in one classroom.

Teachers in our sample are good practitioners, whose affective impact upon students is only moderate. Marx, Grieve and Rossner (1988), writing about students in B.C., find that few of the students they interviewed think of school as occupying a central place in their lives. Some students indicated that 'a particular teacher did cause them to be actively involved'. But the authors believe that such teachers are rare in the experience of students. Our evidence supports this conclusion.

The implications for school improvement

Teachers in British Columbia are amongst the very best-trained (in terms of years of preparation) and best-paid teachers in the world. Many have experi-enced teacher training programs that emphasize the affective dimension of teacher–student relationships.

A random experience in the teacher training program at Simon Fraser Uni-versity will illustrate this. A classroom used for the program was recently the site of a meeting. The room was 'decorated' with signs that were obviously the outcome of a brainstorming session on what constitutes a good teacher/good classroom. The signage referred to the following desirable qualities of teacher/classroom:

teacher reflective/empathetic	active learners	exciting/challenging atmosphere
safe and trusting environment	teacher accessible/approachable	mutual respect

These are no doubt desirable emphases in a pre-service teacher training pro-gram. Yet such teachers and classrooms remain rare in the experience of middle-school students. Assuming that these pre-service student teachers believe what they say, some considerable change occurs when they become classroom teachers. We will return to this issue in the final chapter.

A most important methodological point follows from this chapter, repeating a conclusion already stated for Chapter 6: **case study analyses alone cannot provide guidance for either policy or practice.** Unless the inferences which emerge from case studies are tested by some alternative means, as they have been in most of the analyses presented here, they cannot be relied upon for guidance. With respect to school improvement, there are now hundreds of empirical studies in print which purport to guide policy and practice on the basis of case study analysis. They constitute a serious threat to the credibility of empirical research, and to the welfare of teachers and students.

On the other hand, survey research alone is also a weak guide to policy, since it is rarely interpretable in ways which have direct relevance. The typical research finding – school achievement is correlated with family education level – is often used as a guide to policy, with additional funds being allocated to what are seen as disadvantaged communities.

In fact as we have seen family education or income level is a weak proxy for the kinds of supportive family activities described in detail in our case studies in Chapter 3. That is why effective schooling is 'what money can't buy' (Mayer, 1997), and 'there is no strong or consistent relationship between variations in school resources and student performance'. (Hanushek, 1997, p. 141) In the final chapter I will attempt to outline a school improvement strategy which builds upon the findings of this and previous chapters, and acknowledges the difficulties outlined in this discussion of the implications of this chapter for school improvement.

10

Changing Teacher Collaborative Practices

Gladly wolde he lerne, and gladly teche.

(Chaucer)

In this chapter we return to a topic already discussed in Chapter 5, the impact of an attempt to change teacher practices of parent involvement. In this chapter we analyze a larger group of classrooms with more variability between teachers (from a later year of the study – Year 5) and include a measure of teacher practices based upon teacher, student, and parent perceptions.

The questions we pose are:

Is there evidence in the student or parent interviews of home or school experiences that positively influence student attitudes?

Are such experiences clearly related to changes in teacher and/or parent practices attributable to the Coproduction Project?

TEACHER PRACTICES AND PARENT AND STUDENT ATTITUDES

As we argued in the previous chapter, student participation/commitment is vital to classroom and school effectiveness. Relationships with teachers, as perceived by students, have a very significant impact upon student commitment, as we showed in the model in Chapter 1, and in detail in Chapter 9. In Chapter 4 our analysis of interviews with parents showed that certain teacher practices, which we summarized in the notion of the Coproduction Classroom, were likely to strengthen family collaboration, and hence positive student attitudes. These become the recommended teacher practices, the intervention we attempted in this year of the overall project. (See Figure 10.1 in the Chapter Notes.)

HOW WE TESTED THE EFFECTS OF OUR ATTEMPT TO CHANGE TEACHER PRACTICES

We began with an analysis of the teacher interview data. We focused on teacher reports of:

1. attempts to strengthen parent involvement in instructional activities (TRIAD);
2. instances of teacher/student collaboration (T/ST COLL); and
3. instances of practice change (PR CHANGE) judged likely to affect student commitment.

(See Chapter Notes for detailed discussion.)

Our original intent, to measure change in practice, was challenged immediately, since the practice change measure does not coincide with the overall ranking of the classrooms. We had to decide what was really important – the degree of collaboration reported, or the amount of practice change reported. We opted to combine both measures in the rankings in Figure 10.2 (see Chapter Notes). This table is of course based on teacher self-report data; we have learned not to rely on single source data.

Similar data for parent and student perceptions is presented in Figure 10.3 (in the Chapter Notes). The emphasis is on any collaborative activities between the dyads. Figure 10.4 summarizes the rank-ordering of the classrooms based on all of the interview data. The practice change measure is given, since it was the original focus; it is sometimes but not always a good predictor of overall ranking.

The rank-ordering of classrooms by parents and students roughly coincides with that based upon teacher reports alone: classrooms 22, 29, 62, and 73 are seen as strongly collaborative, and 25, 28, 77, and 78 are seen as relatively weak in collaboration. The major difference is the change in status of classrooms 28 and 29. Based upon teacher self-reports, the first was relatively high in collaborative activity, the latter relatively low. But based upon parent and student reports, their positions reverse almost precisely. (Classroom 79 also moves substantially, up from 9 to 4.)

CLASSRM NUMBER	TCHR PR. CHANGE COUNTS	TCHR COLLAB/ RANK	PAR./STUD. RANKS	OVERALL RANK
22100	19	03	04/02	HI
25100	13	07	11/12	LO
28100	17	04	10/07	MOD
29100	04	10	01/04	HI
62100	05	02	07/03	HI
63100	04	08	12/05	MOD
72100	13	11	06/09	LO
73100	08	01	02/01	HI
74100	08	12	05/08	LO
77100	05	05	08/10	MOD
78100	02	06	09/11	LO
79100	02	09	03/06	MOD

Figure 10.4   Ranking of classrooms based on participant interviews

With respect to the student data, the sum of student perceptions of teacher/ student, student/parent, and teacher/parent collaboration is labelled student commitment. We can illustrate these three collaboration elements from the student interviews. Student expectations of teachers are fairly simple, as we saw in the previous chapter. They include fairness, ability to help the student (which seems to involve explaining things clearly), interest in individual students and their opinions, and maintaining classroom order, particularly quiet.

S73304, favourite t chars, 4,
FS: Mrs M.; she has really good ways of – easy ways to make, to try to help you out. And she always has really really good ideas.
I: Do you learn lots in that room?
FS: Oh yeah lots and lots and lots.

S73306, class lrng env pos, 10,
She always has people say what they feel whenever – like if they're angry at something, she always wants to fix it; she always wants you to feel good about yourself.

S63304, st coll pos, 12,
He talks to you about things you do outside of school, probably sports or stuff; he is interested in what we do. He expects us to know what is good, what we should do and what is bad. He pays attention to our opinions.

S25301, cl could be diff yes, 3,
I would make sure the noise level was down so people would work.
(Asked what he would do if he were the teacher.)

S79307, class lrng env pos, 4,
It's quiet and you can concentrate. It's fine for me; it's quiet.

S61301, class lrng env mixed, 2,
It's easy to work, except when there is lots of noise. You can't really concentrate or anything.

The second contributor to commitment, collaboration with parents, largely involves the curriculum of the home, divided into general encouragement and specific assistance with school work.

S29304, curr of home gen comm, 1,
I: What about your parents, how can your parents help you to prepare to get ready if you are going to be a teacher or a nurse?
FS: Um. They can encourage me to keep doing well and stuff.

S79307, curr of home pos, 7,
MS: If I don't understand it and it's something that's hard; like we're doing grade seven math and I needed help.

The curriculum of the home is as likely to involve the father as the mother in two-parent families (the norm although not the rule in our sample). Note also the importance of other family members. Students usually report enjoying this opportunity to work with parent(s); sometimes there is less tension than in school, and it is always quieter.

S72307, curr of home pos, 19,
And then I have homework. At home my dad usually explains it to me. I think I like it the best when my dad helps because I'm not afraid to say no if I don't understand – she (mother) usually helps sometimes but it's usually my dad. But he usually teaches me things ahead like algebra. He started teaching me just for fun.

S62307, curr of home pos, 12,
MS: Yeah, sometimes we go out on walks and like I talk to them about maybe at school or if I were in trouble at school I talk to them usually on our walks where we are more relaxed walking.

I like working with my parents on school work. They really help and they never have a negative attitude about how I should do.

Well my grandpa he usually, when he comes over, gives me a long, long talk about university and making the right decisions and things. We usually have about an hour talk.

The two outlier classrooms seem to be 73 and 25, and a comparison of some illustrative student quotations clarifies the differences students feel, with respect to (a) teacher/student relations; (b) teacher/parent relations. The key themes in the first area are teacher helpfulness (supportive/anxiety-reducing). Helpfulness is a very important issue for students, and teachers 73 and 25 have very different impacts upon them.

S73304, st coll pos, 12,
FS: Yesterday she said if anybody needs help in long division to come up to the board and she would help them on it and I can't do long division very good and so she really helped me.

S25305, class learn env neg, 9,
FS: Sometimes I think she expects too highly of us. I always feel that I am not allowed to make mistakes . . . like if I make a mistake then she will be mad or something.
I: You feel that way or that happens?
FS: No, I just feel that way.

Helpfulness seems to go together with fairness, and paying attention to student feelings. Clustering of attitudes in this way is a common finding in this work.

S73304, t char pos, 1,
I: Is your teacher fair to students?
FS: Yeah, oh yeah. And she always, if she's not fair, she always tries to fix it. And it usually always works.

S73306, class lrng env pos, 10,
FS: She always has people say what they feel whenever, like if they're angry at something, she always wants to fix it . . . she always wants you to feel good about yourself.

S73306, st coll pos, 8,
I: She pays a lot of attention to students' opinions?
FS: Yes she does.

S25305, st coll neg, 9,
FS: Sometimes I get nervous when I'm talking to Miss An.[present teacher] but I didn't get nervous when I was talking to Mrs Au. [previous teacher]

S25305, t char neg, 4,
I: What happens when you make a mistake?
FS: Well, some people she kind of, if they have been making really stupid mistakes, sometimes she kind of ridicules them a bit.

S25305, t char neg, 4,
I: When she ridicules people, how are you feeling about that?
FS: Um, I don't think it is really fair. Sometimes, it was kind of a stupid answer so.

There are other features of classroom 73 worth attending to, as part of the cluster of attitudes which elicit very positive responses from students. We can best do this by showing parallel views, teacher and students, about student decision-making and responsibility.

t73, st decision
I do try to as much as I can, give them a feeling of owning their own work and being part of this class, consulting with them, so this isn't all being done 'to' them, but they're a part of the decision-making process

t73, st choice instance
Friday they plan their own day which they will be doing today.
They get an outline of all the things which are scheduled, they have an outline of all of their assignments, and . . . they decide what they're going to do . . .
They are so disappointed if they can't plan their own Friday. I've expected responsible choices and so they have an outline and they fill it in and they evaluate how they have spent their day and this changes over the months in their evaluation of them – initially wasting their time or they weren't focused or they didn't allow enough time, and these are their own comments.
They are responsible for all of the things that they are learning, their behaviour, the results of their behaviour, a lot of them didn't like to hear that at the beginning of the year and now they're accepting it and . . . they act in responsible ways.
I was checking these planners every day at the beginning of the year, I'm no longer doing that . . . they're learning to look ahead and to take responsibility [for] planning [and] time management.

student 73304, favourite t
Mrs M.; she just has really good ways of; easy ways to make . . . to try to help you out. And she always has really good ideas.
I: Do you think you learn lots in that room?
FS: Oh yeah lots and lots and lots . . .

student 73304
Sometimes she goes 'do you like doing it or do you want to switch?' Like if we're doing art and we were really into it, she'd ask if we wanted to still do it some more before she would go into a different activity.

student 73304
I: On projects do you get choices?
FS: Yep. Lots of time in art she gives us about four things that we can do and we can choose which one we want to do. . . . Social studies we did Peru and we had to put up our hands and then she picked which ones would be in each group and so we could be in a group that we wanted to be in, with people we wanted to be in it with.

Another major issue for this teacher is modelling behaviour, particularly treatment of others. This results in a classroom environment that is a pleasure for students to work within – almost uniquely in our years of interviewing students, this classroom is said to be quiet when necessary.

t73, t respects st modelling beh
I show respect for students; I try to do
that by listening to them. I guess to
allow more time to that stimulus and
response when kids do things disruptive
[I] try to model that myself and that
means without calling them down as I
expect them not to put others.
I: The ideal relationship teachers and
students?
t73: Again, respect, openness, caring. . . .

t73, t reaching st
I: What about reaching all the students; do
you have a problem with that this year?
FT: Let's just say that I try to do it, but
I'm sure that I'm [not] 100% successful,
because when I'm making a particular
effort to reach certain students, I'll often
reflect that I'm missing others. But I do try
to look at their individual styles and their
individual ways of doing things, make
room for them to work within those ways.

S73306, class env friends pos
I think my classmates really enjoy our
classroom; there's no doubt about that
one.

S73306, class lrng env pos
[On working in class here] Well it's a
lot easier, unless my class is talking a lot
but usually it's nice and silent.

S73306, class lrng env pos
The class is really good for being quiet
when I have to [work].

S73306, class lrng env pos
I didn't really have a good year there
[another school] . . . Down here it's not
like that, they treat you with respect.

S73306, class lrng env pos
Source material: she always wants you
to feel good about yourself.

In the second area general teacher/parent collaboration, and the use of student
planners to facilitate this are key themes. With regard to parent contact, there
are sharp differences between the classrooms in both references and types of
reference by the students (these points could be as well illustrated by reference
to the parent comments).

The student planners elicit much very favourable comment from students in
classroom 73.

S73304, s engagement pos, 9,
FS: The student planner, we really like that thing. I love that thing, I couldn't live
without it. I always forget what I have for homework and if you just look in it it tells
you what you've got for homework and when it's due.

S73306, t init pt coll, 6,
I: What about, your teacher talking to your parents. Do you think she has ways of
letting your parents know what you are learning?
FS: Yeah, I think she does. She uh, if you're having trouble in class . . . like if you
missed a lot of homework, she phones our parents and she talks to them about it so
we can fix it.

The lack of teacher/home communication is as obvious in Classroom 25:

S25301, t init pt coll neg, 2,
I: Does your teacher have ways of letting your parents know what is going on in the
classroom?
MS: Not really, she doesn't usually phone or anything.

S25301, t init pt coll neg, 2,
I: Do you have interviews?
MS: No, not usually.

TESTING OUR CLASSROOM PORTRAITS

The comparative classroom portraits summarized in Figure 10.4 (p. 133) combine the perceptions of all three triad partners. We follow our normal cross-checking pattern, and undertake a final check of the rankings using the quantitative data (Table 10.3 in the Chapter Notes). We use the summary judgments (the last column) from Figure 10.3, of parents on collaboration, and of students on commitment, to present some of the attitude scales of both parents and students, those most likely to be influenced by teachers.

The summary portraits in these tables differ somewhat from the originals, drawn from the interviews alone. But there is little doubt about the relative strength of classrooms 73 and 78, and the weakness of classroom 25 and others, by comparison.

The general pattern revealed in this chapter is that:

1. some teachers have consistent positive impacts upon the attitudes to school of many students **and their parents;**
2. these teachers shape **both home-based and school-based attitudes,** and
3. other teachers have equally consistent effects on the low end of the attitude scales.

The pattern suggests that **student commitment can indeed be sustained and strengthened by teachers and their attitudes and practices, but strong connections with the home are needed to accomplish that task.**

THE POWER OF TEACHER PRACTICES

Our questions were:

Is there evidence in the student or parent interviews of home or school experiences that positively influence student attitudes?

Are such experiences clearly related to changes in teacher and/or parent practices attributable to the Coproduction Project?

What the chapter tells us

We have seen that some teachers have consistent positive impacts upon students and their parents. **They model collaborative practices in their dealings.** Other teachers have consistent negative effects, modelling a kind of professional distance. In classroom 25, negative comments outweigh positive comments from students about student/teacher collaboration by 42 to 28 (Figure 10.3). On the other hand, **the teacher in classroom 73 elicited an astounding 120 net positive comments from students.** On the parent measures also this classroom ranked at or near the top.

Yet this classroom was only moderate in reported practice change (Figure 10.2). It was strong with respect to reported triad involvement, and teacher/

student collaboration. The student reports, indeed, are quite distinctive: we must conclude that practice change is not the best measure. Indeed, teacher practice itself is probably of less importance than we had thought. Rather, it is general teacher attitudes expressed in the daily treatment of students which is of importance to students. This is, of course, consistent with the previous chapter, in which we found relationships more important than practices.

Our main conclusion becomes: **student commitment can indeed be sustained and strengthened by collaborative teacher attitudes, expressed in and through their practices; strong connections with the home are essential to the task.**

As Chaucer noted in his portrait of the Clerke of Oxenford ('gladly would he lerne, and gladly teche') modelling behaviour is at the heart of teaching – the attitude of the learner/teacher is as important as what is taught. Our teacher 73 communicates collaborative attitudes, by modelling, to students in all that she does:

student 73304, favourite t chars
FS: Mrs M.; she just has really good ways of; easy ways to make . . . to try to help you out.
I: Do you think you learn lots in that room?
FS: Oh yeah lots and lots and lots.

student 3 73304, st coll pos
I: Do you talk to her individually; just you and her?
FS: Uh huh – if there's a problem that I have or a student is getting more attention than everybody else is, then I can usually talk to her. The whole class can.

In the previous chapter we spoke of the duality at the heart of student perceptions – good practices/technical skills together with good personal relationships with students make up the good teacher. Here the emphasis is upon a similar duality in instructional practice – teachers who combine challenge with support. In our experience, few students encounter such teachers.

The implications for school improvement

The upper elementary years are particularly important to students since it is here that the relationship between home and school, and hence student 'bonding' to school (Finn, 1989), can break down. To maintain positive student attitudes requires stronger collaboration between triad members than is typically found in schools in British Columbia or, we suspect, elsewhere. It is hard to imagine how schools can be improved without addressing this fundamental issue.

Yet it is not very difficult to strengthen perceived collaboration. Increasing teacher awareness and encouraging a few modest and not particularly demanding practice changes may help. However, underlying the practices of successful teachers are attitudes towards students and their parents which are not common amongst teachers in British Columbia. Developing and modelling such attitudes, and the practices that exemplify them, may constitute a much more serious challenge for many teachers.

Note that the teachers in our sample, and probably in the province, are competent practitioners. Few parents and students have experienced teacher incompetence of the kind described, for example, by Bridges (1986). They do encounter some teachers who do not engage students emotionally in learning.

The most successful teachers in our sample are modern exemplars of the Clerke; they model cheerful learning and teaching. They create classrooms **which are both productive and happy workplaces** for students and teacher alike. In the UK, based on a very different kind of study of effective secondary schools, Sammons, Thomas and Mortimore (1997, citing Hargreaves, 1995) speak of a school culture which is 'demanding but enjoyable' as optimal. Our most successful teachers create such a climate in their classrooms.

They also enjoy very successful careers, because students respond positively to their invitation to work collaboratively and to enjoy learning. Without such a sense of willing student collaboration no teacher can be or feel truly successful (McLaughlin and Yee, 1988).

11

The Power of Three: Lessons for School Improvement

The nature of things is in the habit of concealing itself.

(Heraclitus)

In this final chapter, I will first draw together the various analyses into a composite portrait of the power of three, describing how this collaboration works (or doesn't). Second, I describe some unhelpful myths about parents and schools. Discussion of these myths are used to summarize the general significance of our work, and compare it with the views of scholars in other countries. Third, I describe some proposals for school improvement arising from the work described here. Then, fourth, I present the broad outlines of a plan for school improvement, appropriate to middle schools.

HOW PARENT AND STUDENT ATTITUDES ARE SHAPED

The major questions posed and responses given, by chapter, are:

Chapter 3: How do families shape the commitment of children to school?
Parent mediating and intervening activities play a vital part in forging that connection with school and schooling which predicts the educational future of the child. When school and home are connected, schools can reinforce positive attitudes brought by students from the home. Teachers can compensate for home attitudinal disadvantage by forging strong links with students.

Chapter 4: What do parents regard as a 'good teacher'?
Teachers must (1) realize that parent collaboration is often dependent upon teacher invitation; (2) legitimize parent collaboration by recognizing parent rights and responsibilities; (3) facilitate collaboration through parent/teacher dialogues, informing parents about curriculum and methodology; (4) encourage collaboration by providing activities which parents and children can do together; (5) acknowledge parent collaboration by providing good, timely information about student performance.

Chapter 5: Can teacher collaborative efforts with the home be strengthened?
Teachers wishing to improve their practice with respect to collaboration, need

141

to make changes in their attitudes and practices consistently and obviously over a whole school year. Few, small and temporary changes are not helpful. Both breadth of change and persistence in the change are essential.

Chapter 6: How do more collaborative teachers differ from others?
Collaborative and non-collaborative teachers differ in the extent to which power to influence the triadic relationship is left to the student. The former group takes the responsibility for establishing links between home and school. Students are held accountable (for example, for having homework books signed). But they are not the sole link. Collaborative teachers believe that when parents are involved, it makes education easier for the kid, the parent, and the teacher.

Chapter 7: How do students and parents view teacher collaboration?
Teacher attitudes and practices affect the sense of partnership that can be generated amongst parents and the sense of teacher/student collaboration which can be generated amongst students. Even subtle differences between practices are perceptible to parents and students; some practices are strongly preferred. Teacher attitudes which predict collaboration are: a valuing of parental assistance; a realization that students and parents collaborate at home; and an acceptance that student classroom attitudes reflect parent attitudes to school and teacher. These attitudes differentiate between teachers.

Chapter 8: Can home and teacher work together to develop student acceptance of responsibility?
The development of student responsibility tends to be a function of the attitudes and practices of all three parties. The vital elements are (a) for teachers, beliefs about parental involvement, student capabilities, and deliberate teaching of responsibility; (b) for students, communication with parents about school, valuing school, and collaboration with teachers; (c) for parents, valuing school, an 'invitational' teacher attitude, and communication with students about school.

Chapter 9: How do relationships with teachers affect student commitment?
Student commitment to school is predicted by the student's general valuation of the importance of schooling (a home element), and the student's experience of collaboration with a teacher, based on the perception that the teacher cares about the student. Students do not experience such teachers often. But teachers who 'reach' students are powerful and memorable for students and their families.

Chapter 10: Do teacher attitudes/practices strongly influence student commitment?
The portraits of more and less successful classrooms suggest that (1) some teachers have consistent positive impacts upon many students and their

parents; (2) these teachers shape both home-based and school-based attitudes, and (3) other teachers have equally consistent effects on the low end of the attitude scales. Student commitment can indeed be sustained and strengthened by teachers and their practices, but strong connections with the home are usually needed to accomplish that task.

In what follows these specific findings, together with more general conclusions from the research study, are reshaped into lessons relevant to the school improvement effort.

FOUR MYTHS ABOUT PARENTS AND STUDENTS

Four myths about parents and their children, apparently believed by educators in many countries, can be dismissed on the basis of our findings, and those of scholars in other countries.

Myth 1: Some parents (and their children) don't care about school and schooling

This is often heard in school staffrooms as 'you can't expect those kids to be interested in school – look at their homes and/or parents' (often a single parent family is the referent). A less obviously biased version is 'this school serves a disadvantaged community'. In the USA and the UK the hidden reference here is to disadvantages of ethnicity and class. In Canada it is usually to poverty. Although these statements seem quite different, **the disastrous educational consequences of the two forms of the statement are the same – low expectations for student achievement, and no expectations for parent involvement.**

One of the strongest conclusions from our work is that **all parents care.** The most universal comment in our interviews concerned the importance of education: virtually every student we interviewed said that schooling was important to their future lives. The vast majority said this in response to home influence, and parent concern and guidance. In the UK, amongst ethnic minorities 'parents are acutely aware that without educational credentials their children may be deprived access to higher levels of education and training and may thus remain in unskilled employment or unemployed.' (Tomlinson, 1989, p. 16). Perhaps as a consequence of such parental beliefs, the attainment of ethnic minority children now exceeds that of white children (Sammons, 1995, p. 481).

Because all parents care, **all students care.** In the UK, 'behind the public mask of nonchalance that some pupils wear to hide their anxiety about the future is a concern to succeed and some realization of the consequences of not making the grade' (Rudduck, Chaplain, and Wallace, 1996, p. 3). Of the hundreds of students we interviewed, a few children asserted that they did not care about school. But children in middle schools wear their hearts on their sleeves: they were clearly saying that **school did not care about them.** Usually this was in the context of a particular classroom, and even of interactions with a particular teacher. As we showed in Chapter 3, in very unusual cases where homes have not provided good attitudinal preparation, teachers can make a great difference to children's attitudes to school, for good or ill, by demonstrating that the child's future mattered to them.

Earlier we argued that **it is not who parents are that matters, but what they do** (with respect to schooling). Recent work by Mayer in the USA has shown that money (beyond the bare minimum) cannot buy improved life chances for children: 'Once basic material needs are met, factors other than income become increasingly important to how children fare' (1997, p. 148). She demonstrates that: 'the amenities that are important to children's outcomes are weakly related to parents' income, whereas the amenities that are strongly related to parents' income are not very important to children's outcomes' (p. 10). The relationship between parenting practices and parent income is also weak (p. 11). Yet parental effects upon children's learning are strong.

Mayer quotes a teacher working in a school serving a poor community:

> One of the most astounding things to me since I've been here is how few parents there are – in fact I could only think of one or two if I thought real hard – that don't seem to care. Folks care. They want for their kids.
>
> (1997, p. 151)

It is very sad that this insight of the teacher is seen as 'astounding'.

Myth 2: Some parents cannot help their children to be successful in school

This is obviously related to Myth 1. Mayer demonstrated that low income and single parenthood together are associated with poor schooling outcomes for children. However, they may be correlated with poor outcomes 'because they are proxies for unmeasured parental characteristics' (1997, p. 155). We have labelled these 'unmeasured characteristics' (which have in fact been measured by many social scientists) 'family environment' and 'the curriculum of the home', and have described them in detail (Chapters 3 and 8). Clark (1983) has provided excellent descriptions of the 'unmeasured characteristics' for poor Black families in the USA. Some of these families have high-achieving children, some have low-achieving children. Clark examined the family dynamics which differentiate them:

> No matter whether the family unit consisted of one or two parents, specific psychosocial orientations and home activity patterns were seen clearly time and again in the high achievers' homes. These recurring processes and patterns, as a group, represent parents' styles of helping their children adjust to the student role by 'sponsoring' or grooming them for that role. The interpersonal communication patterns in these homes tended to be marked by frequent child–parent dialogue, strong parental encouragement in academic pursuits, clear and consistent limits set for the young, warm and nurturing interactions, and consistent monitoring of how they used their time.
>
> (1983, p. 111)

The result of such parenting is children who have 'developed an inner belief that they are capable of acting on (and ordering) their world' (1983, p. 118). In our analyses this 'inner belief' is labelled student efficacy; it parallels parent and teacher efficacy as important predictors of behaviour.

In the UK the importance of parent attitudes was demonstrated long ago – an investigation for the Plowden Committee (1967) 'showed conclusively that it was not material home circumstances but parental attitudes which accounted for the greatest amount of variance in pupil achievement' (Solomon, 1994, p. 565). Within the general attitude set, it was parental aspirations for their children which made the greatest difference to achievement.

Again, **it is not who parents are that is important, but what they do, with and for their children, to prepare them for success in school.**

Our other myths concern the present situation and the motivations of parents with respect to schools and schooling.

Myth 3: Parents are involved and influential in schools at present

There are public schools in British Columbia in which signs are posted at the entrance to advise parents that they cannot bring their primary school children into the school – they must leave them at the door. There are schools in which teachers have barred individual parents from the school, because they are 'troublemakers' (that is, concerned about the welfare of their children, and not convinced that the school is serving them well). These schools are unusual, at the moment, but **represent a teacher ethos which sees parents as the enemy – in a public school system.**

The body of knowledge associated with a profession is sometimes used to distance members of that profession from those they serve. We have seen many instances in our data of parents commenting on this distancing, which they feel strongly. Sykes (1990, p. 81) argues that teachers:

> must share responsibility with parents, and this means reducing social distance and demystifying school knowledge. In other fields, social distance and mystification enhance the claim to expertise, and possession of the knowledge contributes to social distance. This circular relation builds professional status but is impermissible in teaching.

Yet the wish to keep parents at a distance seems characteristic of educational systems everywhere. In the UK, Vincent and Tomlinson argue that 'there are few opportunities for collective parental participation at any level of the education system' (1997, p. 366). The experience of some of our parents, described in Chapters 3, 4, and 6, strongly resembles the European norm for relations between parents and schools. The universal perception of 'distancing' is matched by as universal a desire for a more productive relationship between home and school. Both are illustrated in these statements:

> The school structures in Austria, Germany and Switzerland enable teachers to be able to keep parents at arms length. It is these structures that cause parents to bemoan, just as they did 150 years ago, 'What can I do: I've got a hostage at school.' What ought to be the most important proper expectations? A school constitution forcing teachers to do what is expected of them . . . . : to try everything possible to enable the children in their care to learn to the best of their possibilities both inside and outside of school.
>
> (Krumm, 1994, p. 23)

There is an increasing opposition in Italy to what might be described as the 'fictitious pedagogy' of the 1970s which viewed schooling as the totality of education. . . . Its results were:

- the diffusion of prejudicial suspicion about the educational capacities of parents and, when schools failed to live up to expectations, of teachers as well;
- impotent feelings among relevant adults and a mistrust of their own capacities and resources;
- impatience and resentment by parents and teachers at the scapegoat role being allocated to them;
- loss of prestige of both family and school.

If construction of identity begins in the family and if the family mediates between the individual and society, then the family needs constant reinforcement from social agencies, including the school. It also requires the continuous example of those adults who are significant to the child. These, again, point to partnership between school and family.

(Scaparro, 1994, p. 31)

Two kinds of strategies should be developed by the schools and the Parents' Associations at school in order to increase parent–teacher cooperation. The first has to do with informative and consultative actions; through them parents and children could acquire relevant information about family issues that influence parent–teacher relationships, parent–children relationships, learning processes and school achievement. The second ones have a formative nature; they are more structured and long-term, and should be contextualized in the school. They are related to implementing programs in schools to increase parents' involvement. Through formal and informal activities performed at schools, these programs would allow parents to understand better the educative reality of the schools and to feel they belong to them.

(Martinez, Marques, and Souta, 1994, p. 54; speaking of Portugal and Spain)

Teachers often wish to do their job independently; they find it difficult to have parents watching over their shoulders. On the other hand, parents want the school to reinforce what they themselves transfer to their children at home. . . . 'The school to the parents' is a maxim that is practically never realized. The formal school system should leave more room for parents to substantiate their responsibilities for their children. It would only be to the advantage of teachers and students alike.

(Smit and van Esch, 1994, p. 66; speaking of the Netherlands)

Too little effort, in my opinion, is made to develop joint learning processes involving parents, teachers and children on equal terms, while admitting their different qualifications, capacities and institutional roles to be developed and applied. Mutual influence and dependency offers opportunities for using the manifold resources in creating a common ground on which to develop new joint learning processes.

(Ravn, 1994, p. 77; speaking of the Scandinavian countries)

The aspect of parental involvement which is more significant *educationally* (italics in original) concerns parents' contributions to the learning of their own individual child. If significant learning happens inevitably in the family and significant learning (of a different nature and differently provided) also happens in the school, then it may be argued that educational partnership should involve both elements of learning. . . . Once home-learning is seen to be an inevitable and remorseless element of every child's education and influential upon teachers' effectiveness, then a powerful *professional* (italics in original) reason for educational partnership emerges. The challenge is to find ways to harness home-learning without disrupting the established systems or putting undue pressure on parents.

(Macbeth, 1994, pp. 84, 85)

Our parents are conscious of the difficulties that teachers face daily. When they have an opportunity to visit or work in classrooms their normal reaction is 'I don't know how they do it', i.e. cope with the varying needs of many energetic students for hours at a time. They have no wish to disrupt what they see as a delicate and finely balanced system, which depends on the energies of dedicated teachers.

Parents are widely supportive of schools and teachers in Canada (Livingstone, 1995; Barlow and Robertson, 1994) as in other countries (Hughes, Wikeley, and Nash, 1994 describe the feelings of parents in England). This is certainly true for our parents; yet **parents are conscious that much more could be done to help their students learn, in classrooms and in the home, if their own willingness to help was not discounted and undervalued.**

Associated with Myth 3 is another, never far beneath the surface of teachers' concerns:

Myth 4: Parent involvement is a way for parents to control schools

There are scholars who believe that the only way to change schools is to bring parents into positions of control. Raywid (1990) proposes 'schools of choice' as the only way to open schooling to parental influence (I concur; see Coleman, 1994). Sarason (1995) believes that the existing governance system should be abolished. He describes a series of meetings with teachers, in which teachers complained about parents:

> It would be unfair to say that these teachers were, so to speak, antiparents (i.e. wishing that they would go away and stay away). What was nettlesome to them was when parents, directly or indirectly, challenged their professional knowledge and practices, and sometimes the scope of their authority. That response is not peculiar to educators; it is a response quite characteristic of those in all the professions.
>
> (1995, p. 23)

Sarason proposes a political principle for the governance of schools: 'the decision-making process should reflect the views of all those who will be affected by the ultimate decision' (1995, p. 39).

In Canada Lawton believes that revolutionary change in the public school system is imperative. He argues for privatization, based on the principles that 'parents must be able to ensure that their children are educated in accordance with their family's values' (1995, p. 98); that 'no group should be given a monopoly within the education system'; 'parents and school-community members must control the governance of individual elementary and lower-secondary schools' (p. 100). Such views emerge from considerable parent frustration, as we have shown for our own parents in Chapters 3, 4, and 8.

However, there is little evidence so far that parents can successfully govern schools. The Chicago experiment with universal school-based management by parents (Bryk *et al.*, 1994) has encountered serious management problems. In the UK, parent governors rely heavily upon educational professionals, notably heads. Filling parent-governor positions is difficult for schools (Macbeth, 1989, p. 143). British parents are primarily focused upon the quality of relationships in the school, and the general climate, rather than on control issues (Hughes, Wikeley, and Nash, 1994, pp. 99–104).

Nothing in our Canadian data suggests that ordinary parents here are interested in school governance. Parent Advisory Committees are viewed negatively. School Boards are never mentioned at all in hundreds of lengthy and very wide-ranging interviews. Principals are mentioned rarely (with a few exceptions). Our parents describe the source of both positive and negative schooling experiences for children as the classroom, not the school. There is little sense that changes at school level would change the teacher/student and teacher/parent relationships which parents see as vital.

They are probably correct in such skepticism. Our study sites included one private school, which was fully parent-controlled, financially and managerially, charging high fees and enrolling students from families with considerable financial and professional resources. Parents were required to devote some time to volunteering in the school. Yet we were unable to see any consequences of this governance model for the classroom experiences of students and parents (see Chapter 7). These parents seemed just as frustrated with their experiences in trying to help their children as public school parents.

Our parents generally dismiss parent governance as necessary or useful, **because they see little connection at present between governance arrangements and teaching and learning activities. They believe these are entirely controlled by teachers.**

Discussing the current international education reform movement, Levin argues that

> the kinds of strategies that might really change the educational basis of schooling – in particular placing students and their schooling at the center of the educational process – have not been at the center of government-sponsored reforms. Partly this may be because they are so difficult to put into practice. We know how to pass laws changing governance but we don't know much yet about how to change instructional practices. Partly it may be because such changes are less visible than testing and governance changes, and so lack immediate political appeal. Whatever the reason, **it is hard to believe that programs of reform will lead to better outcomes, in any sense, if they do not center around what students do.**
>
> (1997, p. 264; my emphases)

Indeed. I now address some changes which I believe do have the potential to improve schooling, because they do place students (and their parents) at the heart of the matter.

PROPOSALS FOR REFORM BASED UPON OUR RESEARCH

I will first state a series of proposals. These proposals derive from my view of the purposes of schools, which rest upon the assumption that the family has the moral and legal right to decide what is in the best interests of the child (Macbeth, 1989). This right is, for example, enshrined in the provisions for programming for special education ('statemented' in the UK) children; such individualized programs require the written consent of parents almost everywhere.

Purposes

In recent years policy analysts formulating the purposes of public education have given precedence to broad policy (government) purposes, such as equity, excellence, and efficiency (Mitchell and Encarnation, 1984), without any reference to the needs of families and children. But the most important outcomes of a good school are not social levelling, or supporting the expansion of the national economy, or creating docile citizens, but rather student commitment to education and learning.

A commitment to serving the educational needs of families must come first; the societal benefits that typically flow from education cannot be achieved without this commitment:

1. The proper purpose of schools is to provide an educational service to families. (The label 'educational service' is common in the UK, but regrettably both the label and the notion seem entirely absent from most discussions of schooling in North America.)
2. The most important outcomes of a good (middle) school are student commitment to education. This commitment is typically associated with good results in tests and examinations (Sammons, Thomas, and Mortimore, 1997, p. 174), and with the continuation of schooling to graduation, as opposed to 'dropping out'. It usually results in later 'success' as defined by family and student.

'Success' for us includes 'career success', 'life enhancement', the learned ability to enjoy a wide range of civilizing and enriching activities; and 'good citizenship', participation in the political and social life of the community. Large-scale longitudinal studies in the USA have demonstrated that these and other forms of success are indeed associated with perseverance in formal education (Hyman, Wright, and Reed, 1975). Such studies demonstrate the multitude of ways in which the larger society benefits from the success of individuals; indeed, without the educated citizen democratic governance is impossible.

Proposals

Our proposals include three forms of collaboration, all justified by our findings:

1. more inclusive models of learning, in which parents become co-teachers and co-learners with teachers and students;
2. consistent teacher modelling of collaborative practice in classrooms; and
3. school-wide development activities, themselves conducted in a collaborative way.

Building communities of learners
The theme of Chapter 3 was 'making connections', the ways in which families help their children to 'connect' with school and schooling. The analysis

demonstrated the power of the family to form students' school careers. Both mediating and intervening activities were common. Many of the parents described in this chapter have not been encouraged to participate by the school, and must derive efficacy from other sources. Typically this source is a keen sense of their parental obligations. Hoover-Dempsey and Sandler suggest that such a parental role-definition, plus experience of success, generates efficacy, which can then be sustained by school invitations to get involved (1997, p. 28).

Chapter 4 concluded with a series of suggestions for teachers, intended to help them to maximize their positive impact on the children in their classrooms. We suggested that teachers facilitate and encourage parent collaboration through some simple practices, all well-known but not implemented consistently in any of our schools (or we believe in many schools anywhere). However, the practices are less important than teacher attitudes. The teacher who accepts the importance of parental support in the effort to strengthen student commitment, and also takes responsibility for sustaining parent efficacy, is vital to school improvement.

Together these chapters suggest that the parents in the school community constitute the most important resource the school has for school improvement, when this is defined as raising the level of student commitment. Student engagement, or the lack thereof, is the most pressing problems facing schools (Newmann, 1992, pp. 2, 3; Metz, 1993; Talbert and McLaughlin, 1993, pp. 184, 185).

The first task of the school as learning community is to strengthen collaborative links between teachers and parents. This work must be done both by school leaders, acting to shape school climate or ethos, and by every classroom teacher.

PROPOSAL 1: the most important task facing the school at present is collaboration with parents in building active communities of learners. The school that is concerned about student commitment, and all should be, will focus upon strengthening collaborative links with parents as instructional supporters of their children.

Modelling collaborative practice

One consistent classroom-level difference between more and less effective schools has emerged: 'teachers in an effective school displayed almost double the mean percent of interactive teaching as that displayed by teachers at an ineffective school' (Teddlie, Kirby, and Stringfield, 1989, p. 3).

In Chapter 6 we saw that collaborative teachers create a classroom setting that reflects many of the characteristics of the effective school (Chrispeels, 1992, pp. 9, 10). They convey to students and parents that in their classrooms students work hard and 'learn lots' (opportunity to learn). Students are kept informed of what is expected of them (high expectations) and how well they have achieved those goals (frequent monitoring of student progress). The collaborative teacher extends learning opportunities by keeping parents informed about how parents can support learning at home (student time on task; positive home–school relations). Additionally, collaborative and non-collaborative teachers differ in the extent to which power to influence the triadic relationship is left to the student. The former group of teachers takes on the responsibility to establish links between the two adult members of the triad. Students in these classrooms are not the sole link between home and school.

Collaborative teachers believe that when parents are brought into the relationship, it makes education 'easier . . . for the kid, the parent, and the teacher.' Other teachers convey professional distance, usually wordlessly; as one parent observed: 'he figures he can handle it himself better.'

In Chapter 7 we found that even subtle differences between teachers' practices are perceptible to parents and students and some practices are strongly preferred. The teacher attitudes predicting collaboration with parents were: a valuing of parental assistance; belief that students and parents do collaborate at home; and an understanding that student classroom attitudes reflect parent attitudes.

In Chapter 8 we found that when the development of student responsibility occurs it is a function of the attitudes and practices of all three parties. The teacher attitudes to students that predict collaboration can also be summarized. Because both academic interactions and social interactions are important to students (Wang, Haertel, and Walberg, 1993, p. 277), collaborative teachers maintain a balance between both aspects: 'he's nice, and he helps me'; 'the teacher is real nice and she teaches, she doesn't play around and play games, she teaches'. In Chapter 9, we find that preferred teachers listen to students; know student needs; empathize with students; are serious about teaching, with high expectations; and help students individually. Few classrooms contain such teachers; in other words, few teachers reach all, or nearly all, the students in their classrooms.

In Chapter 10 we find that some teachers **model collaborative practices in all their dealings with students.** Other teachers have consistent negative effects, modelling a kind of professional distance, eliciting as many negative comments from parents and students as positive ones. But teacher practice itself is of less importance than we had thought. Rather, it is general teacher attitudes expressed in the daily treatment of students which is important to students. Modelling behaviour is at the heart of collaborative teaching.

This is essentially the way in which our Teacher 73 conducts her classes (Chapter 10); the way in which our preferred teachers in Chapter 9 are seen to function by their students; and the way in which our most successful exponent of teaching responsibility in Chapter 8 deals with students.

These are not new findings for B.C. A few of the students interviewed in a study of 'The Learners of British Columbia' (as part of a Royal Commission Report; Marx, Grieve, and Rossner, 1988), indicated that 'a particular teacher did cause them to be actively involved'. But such experiences, and such teachers, are rare.

These writers recommend that teaching methods:

> must require that students be active, that they must talk and work together . . . must ask questions just as much as they answer them. They must provide resources and help for others just as much as they use resources and help provided by others, and they need to work in cooperative environments just as much as they need to work in competitive environments.
>
> (1988, p. viii)

This report also emphasizes the relationship between choice and motivation for students.

Like other workers, for example teachers, students find that being able to exercise control over the conditions and processes of their work enhances their ability to complete it successfully. Much other scholarly work of the last decade suggests that students can and should take responsibility for their own learning (e.g. Good and Brophy, 1987, p. 499; Cohen, McLaughlin 1993). In Chapter 8 we described in detail the practices and attitudes which facilitated that process for our students.

All of the teachers in our (volunteer) sample were good practitioners; yet their impact upon their students was much less than they and we expected to find. Underlying the practices of our most successful teachers are uncommonly accepting and collaborative attitudes towards students and their parents, inside and outside the classroom.

PROPOSAL 2: As part of the 'community of learners' effort, teachers should model collaborative practice. Teacher decision-making in regard to daily, weekly, and long-term instructional plans about classroom activities is guided by one central question: 'in what ways can students, parents, and teachers work together to optimize learning, in and out of the classroom?'.

A school-wide program of practice change: the importance of school climate
In Chapters 5 and 10 we found that the modest changes in teacher practices regarding parent involvement recommended as part of the Coproduction Project and described in Chapter 4 were not consistently and powerfully implemented in any classroom, in ways that would offset general disappointment amongst the parents and students we studied about their school experience over the year.

If teachers wish to improve their practice with respect to collaboration, they must make many of the kinds of changes suggested, and make them consistently over a whole school year. What is needed is **a school-wide program of practice change, with feedback on attitude changes amongst parents and students.**

This proposal may seem contradictory – if the classroom level is of first importance, as I claimed earlier, why bother about school-level activities? However, the better the school, the more interdependent classrooms tend to be.

> The most powerful and enduring lesson from all the research on effective schools is that the better schools are more tightly linked – structurally, symbolically, and

culturally – than the less effective ones. They operate more as an organic whole and less as a loose collection of disparate subsystems.

(Murphy, 1990, p. 9)

Individual classrooms need to change – yet for teachers planning and changing together with colleagues is more likely to be effective than trying to change independently. Students need the support of parents and teachers to become more effective learners; teachers need the support of peers and school leaders to become more effective teachers (Fullan, Bennett, and Rolheiser-Bennett, 1989; Louis and Smith, 1992).

Sammons, Thomas, and Mortimore (1997, pp. 165–7) point out a variety of ways in which levels interact. They summarize their findings thus:

Behaviour policy and practice, leading to a safe orderly working environment and an academic emphasis, are necessary for task achievement (effective teaching and learning and thus students' academic progress) while the student-focused environment concerns social cohesion and creates a positive climate for learning. The school experience thus becomes both demanding and enjoyable for teachers and students alike.

(1997, p. 179)

Their model of secondary school effectiveness (1997, p. 170) emphasizes inter-actions between levels, what we have described as 'the web' (Coleman and Collinge, 1991). They argue that there are many ways for schools to be ineffec-tive, but one mode of effective school (p. 178), and it is tightly linked.

I (with LaRocque) have argued that tight linkages distinguish good from bad school districts:

The levels within a school district are to a large extent autonomous, but in high-performing districts there is a monitored aspect to this autonomy; the professional freedom to operate schools and classrooms is bounded by the prevailing norms and practices of the district which are summarized in the notion of productive ethos. Productive ethos at the district level both constrains and facilitates; that is, it provides a kind of 'Supported-Enforcement' (Huberman and Miles, 1984) element to the work of principals and teachers.

(1990, p. 197)

The most important form of linkage between levels (for us, between classroom and school) is summed in the notion of school climate ('culture' or 'ethos' to describe professional culture). Thus, for example, school climates support some classroom emphases by teachers, and challenge others.

The duality of personal relationships between good parents, good teachers and students – 'pressure and support' (Figure 2.1), or 'challenge and caring' – is matched by descriptions of school climates emphasizing both social control and social cohesion. In such schools, 'for both teachers and students, school is a demanding but very enjoyable place' (Hargreaves, 1995, pp. 28, 29).

A school-wide program of practice change: the importance of monitoring
Since the major difficulties with school development planning in many places have concerned evaluation of success (Haylow and Coleman, 1991; MacGilchrist and Mortimore, 1997, p. 212), I propose a school development

model linked to affective outcomes, specifically **the tracking of changes in student and parent attitudes towards school practices and climate.**

The importance of feedback to teachers cannot be overstressed (see Sammons, Thomas, and Mortimore, 1997, p. 184, on the use and misuse of achievement scores for this purpose). One distinctive feature of 'the intelligent school' (MacGilchrist, Myers, and Reed, 1997) is the use of data to monitor change efforts. In any attempt to raise student commitment what must be fed back to teachers is data on the trends in student and parent attitudes, classroom by classroom.

The surveys we used in the study described here could easily be adapted for this purpose. In the Chapter Notes I provide some of the scales (lists of items) most likely to be useful. Note that our measures are all taken in schools in which attempts are being made to strengthen home–school collaboration. Yet there is still a slight tendency for scores to decline over that school year. Schools using our measures should not expect immediate school-wide improvement – rather, classroom by classroom changes, some positive, some negative, are more likely (see the Chapter Notes).

> **PROPOSAL 3: Both breadth of change and persistence in more collaborative practices are essential. A school culture supporting such changes in teacher practice is essential. Continuing feedback on attitude changes amongst parents and students is also required. As a consequence, whole-school implementation guided by monitoring of attitude changes is necessary for significant improvement to occur.**

GETTING FROM THE SCHOOLS WE HAVE TO THE SCHOOLS WE NEED

How are schools to be improved? Despite many years of research, there are still no clear answers to the question. Consider the current and very extensive effort at school improvement under way in Memphis, Tennessee, described in a recent special issue of the journal *School Effectiveness and School Improvement* (Stringfield *et al.*, 1997).

Virtually all the models being tested focus on changing pedagogy (as opposed to changing relationships). Student engagement and the **instructional relevance of parents** are ignored, although the 'support' of the community and of parent volunteers within the school is cited as a resource (Ross *et al.*, 1997). The choice of model to implement in various schools was made by school staffs, without reference to parents and students (*ibid.*) Teachers are unlikely to choose reform models emphasizing the strengthening of parental contributions to student learning, or of levels of student commitment.

The Memphis effort is being mounted 30 years after James Coleman and colleagues demonstrated that in-school factors are modest and inconsistent in their impact upon student achievement compared to the effects of home influences (1966), and shortly after one of the most extensive reviews of research ever reported (Wang, Haertel, and Walberg, 1993) concluded that proximal factors such as family influence (and the student characteristics closely related to them) are **virtually the only strong and reliable influence upon student commitment and achievement**. By contrast, many studies have demonstrated the weakness of the variables being addressed in Memphis (Hanushek, 1997). The 'nature of things' with respect to schooling outcomes continues to 'conceal itself'.

The proposals here, in brief, were:

1. **collaboration with parents in building communities of learners;**
2. **teacher modelling of collaborative practice in classrooms;**
3. **school-wide implementation and monitoring of change efforts.**

Each of these proposals requires changes in the ways schools normally operate. Parents, teachers and students must think about their roles and responsibilities in different ways. So must school leaders – rather than buffering schools from parents, leaders must find ways of opening schools to parents.

Detailed planning must be done at school level, but four issues which must be attended to in order to maximize the chance of success can be sketched.

School improvement and parent involvement

Parents have a substantial contribution to make to collaborative efforts, as we have demonstrated. Chrispeels (1996, p. 305) has shown the very close correspondence between family practices which support children's learning, and characteristics of effective schools such as: 'time on task', 'clear mission and academic focus' and 'high aspirations/expectations' aptly describe the attitudes communicated by many of our families, and match descriptions of effective schools.

The impact of parent involvement on school climate has been less studied. The assumption of researchers is that teachers require 'buffering' from parents. However, a large-scale (86 schools) study specifically of middle schools found that 'Although teachers desire buffering from the outside . . . pressure from parents and the community seem to facilitate rather than hinder' (Hoy and Hannum, 1997, p. 304), Such pressure was associated with higher student achievement. The researchers are surprised by this result; our interventionist parents in Chapter 3 would not be surprised at all.

In sum, then, the main contributions of parents are (1) the attitudinal preparation of students; and (2) maintaining pressure on the school for higher levels of student commitment. Obviously, no attempt to improve schools using the ideas suggested here can be successful without prior consultation with parents, which elicits genuine parent enthusiasm and commitment to helping in the school effort.

Teacher practice change and student involvement

It is unlikely that schools anywhere can be improved without teachers who accept the view that the work of teaching has a dimension that goes beyond techniques or practices, beyond professional status, and beyond union rules. In good schools teachers assume broader responsibilities for students than the narrowly curricular (Wehlage *et al.*, 1987, p. 45). Some have described this as 'a culture of inclusion' (Newmann, 1992, p. 183), others as 'the ethic of care' (Marshall *et al.*, 1996).

The impact of such a school-wide climate upon students has been demonstrated: student outcomes improve when they 'experience the school as a caring and supportive environment in which they actively participate and have opportunities to exercise influence' (Battistich *et al.*, 1995, p. 649). A school community of this kind 'both conveys a set of values and helps establish the motivation to abide by them' (p. 649).

The best illustration of an attempt to implement a 'community of learners' approach in the literature is a report on the outcomes (in achievement and attitudes) of cooperative learning, adopted school-wide. The results were unequivocally positive for many different kinds of learners.

> This study is the first and only evaluation of a cooperative elementary school. It is not merely another study of cooperative learning; it is the only study to evaluate cooperative learning as the focus of school-wide change, the only study to evaluate cooperative learning in many subjects at once, and one of the few to show the effects of cooperative learning over a multiyear period.
>
> (Stevens and Slavin, 1995, p. 347)

The model of cooperative learning chosen is all-important. Projects which provide solely for group accountability for outcomes are rarely successful, because of the 'free rider' effect; capable students find themselves doing all the work for the group. But **models which provide for both group goals and individual accountability** have been very successful (Stevens and Slavin, 1995; Madden *et al.*, 1993). This is just one approach to developing a classroom community; the essential elements, for students, have been described in some of our chapters, particularly in Chapters 9 and 10.

Perhaps of greatest importance is 'fairness' – the perception that the teacher treats each student appropriately (not necessarily equally – students are conscious of differing needs amongst their peers). We have shown the collective sense of classroom well-being amongst students. The 'caring' scale we constructed for Chapter 9 included items referring to teacher relationships with all students.

The 'community of learners' approach has been described as one 'in which shared goals and standards, an atmosphere of mutual trust, and norms for behaviour support students in taking the risks and making the sustained efforts entailed in serious learning' (Talbert and McLaughlin, 1993, p. 169). Some of our students have experienced a 'community of learners' at classroom level (Chapters 8, 9, 10). There is no doubt about its power to influence them. Unfortunately all of them have experienced disruptive classrooms in which the irresponsibility of the few makes learning difficult for the many.

In sum, then, the 'community of learners' approach includes (1) a school-wide 'culture of inclusion' in which all students participate and have influence;

and (2) opportunities for students to work collaboratively with others, in classrooms in which teachers are fair, and where shared standards for work and behaviour are developed and implemented.

Implementing school-wide change: school leadership

Zeldin has commented that 'forming productive coalitions is the new art of leadership' (Zeldin, 1994, p. 155). We need such leadership to bring about more collaborative schools. But reliance on administrative leadership alone is likely to be disastrous. Careful case studies of school change (Huberman and Miles, 1984; Prestine and Bowen, 1993; Chrispeels, 1992) demonstrate that school administrators move from position to position frequently (and often unwillingly) and change efforts which rely on individual administrators are fragile as a consequence. One solution is 'systemic leadership' in which collective responsibility for leadership exists (Prestine and Bowen, 1993, p. 308).

Although 'systemic leadership' is usually taken to mean teacher leadership, that is too narrow a view. Change efforts are often disrupted by resistance from parents and students who feel aggrieved when changes are made without their knowledge and support, just as teachers do (Fullan, 1991). Teacher leaders, parent leaders, and student leaders must be included in the 'productive coalition' since all members of the school community have a part to play in implementing change.

Educators may question student participation at middle school level; however, Shedd and Bacharach argue that 'if schools are to teach creativity and problem-solving and cooperation and involvement, they must practice them, not just in the classroom but at all levels of the system' (1991, p. 193, 194). We have shown in Chapters 8 and 10 that some teachers work hard to provide choices for students, as opportunities to act responsibly, with positive consequences.

In most schools, the preference for more collaborative teaching and learning will be stronger amongst parents and students than amongst teachers. But they are powerless to make significant changes. The commitment of teacher leaders, and the transformational leadership they offer to colleagues, will be vital to the changes suggested here.

Transformational leadership redefines mission and vision, renews commitment, and restructures for goal accomplishment (Roberts, 1985). In a school willing to reconsider its mission, and to place collaboration at the centre of the collective vision of the good school, restructuring both school-wide attitudes and school-wide practices becomes the key to success. The 'productive coalition' will be both evidence of new attitudes, and an important model for classroom change.

Implementing school-wide change: teacher development

Such restructuring requires teacher learning, as well as cooperation from students and their parents. We saw in Chapter 8 how parents respond to collaborative classroom practices when they are involved as participants. They appreciate the skill and commitment of teachers who can teach students not only curriculum content but more responsible ways of managing their own learning:

> I find it amazing when I go in there and it's just about time to quit . . . and each child manages to say how they felt about the day – and there's nobody shouting and there's nobody pushing in – and then she goes around and does all of the diaries [homework books] and everything. So there's certainly a real feeling of cooperation and of respect.

The notion of the community of learners implies that all participants are on occasion learners; all on occasion teachers. The cliché form of this idea in North American schools is the sign often seen on the Principal's door: HEAD LEARNER. If this is a genuine belief, which is modelled as well as publicly espoused, it can serve as an important statement to all, since if we are to have more collaborative schools, teacher learning is essential.

But effective teacher learning depends upon professional efficacy (Smylie, 1988). This sense of professional competence is shaped by students (Metz, 1993, pp. 104, 105) and also by colleagues willing to share their expertise. More effective schools report higher levels of teacher sharing, and more consistency in practices between classrooms (Teddlie, Kirby, and Stringfield, 1989; Virgilio, Teddlie, and Oescher, 1991). Indeed, teacher commitment 'flows out of teachers' opportunities to learn, be challenged, and contribute together as a team' (Kushman, 1992, p. 38).

There is also some evidence in our work that parent involvement contributes to teacher efficacy; our teachers spoke of the satisfaction they felt when meetings with parents resulted in new levels of understanding of curriculum and student work. This was common in the context of both homework books, and three-way conferences as a means of reporting to parents on previous student efforts and attainment and on setting new growth targets.

Rosenholtz uses the term 'teacher certainty' rather than efficacy, but the notions are very similar. She finds that it is supported by parent involvement, teacher collaboration, and student behaviour (1989, p. 114), **all acting as independent influences.**

What is not often noted is that more consistency in teachers' practices between classrooms **requires a decline in teacher autonomy** (Smylie, Lazarus, and Brownlee-Conyers, 1996), which goes together with the following characteristics: more participative decisions; more organizational learning opportunities for teachers; instructional improvement; improved outcomes for students; and increased accountability for teachers.

Collaborative learning communities offer much for teachers whose efficacy has been threatened by hard-to-reach students, remote parents, and professional isolation (that is, almost all teachers). But such communities require teachers to give up high levels of autonomy. This trade-off for teachers is the down side of the collaborative learning community recommended here.

Implementing change over time: monitoring attitudes

The great weakness of school development plans has been monitoring. A new emphasis upon monitoring attitudes is emerging in Canada as part of the 'school accreditation' process (Gray and Maxwell, 1995), and in the UK as part of school inspections (Coleman, 1992).

I suggest that schools wishing to become collaborative learning communities adopt a change model which I label 'monitored implementation of affective change'. This model is characterized by:

1. collective (school-wide) specification of attitudinal goals and measures of collaboration/commitment, but classroom-level specification of practice change aimed at improving student commitment; i.e. collective goals but individual or small-group actions to attain them;
2. tightly focused staff development activities which emphasize teacher research, i.e. 'piloting' classroom practice changes and tracking the results, in preparation for school-wide adoption;
3. monitoring that measures what you are trying to change, matched with attempts to change that which you are trying to measure, i.e. 'teaching to the test';
4. wide sharing of data, together with careful development of skill in analyzing/interpreting data by all members of the school community (see Chapter Notes for more on monitoring).

Specific suggestions for improving levels of collaboration have been made in some of the chapters (in particular Chapter 4). For North America, Swap (1992) has provided detailed suggestions, as have Walberg and Wallace (1992). Macbeth (1989) has provided similar guidance in the UK. Kellaghan and colleagues have described some ambitious plans from various places (1993).

Although these guidebooks are likely to be helpful to schools, what will work best in a school must be determined by the school community. Many approaches are worth trying – I personally favour the careful use of homework books and three-way conferencing as key practices with respect to collaboration with parents and student responsibility, but there are many other possibilities. There is much to be learned from diversity of practices **if these efforts in individual classrooms are:**

1. maintained in intensive form for the whole school year; and
2. carefully monitored by measuring student and parent attitude change.

Much can be learned from other attempts to change. These comments (from Prestine and Bowen, 1993), drawn from school experience, constitute good advice on change efforts:

> The focus at all levels must be on essential school change efforts and everything that is done must be commensurate with that focus.
>
> (p. 306)

Small limited pilot project efforts, while possibly having some utility early in the change process, had to be replaced by more ambitious, systemic, and enduring changes.

(p. 307)

The longer the school waits in establishing observable and sustained change, the greater the buildup of resistance and inertia to such change.

(p. 307)

Once the school achieves a consensus understanding and solid systemic change, all participants, whether proponents or opponents, are drawn into the larger changes by the very fact of being within the school.

(p. 308)

The change process is understood as an active, systemic, and continuing learning process for the individuals as well as for the school as a whole.

(p. 310)

Despite many years of research, the power of three – that is, parent(s), student and teacher – working together remains concealed from most scholars and practitioners involved in school improvement. But collaborative learning communities are emerging (Chrispeels, 1992), if slowly.

Such tightly linked schools, focused on providing good educational services to families, and explicitly addressing the problem of student engagement through collaboration with families, constitute the best long-term solution available for the educational and social problems associated with alienated and under-educated students, with drop-outs, and with unemployed and unemployable youth.

Appendix

Quantitative and Qualitative Methodologies

Our methods for studying the interactions of schools and families were chosen to reveal both the details and the general picture. Our focus moves from close-up (interviews with individuals) to landscape (the statistical analysis of survey data), or in the reverse direction, often within each chapter. Over the six-year data-collection span we were consistent in the main dimensions – how the data were collected and recorded – but varied the process of analysis to look at the data in different ways. We here describe the consistent elements, particularly the triad concept as organizing framework for our thinking about teacher, parent and student collaboration, and as guide to data collection.

THE GENERAL APPROACH TO DATA COLLECTION AND ANALYSIS

There is considerable variation in school organization in British Columbia; we studied the upper grades in various elementary schools – students in grades 4, 5 6, 7 and 8 were included in different sites; their ages would generally fall between 10 and 14 years.

Care was taken to ensure that schools were representative of schools throughout the province of British Columbia. Thus, both urban and rural schools were asked to participate as were schools accommodating children from a variety of socioeconomic circumstances. Once a school had been identified as a potential site, school-district approval was sought and obtained.

The site descriptions that follow are those of the first year participants, but are broadly illustrative. The schools in other parts of the province which participated in subsequent years were similar to the schools described here.

Typical sites

Site Alpha is a relatively large district, in terms of both the student population it serves and its geographic range. It serves a community with a resource-based economy, in this case forestry. Although the administrative office and most of the schools are clustered in and around the district's one main population centre, there are three communities at a considerable distance from the district's administrative centre, each with its own elementary and high schools. In addition, there are a number of very small outlier schools scattered throughout the district. The socioeconomic level of each of the neighbourhoods varies widely. Many students are bussed to school. Five elementary schools in Site Alpha participated in this study.

School A offers a French Immersion track (a program in which French is the language of instruction). Students in the English track can walk from their homes, but many students in the French program are driven to and from school by their parents.

School G is a smaller school. Many of the children come from families in the lower socioeconomic bracket, but the school does draw students from some newly developed middle class neighbourhoods. The student population has a reputation of being challenging; teacher turnover is•high.

School H serves a middle class residential community. Teacher turnover is low, and the school has a reputation in the district for having fewer discipline problems than other elementary schools. The school has a reputation for having an active parent community.

School N is located in a rural community approximately thirty kilometres outside the district's main population centre. Most of the approximately 200 children who attend this school are bussed in, some from a considerable distance. School N has a reputation in the district for having strong support from a fairly tightly knit community.

School S is sited near the district's main population centre. The student population represents a broad cross-section of socioeconomic backgrounds. The school has a good reputation among parents, and the community is very supportive of the school.

Site Beta is a medium-sized suburban school district located just outside a large metropolitan area. Most residents commute to jobs in the city; some are employed in the town. Most of the schools in the district are located within the main population centre, with a few scattered in the rural areas. The community has grown rapidly over the past years.

School A opened three years ago in a newly constructed subdivision approximately two kilometres from the town centre. The school serves a middle class community. Most students walk to school. The school has a reputation for being fairly progressive, with supportive parents.

School B is located approximately one kilometre from the town centre, in a residential area. The district's largest high school is directly across the street. The neighbourhoods surrounding School B are older than those around School A. School B serves families from a broad range of socioeconomic backgrounds. The student population is regarded as somewhat challenging.

Although we speak of school sites as our hosts, in fact the classroom was the focus of our study: 'schools are not really the units of instruction . . . the productive technology, where materials are actually put to use, occurs in the classroom' (Bossert, 1988, p. 349).

Our assumption was that what occurs in classrooms is critical to student development, and that schools improve as the classroom-based triadic relationships amongst teacher, parent, and child become more collaborative; other routes to school improvement, for example through curriculum development, are much less likely to affect students directly and hence to produce changes in them.

THE ADVANTAGES OF MIXED METHODS

The general methodology involved mixed quantitative and qualitative methods, in which various interactive techniques are used to ensure that each data set added to the credibility and significance of the other. Many alternative ways of mixing methods are available; most investigations use a small subset of the possibilities available. The analyses that follow in the various chapters use most of the possibilities suggested by Caracelli and Greene (1993).

Mixed methods approaches have several advantages; they provide for:

- **triangulation** – the comparison of results across data sets and analytic approaches;
- **complementarity** – the measurement of distinct but overlapping elements;
- **development** – the sequential use of the qualitative/quantitative approaches to inform/improve the use of the other method;
- **initiation** – the generation of new hypotheses or research questions;
- **expansion** – the broadening of the range of the inquiry to encompass unanticipated findings.

AN INITIAL QUANTITATIVE ANALYSIS: THE PREDICTORS OF STUDENT COMMITMENT

The research reported in this analysis is limited to data collected from two groups, students and parents. We focus upon the perceptions that affect the rating given to a school by these participants.

The data analyzed here are drawn from Year 1 of the project. In this phase, we attempted to disentangle the complex of attitudes and values within families and between families and schools that affect the ways in which the parent and student participants rate schools. This preliminary stage was intended to clarify the main ways in which teachers could change aspects of their practice to improve parent and student perceptions. Our initial assumption, based on previous research (e.g. Epstein, 1986), was that teacher practice change would contribute substantially to the coproduction effort.

Four detailed questions shaped this portion of the study:

1. Do groups of parents and of students share similar attitudes to schools, classrooms, and teachers that affect ratings of school?
2. Do some attitudes seem to affect ratings more strongly than others?
3. Are the attitudes of students and their respective parents congruent?
4. Do these perceptions vary over time and between classrooms?

Sample, data collection and analyses

The data were gathered in 12 volunteer classrooms in 7 schools from 2 school districts (the sites described above). Parents (or guardians where appropriate) gave permission for their children to participate; about 30% of parents contacted declined. Parents, students, and teachers responded to surveys. Within our group of families there were quite large variations in family education and income, covering most of the socioeconomic range found in the province. One feature of this first and all subsequent analyses is **the failure to find any strong association between the socioeconomic data and any other variable; the attitudes to school of parents within our samples are not shaped by socioeconomic differences.**

The surveys used Likert-type scales (Borg and Gall, 1990, p. 311); respondents were asked to choose between Agree Strongly, Agree, Not Sure, Disagree, Disagree Strongly for a series of questions. Response data for parents and students were lightly edited; for example, inappropriate response codes appeared occasionally. Very few changes were required.

The student questionnaire consisted of 51 items forming 6 scales (see list in Figure A.1). An additional item asked students to rate their school on a 10-point scale. The parent questionnaire consisted of 61 items forming 9 scales. Additional items asked parents to rate the school on a 10-point scale, and requested some demographic data, including family education level. The teacher questionnaire consisted of 46 items forming 6 scales: parent involvement; teacher collegiality; collaboration with students; parent efficacy; teacher efficacy; and student responsibility.

These instruments were administered twice during each year of the study. For this analysis the dates were fall, 1990 (Time 1) and spring, 1991 (Time 2). A variety of basic analyses were conducted. The first, Cronbach's Alpha, demonstrated the internal consistency of the scale items. Subsequently these scales were marginally improved by rewriting, adding or deleting items. All were judged adequate by accepted standards, with typical Cronbach Alpha scores for the scales approximating .80.

We used the scale scores for individuals (calculated by summing all the responses to items in a scale and finding the mean value) to develop a correlation matrix showing the general statistical relationship between the various scales, for individual respondents. Then we developed speculative 'path analyses' – causal relationships linking student and parent attitudes to the ratings of school quality.

LIST OF SCALES

Parent perceptions of

Sc 1. student/teacher communication
Sc 2. student/parent communication
Sc 3. teacher/parent communication (instruction)
Sc 4. teacher/parent communication (general)
Sc 5. teacher concern about parent involvement
Sc 6. parent/school communication
Sc 7. parent values schooling
Sc 8. school climate
Sc 9. parent efficacy

Student perceptions of

Scale A. communications with parents.
Scale B. student values school.
Scale C. school/home communication.
Scale D. personal efficacy.
Scale E. student/teacher collaboration.
Scale F. parent valuing school.
Scale G. peer group values.
Scale H. school climate (not used in Yr 1).
Scale J. student responsibility (Chapter 9).
Scale K. teacher caring (Chapter 10).

Figure A.1 List of scales used

We found considerable overlapping of variables – for example, each of the parent attitudes is quite strongly associated with many of the others. However, the two domains of parent and student attitudes are far more separate than we had expected.

Responding to the research questions

With regard to Question 1 (Do groups of parents and of students share similar attitudes to schools, classrooms, and teachers that affect ratings of school?), we found that parents and students share attitudes toward teachers and schools that might influence their perceptions of school quality.

The quality ratings are more strongly associated with some attitudes than others (Question 2). For example, for parents the general perception of school climate seems very important. For students, the perception of student collaboration with the teacher seems important.

With regard to Question 3 (Are the attitudes of students and their respective parents congruent?), the scarcity of associations linking student and parent attitudes suggests that attitudes are either largely independent or linked in ways that are not obvious from our data.

Question 4 was 'Do these perceptions vary over time and between classrooms?' The same steps were taken with Time 2 data, to create scale scores. Then we compared the scores for individuals in Time 1 and Time 2. There were almost no significant differences between the Time 1 and Time 2 scores (T-test; $p < .001$). Over time these are stable perceptions.

Between-classroom variations are of particular importance since our initial phase included some modest interventions that were differentially implemented in classrooms. Interclassroom variations in mean score were very modest for Time 1 (tested via ANOVA), suggesting that within our geographically and socially diverse group of schools and classrooms there were standard patterns of teacher/parent, teacher/student, and student/parent relationships. For Time 2, for parents, interclassroom variations in rating of school and 6 of the 9 mean scale scores were significant (at the .05 level), suggesting that some changes had been perceptible to parents. For students, 3 scale means showed significant variation.

Our general inference is that within these quite diverse groups of parents and students, located in different classrooms, in schools some of which are hundreds of miles apart, the basic attitudes towards school **are very consistent and strongly established, and the experience of schooling during the year confirms rather than modifies them.** There is collective stability, although within this there may well be individual change.

Additional analysis

The second research question is in many ways the most important: Do some attitudes seem to affect ratings more strongly than others? We used an analytic technique called structural equation modelling, a version of path analysis that simultaneously tests a group of regression equations that constitute a model of causal relationships (the program used was EQS, Bentler, 1989). The technique clarifies causal paths by eliminating overlapping variables, and ordering the variables into those linear arrangements that best explain causal connections.

The paths produced by this technique are shown in Figure 1.2 (in Chapter 1). The adequacy of this set of causal relationships is described in terms of the 'fit' of the model to the data. For the parent data, the left side of the figure (including the 'crossover' relationships shown with broken arrows) the comparative fit index was .974; for the student side, the fit was .988. These are considered good fits.

Table A.1 The scales for the Time 1 analysis, with analytic data

PARENT SURVEY Time 1

Scale 1. Parent perception of student/teacher communication.
Cronbach's Alpha: .66. Items with corrected item-total correlations:

.37 16. My child's teacher(s) makes sure my child understands homework assignments.
.55 23. My child feels comfortable approaching teacher(s) with schoolwork questions or concerns.
.54 46. My child feels comfortable asking the teacher(s) for help.
.48 48. My child feels that her/his learning is important to the teacher(s).

Scale 2. Parent perception of student/parent communication.
Cronbach's Alpha: .82. Items with 'corrected item-total correlations':

.56 3. My child keeps me informed about classroom activities.
.47 8. My child talks to me about his/her plans for schooling in the future.
.63 12. My child lets me know when s/he is having problems in the class.
.65 13. My child usually discusses homework with me.
.69 17. My child keeps me informed about school activities.
.56 55. My child lets me know when he/she needs help with a homework assignment.

Scale 3. Parent perception of teacher/parent communication (instruction).
Cronbach's Alpha: .72. Items with 'corrected item-total correlations':

.60 5. My child's teacher(s) provides information about instructional programs so that I understand my child's schoolwork.
.55 7. My child's teacher(s) keeps me informed about homework assignments.
.55 15. My child's teacher(s) keeps me informed about what my child is learning in the classroom.
.36 53. My child's teacher(s) gives me information which allows me help my child with homework.

Scale 4. Parent perception of teacher/parent communication (general).
Cronbach's Alpha: .65. Items with 'corrected item-total correlations':

.54 6. My child's teacher(s) keeps me informed about classroom activities.
.43 19. My child's teacher(s) informs me when my child is doing well in class.
.28 33. I feel satisfied with my interviews with my child's teacher(s).
.36 56. My child's teacher(s) often asks me to help.
.45 61. My child's teacher(s) work hard to interest and excite parents.

Scale 5. Parent perception of teacher concern about parent involvement
Cronbach's Alpha: .81. Items with 'corrected item-total correlations':

.54 27. I am sure that my child's teacher(s) will contact me about my child's work in class, if necessary.
.48 29. I am sure that my child's teacher(s) will contact me about my child's homework, if necessary.
.59 31. I am sure that my child's teacher(s) will contact me about my child's behaviour, if necessary.
.56 37. My child's teacher(s) makes me feel part of a team.

.72 39. My child's teacher(s) seems interested in hearing my opinions about my child.
.50 40. Parents find teachers easily approachable at this school.
.61 44. My child's teacher(s) makes time to talk to me when it is necessary.

Scale 6. Parent perception of parent/school communication
Cronbach's Alpha: .78. Items with 'corrected item-total correlations':

.38 2.   I call/visit my child's teacher(s) to talk about my child's progress.
.43 9.   I talk to my child's teacher(s) about the instructional program in the classroom.
.45 18. I make sure to tell my child's teacher(s) when I think things are going well.
.64 21. I feel free to contact my child's teacher(s) about my child's work in class.
.67 22. I feel free to contact my child's teacher(s) about my child's homework.
.71 25. I feel free to contact my child's teacher(s) about my child's behaviour in class.

Scale 7. Parent values schooling
Cronbach's Alpha: .54. Items with 'corrected item-total correlations':

.41 1.   I talk to my child about school events/activities.
.35 4.   I encourage my child always to do his/her best work in school.
.38 59. I talk to my child about schoolwork quite a lot.

Scale 8. Parent perception of school climate
Cronbach's Alpha: .81. Items with 'corrected item-total correlations':

.38 10. The instructional program in our school helps to motivate students.
.55 24. Students are excited about learning in this school.
.46 26. Students in our school have the necessary ability to achieve well in basic skills.
.50 28. The academic emphasis in our school is challenging to students.
.63 30. Students are proud of our school.
.53 32. Our school reflects the values of the community in which it is located.
.53 36. Teachers make schoolwork interesting for students in this school.
.46 45. Our school is an important part of the community.
.51 47. Our school makes visitors feel welcome.
.34 57. My child feels comfortable in class.

Scale 9. Parent perception of parent efficacy
Cronbach's Alpha: .45 (T2: .61). Items with 'corrected item-total correlations':

.40 38. My own education prepared me well to help my child with schoolwork.
.28 49. I usually feel able to help my child with homework.
.15 50. Parents are given lots of good information from the school about what the children will be learning.
.13 51. I wish I could do more to assist my child with schoolwork.
.23 52. I make a strong contribution to how well my child does in school.
.38 54. My child's family has strengths that could be tapped by the school to help my child succeed.
.19 60. My child and I find it difficult to work together on schoolwork (REVERSED).

STUDENT SURVEY T1

Scale A. Student perception of communications with parents.
Cronbach's Alpha: .77. Items with 'corrected item-total correlations':

.58 1.   I let my parent(s) know about school events and activities.
.59 3.   I let my parent(s) know about things that happen in class.
.52 11. I let my parent(s) know what homework I have.
.47 12. I talk to my parent(s) about my plans for the future.
.38 13. I feel comfortable asking my parents for help with my homework.
.66 17. I feel comfortable talking to my parents about schoolwork.

Scale B. Student values school.
Cronbach's Alpha: .70. Items with 'corrected item-total correlations':

.50 26. It is important to my friends at school that they have their assignments done on time.
.45 27. I don't stay home from school unless I'm really sick.
.36 28. It's important to me that my teacher knows that I am doing my best in school.

.55 29. My friends don't stay home from school unless they are really sick.
.32 32. It's important to me that my parent(s) know that I am doing my best in school.
.34 33. It bothers me if I am late handing in assignments.
.34 41. I stay away from school whenever I can (REVERSED).

Scale C. Student perception of school/home communication.
Cronbach's Alpha: .73. Items with 'corrected item-total correlations':

.34 2. My parent(s) feel comfortable talking to my teacher about my progress in school.
.62 4. My teacher lets my parent(s) know about our work in class.
.57 5. My teacher lets my parent(s) know about what I am learning in the classroom.
.56 6. My teacher lets my parent(s) know about my homework assignments.

Scale D. Student perception of personal efficacy.
Cronbach's Alpha: .75 (T2: .82). Items with 'corrected item-total correlations':

.40 39. I enjoy helping other students in the class with their schoolwork.
.41 42. If I do well on a test, it's usually because I 'lucked out' on it (REVERSED).
.58 42. If I do well on a test, it's usually because I got lucky on it (REVERSED).
.60 45. When I do well on a difficult assignment it is usually because I worked hard.
.58 47. When I don't do well on an assignment, I usually feel that I can do better next time.
.40 48. When I make up my mind to do well in school I usually succeed.
.45 50. I feel that I have the ability to do well in school if I want to.

Scale E. Student perception of student/teacher collaboration.
Cronbach's Alpha: .72. Items with 'corrected item-total correlations':

.43 7. My teacher spends time talking to me individually about my schoolwork when it is necessary.
.39 15. My teacher gives us opportunities to make suggestions about activities in the classroom.
.44 16. My teacher asks me to help other students with work in the classroom.
.27 20. It is important to my teacher that I understand my homework assignments.
.56 25. I feel comfortable making suggestions to my teacher about activities we could do in the classroom.
.54 30. My teacher is interested in hearing my opinions even when I disagree with her/him.
.33 40. I get help from my teacher when I need it.

Scale F. Student perception of parent valuing school.
Cronbach's Alpha: .72. Items with 'corrected item-total correlations':

.28 (REVERSED) 9. My parent(s) rarely talk to me about how well I am doing in school.
.40 10. My parent(s) want me to participate actively in all classroom activities.
.37 23. My parent(s) expect me to tell them when I am having problems in the classroom.
.31 35. My parents remind me to get my homework done.

Scale G. Student perception of peergroup values.
Cronbach's Alpha: .63. Items with 'corrected item-total correlations':

.38 14. My friends and I talk about our future plans, for school and after.
.30 19. When I am having trouble with something in class I feel free to ask other students for help.
.31 26. It is important to my friends at school that they have their assignments done on time.
.41 29. My friends don't stay home from school unless they are really sick.
.40 39. I enjoy helping other students in the class with their schoolwork.

GENERAL MEASURES: ATTITUDE SCALES Time 1 (n = 187)
(1= Strongly Agree – 5= Strongly Disagree; Q62/52 Rating 1–10/lo-hi)

Measure	Mean	SD
PARENTS		
Question 62 Rating of School (1–10, low to high)	6.27	2.13
Scale 1. Parent perception of student/teacher communication.	2.49	0.79
Scale 2. Parent perception of student/parent communication.	2.12	0.74
Scale 3. Parent perception of teacher/parent communication (instruction).	3.03	0.84
Scale 4. Parent perception of teacher/parent communication (general).	2.90	0.75

Scale 5. Parent perception of teacher concern about parent involvement.	2.05	0.61
Scale 6. Parent perception of parent/school communication.	2.16	0.71
Scale 7. Parent values schooling.	1.59	0.53
Scale 8. Parent perception of school climate.	2.33	0.60
Scale 9. Parent perception of parent efficacy.	2.29	0.55

STUDENTS

Question 52 Rating of School (1–10, low to high)	6.01	2.34
Scale A. Student perception of communications with parents.	1.99	0.65
Scale B. Student perception that student values school.	2.17	0.64
Scale C. Student perception of school/home communication.	2.60	0.75
Scale D. Student perception of personal efficacy.	1.95	0.59
Scale E. Student perception of student/teacher collaboration.	2.35	0.71
Scale F. Student perception of parent valuing school.	2.00	0.63
Scale G. Student perception of peergroup values.	2.48	0.65

GENERAL MEASURES: ATTITUDE SCALES Time 2 (n = 162)
PARENTS

Question 62 Rating of School (1–10, low to high)	6.38	1.20
Scale 1. Parent perception of student/teacher communication.	2.52	0.77
Scale 2. Parent perception of student/parent communication.	2.07	0.73
Scale 3. Parent perception of teacher/parent communication (instruction).	2.12	0.63
Scale 4. Parent perception of teacher/parent communication (general).	2.17	0.67
Scale 5. Parent perception of teacher concern about parent involvement.	1.43	0.34
Scale 6. Parent perception of parent/school communication.	2.39	0.63
Scale 7. Parent values schooling.	1.43	0.34
Scale 8. Parent perception of school climate.	2.39	0.63
Scale 9. Parent perception of parent efficacy.	2.49	0.60

STUDENTS

Question 51 Rating of School (1–10, low to high)	5.60	2.36
Scale A. Student perception of communications with parents.	2.01	0.72
Scale B. Student perception that student values school.	2.23	0.66
Scale C. Student perception of school/home communication.	2.80	0.90
Scale D. Student perception of personal efficacy.	1.86	0.62
Scale E. Student perception of student/teacher collaboration.	2.33	0.67
Scale F. Student perception of parent valuing school.	1.95	0.67
Scale G. Student perception of peergroup values.	2.47	0.65

CORRELATION MATRIX Time 1 (n = 187; * p < .001)

PARENTS

	SC 1	SC 2	SC 3	SC 4	SC 5	SC 6	SC 7	SC 8	SC 9
Q62	0.23*	0.04	0.12	0.27*	0.29*	0.19	0.04	0.42*	0.15
SC 1.		0.39*	0.49*	0.52*	0.43*	0.13	0.59*	0.07	
SC 2.			0.17	0.14	0.05	0.19	0.64*	0.17	0.41*
SC 3.				0.78*	0.51*	0.51*	0.14	0.50*	0.13
SC 4.					0.66*	0.60*	0.15	0.63*	0.11
SC 5.						0.54*	0.15	0.66*	-0.02
SC 6.							0.36*	0.53*	0.25*
SC 7.								0.16	0.51*
SC 8.									0.06

STUDENTS

	SC A	SC B	SC C	SC D	SC E	SC F	SC G
Q. 52	0.15	0.35*	0.28*	0.34*	0.37*	0.01	0.38*
SC A.		0.28*	0.24*	0.43*	0.41*	0.38*	0.22
SC B.			0.23	0.40*	0.35*	0.01	0.65*
SC C.				0.12	0.32*	0.12	0.17
SC D.					0.43*	0.22	0.41*
SC E.						0.30*	0.42*
SC F.							0.01

CORRELATION MATRIX Time 2 (n = 162; * p < .001)

PARENTS

	SC 1	SC 2	SC 3	SC 4	SC 5	SC 6	SC 7	SC 8	SC 9
Q. 62	0.32*	0.09	0.38*	0.38*	0.48*	0.32*	0.03	0.58*	0.29*
SC 1.		0.34*	0.49*	0.53*	0.60*	0.41*	0.24*	0.63*	0.36*
SC 2.			0.18	0.15	0.12	0.17	0.46*	0.14	0.41*
SC 3.				0.80*	0.66*	0.62*	0.18	0.65*	0.41*
SC 4.					0.72*	0.69*	0.18	0.70*	0.44*
SC 5.						0.69*	0.21	0.76*	0.44*
SC 6.							0.38*	0.57*	0.48*
SC 7.								0.24*	0.38*
SC 8.									0.47*

STUDENTS

	SCA	SCB	SCC	SCD	SCE	SCF	SCG
Q. 51	0.15*	0.32*	0.22	0.23	0.34*	0.21	0.29*
SC A.		0.42*	0.15	0.51*	0.33*	0.53*	0.39*
SC B.			0.16	0.43*	0.31*	0.34*	0.59*
SC C.				0.04	0.32*	0.33*	0.04
SC D.					0.29*	0.36*	0.48*
SC E.						0.28*	0.35*
SC F.							0.29*

PARENT EDUCATION LEVEL
Correlation Matrix
(n = 213)

	Sc 4	Sc 5	Sc 9
Q70	.18	.18	.20
	p = .004	p = .004	p = .002

Scale 4. Parent perception of teacher/parent communication (general).
Scale 5. Parent perception of teacher concern about parent involvement.
Scale 9. Parent perception of parent efficacy.

METHODS OF ANALYZING THE INTERVIEW DATA

Case studies consist of 'intensive holistic description and analysis of a single entity, phenomenon, or social unit. Case studies are particularistic, descriptive and heuristic and rely heavily on inductive reasoning in handling multiple data sources' (Merriam, 1988, p. 16); they are able to deal with a wide variety of kinds of evidence, are appropriate where phenomena and their context are inseparable, and typically 'concentrate attention on the way particular groups of people confront specific problems, taking a holistic view of the situation' (Shaw, 1978, p. 2) in which the respondents often define for the investigator those aspects which are critical to an understanding of the phenomenon. They produce knowledge which tends to be both concrete and contextual, and which relies upon reader interpretation to fill out the meaning provided by the case (Merriam, 1988, p. 15).

The essence of the case study approach is indeterminacy – that is, such approaches are used when the phenomena under investigation are not well-understood on the basis of previous empirical work. It follows that the interview questions themselves must be open-ended, and that the analysis of the resulting interview data is conducted with an open mind. The 'discovery of new relationships, concepts, and understanding, rather than verification of predetermined hypotheses, characterizes qualitative case studies' (Merriam, 1988, p. 13).

The good case study profits from these characteristics in arriving at conclusions which exceed the knowledge of the respondents – the whole is far greater than the sum of the parts. The teachers in the English schools which were described by Rutter and colleagues as having a strong ethos which distinguished them from other less successful schools (Rutter et al., 1979), the administrators in the American schools in which innovations were successfully introduced (Huberman and Miles, 1984), the teachers in the school districts with exemplary approaches to teacher evaluation described by McLaughlin and Pfeifer (1988) and the administrators in the high-performing Canadian districts described by Coleman and LaRocque (1990) were probably unable to describe the respects in which the institutions differed from others. Yet careful analysis of the data by objective outsiders revealed patterns of activity which unmistakably differentiated these institutions from others and helped to account for their successes.

Qualitative analysis: the problem of validity

There are two main limitations of case studies: first, the nature of the data and the forms of analysis (Miles and Huberman, 1984) are such that there are few constraints upon the researcher: 'an unethical case writer could so select from among available data that virtually anything he wished could be illustrated' (Guba and Lincoln, 1981, p. 378). By contrast, quantitative research tends to provide brute facts, in the form of statistical analyses that resist massage and challenge the preferred interpretations.

Two safeguards are introduced in this study to cope with this limitation of case studies: first, the data collection methods to be described later attempt to collect data which provide naturally occurring forms of 'triangulation', in which 'the flaws of one method are often the strengths of another, and by combining methods, observers can achieve the best of each, while overcoming their unique deficiencies' (Denzin, 1978, quoted in Merriam, 1986, p. 69). (See also Miles and Huberman, 1984; Guba and Lincoln, 1981.) Both the quantitative analyses, and the early qualitative data, helped in this regard. Second, our interviews were conducted by different interviewers, with different experiences and expectations.

The second general limitation of case studies is that the interview, the central data collection tool in most case studies, provides opportunities for inconsistencies: 'what people think they are doing, what they say they are doing, what they appear to others to be doing, and what in fact they are doing may be sources of considerable discrepancy' (MacDonald and Walker, 1977, p. 186). The three main safeguards in this respect were first, the interviewer's willingness and skill in probing, for example by asking for supportive illustrations or examples; second, the comparative analysis of the responses of several respondents, typically within a triad; and third, the comparison of the results of the analysis of interview data with those from the surveys. Many of the specific analyses reported in the main text use the last technique, of comparing interview findings with survey findings as a way of checking the reliability of the analyses.

Qualitative analysis: procedures

Interview schedules were prepared for the three reference groups, plus the principal from each of the participating schools. The topics broached in the open-ended interview questions and their probes reflected the intent of the questions contained in the survey.

Interviews were conducted by all members of the research team. To ensure similarity of approach, designated team members conducted tape-recorded pilot interviews with individuals who were not study participants. These interviews were then analyzed at subsequent research meetings to ensure, as much as possible, a common approach to interviewing.

Three parent/student pairs were randomly selected from each classroom. They were then interviewed usually in the home or, for students, sometimes in a room at the school. The home site provided interesting information regarding the context in which the student lived. The interviewer had an opportunity to observe, for instance, whether there were books in the home or whether the child had a quiet, designated place to study. As well, an interviewer often had an opportunity to observe the nature of the interaction between parent and child. Typically, parents appeared at ease while being interviewed in their own homes and, if the interviews were held in the evening or on a weekend, there was greater likelihood of having both parents present, in those cases where the family included two adults. For parents the choice of location, home or school, seemingly made little difference to the comfort level or the nature of the responses. The interviewers noted, however, that locale did appear to make a difference to students. When interviewed in the home, a parent was often within hearing distance of the child, and this appeared to have an inhibiting effect. Students spoke more freely when interviewed at school.

The interview data in this study were analyzed through 'grounded theory' techniques to provide insights regarding teacher, student, and parent attitudes and their development. The methodology here was guided by Miles and Huberman's work on multi-site causal analysis (Miles and Huberman, 1984). All interview data were taped, transcribed, and 'coded'. We typically used HyperRESEARCH, a computer program to facilitate the coding of textual data (Hesse-Biber, Dupuis, and Kinder, 1991) for coding the interview data. Reports generated by the program included frequency counts, which were used with some caution, largely to identify the most salient issues in the minds of the respondents.

Coding is a process of assigning a brief description to a piece of interview text that summarizes its meaning. The coding of the interview data was conducted on the typical 'grounded theory' basis: that is, we were conscious of the research questions during the process but coded all the data using **emergent codes** that best described what was said, rather than conforming to pre-existing expectations. Codes were established for the first interview coded, and subsequently changed as more interviews were coded, to give an economical but fully descriptive list of codes.

For example, the following comments were made by a student (see Chapter 10):

> Well, lots of times there are kids running around, well not really running around but if you are not in the right class . . . throwing stuff around and stuff like that while you are trying to do your work or if the teacher steps out to go to the washroom or get a drink or something like that.

The comment was coded as 'Disruptive classroom'. These codes were sometimes then used in summary tables to give an overview of respondent perceptions.

For most of the analyses reported later, two coders coded independently, and compared results only after the completion of that stage of the analysis. The overlap of coding categories between the two sets of results is consequently a form of validation.

All the quotations used in the various sub-studies described in the chapters are carefully chosen to be **representative, not situation-specific**. They typically illustrate a category of responses, rather than the view of a particular student, parent, or teacher. However, when individual triads are the subject of the analysis, the quotations do speak to particular situations.

Case studies are important **primarily** to illustrate variety, not convergence. We typically have examined most closely those cases that challenge the kinds of conclusions one would draw from statistical analyses. Thus in Chapter 3 we test our general thesis that parents shape student relationships with school by examining some specific cases in which this turns out not to be an accurate generalization, that is some 'outlier' cases.

Chapter Notes

CHAPTER 3

1. To develop our positive and negative student groups we used student attitude scales that the model (shown in the flow chart in Chapter 1) suggested were causally related to positive assessments of school . They included:

STUDENT VALUES SCHOOL (Scale B –;
Scale E – STUDENT/TEACHER COLLABORATION;
Scale H – STUDENT PERCEPTION OF SCHOOL CLIMATE.

The Cronbach Alpha coefficients for these scales for Time 10 (the data set used here) were, respectively, .81 (10 items); .83 (10 items); and .89 (10 items).

The scores for Scales B and E, those most influenced by the home, were summed, as were the scores on Scale H and Student Rating, to derive new scales labelled Home Influence, and Commitment to School. When the scores on these scales for individual students were rank-ordered, it was possible to select 16 student cases that were above or below the mean on both scales.

2. A detailed coding chart is given as Figure 3.3.

3. Ten vignettes of parent expectations and actions. These vignettes give parent comments of most significance with respect to expectations, mediation, and intervention. A student comment, to represent the student's views, is also provided.

Case 2

We [parent and school] work quite well together.

FP: Academically she seems to be doing very well, so as long as she is doing her best, I really don't look at, it doesn't have to be an 'A' if it's your best, if it's a C+ or a C, you are doing your best, hey, that's fine. So I'm more for the effort put in not the achievement per se. . . . Generally, I think she knows we want her to go on to further education and she wants to go on so I think just from us, her dad and I, you know you gotta get that education, you gotta get it. . . . I'm not really giving them an option in that I really do, really feel very strongly about that post [secondary] education. Just because of the society and the economics we live in, so I don't let her settle for second best, if I think she can do. . . .

FP: Usually at the beginning of the year, we actually go because we go away usually in the fall time and I'll go see the teachers right away and say this is what we're going to do, I need homework and sometimes I find disagreement but we work it out. . . . I can't complain. I mean, I feel like I'm in one of the best schools, where there is one-on-one, where we know each other on a first name basis, so it's good. . . . I've had to take a stand but not for her, yes, I've had to say 'no, this is not the way we do it' and go from there sort of thing. No, we [parent and school] work quite well together.

Student comment (on mother helping): She usually explains everything more so I get a better understanding of it.

CODE GROUPS
codes / counts / cases*

PARENT MEDIATOR ACTIVITIES – med
PARENT CATALYST ACTIVITIES – cata

parent perception of child's progress/commitment to school: positive views –
CODES include:

code	count	cases
ch able learner	15	1,2,3,6,14,16
ch concerned re grades	9	2,4,5,8,9,12
ch responsible does work	36	1,2,3,4,5,6,8,9
ch does plan work	5	2,4,5,14
ch accepts responsibility	17	6,7,9,12,13
ch realistic plans for future	13	1,2,5,6,8,9,10,14,15

activity	count	cases
p helps/supports ch acad	62	1,2,3,4,5,6,7,88,9,10,11,12,13,14,15 MED
p encourages ch/responsibility	46	1,2,3,4,5,6,7,8,9,10,14 CATA
p supports ch plans/cont ed	19	1,2,4,5,6,10,14,15 MED
p encourages sch import	7	1,2,8,9,14,15 CATA
p able/enjoys helping ch wi hw	15	8,9,11,12,14,15 MED

code	count	cases
ch accepts rules re friends	10	1,2,4,6,11,14
ch accepts p values re effort	5	2,9,14
ch asks accepts p help	16	2,3,4,5,6,7,8,9,11,12,15,16
ch enjoys work with p	5	3,7,9,12
ch comm about sch	29	1,2,3,5,6,7,8,9,11,12,13,14,16
ch reaction to p in cl	10	3,5,6,7,9,12,15

activity	count	cases
p and ch solve problems	8	1,4,5,6,14,15,16 MED
p intervened/chose sch	16	1,5,6,8,9,10,11,16 CATA
p collab w t comm/acad	35	1,5,6,7,8,9,11,12,13,14,15,16 MED
p feels welcome in cl/by t	3	1,2,4,5,6,7,8,9,11,12,14,15 MED

code	count	cases
ch always liked sch	9	1,3,5,6,14,15
ch happy at sch	20	1,3,4,5,6,7,8,9,11,12,13,14
ch likes t this yr	8	1,3,4,13,15,16
ch lots of sch friends	11	3,6,8,9,10,11,14,15,16

activity	count	cases
sch/pr welcomes/informs ps	50	1,2,3,4,5,6,8,9,10,11,12,13,15
t facilitates p helping ch	25	1,2,3,6,7,8,10,11,12,14,15
t has empathy/respect for ch	37	2,3,4,5,6,7,8,9,10,11,13,14,15
t maintained p support	49	1,2,4,5,6,8,9,11,12,13,14,15,16

Parent perception of child's progress/commitment to school: negative views
CODES include:

code	count	cases
ch anxious about sch	5	8,10,12,16
ch concern about gr not	2	7,13
ch conflict with ts	7	2,4,10,16
ch did hw in sch	2	2,4,13,15
ch cannot do hw	1	15
ch finds sch hard	3	2,5,8,10,12,16

activity	count	cases
p checks on ch hw not	4	12,16
p encourages ch not	1	16
p enjoys helping ch not	2	13,16
p feels no work wi t necess	5	1,4,8,13,16
p trouble helping ch acad	6	2,12,13,16

code	count	cases
ch grades off social	3	1,16
ch improved a little	1	10
ch less committed to sch	9	3,7,12,15
ch not yet responsible	8	6,7,12
ch plans work not	10	1,2,3,11,12,15,16
ch previous prob in sch	9	3,9,10,11,13
ch not known to t	1	3

activity	count	cases
p inv not/blocked	15	2,3,9,10,12,13,16
p minimal invol soc only	10	1,2,4,8,11,12,13,14
p collab w t blocked	24	1,3,4,7,10,14,15
p collab wi t acad not	12	2,6,7,9,16
p does not know curr	3	13,14
p does not value sch	3	13
p doesnt know t	2	3
p and t conflict over ch	7	10

code	count	cases
ch asks/accepts p help not	4	13,15
ch not comm about sch	13	2,6,10,11,12,15
ch has changed friends	5	8,10,14,15
ch no plans for future	9	2,3,7,11,12,13,15,16

activity	count	cases
t does not keep ps informed	7	6,7,10,14,15
t has empathy for ch not	12	8,10,12,15,16
t does not want p invol	6	2,3,7

Figure 3.3 Parent codes and frequencies for expectations, mediation, and catalyst attitudes and actions

*lists all codes, total counts for the code, and the cases in which at least one instance of the code occurs

Case 4

[On being asked if she felt welcome to call the teacher at need]:
FP: Well, for one thing, I would do it anyways.

FP: I had to help her a lot more last year. I think this year, getting the grades instead of just doing a report card has really benefited her, because she really works for those As, she loves getting them, so most of her work is done at school, she rarely ever has to bring home a thing. . . . The kids love their teacher, and they talk about her with great affection so I think if their teacher didn't show them that respect and affection too, they wouldn't feel that way towards her . . .
FP: Recently K. has been saying that she would like to be a teacher and I think she would be a good teacher, because she has got a lot of patience and she loves to help.

FP: I keep all my kids paced to get their homework done and if I know they have a project I keep asking them, you know, if somebody is doing a project so I think that is probably kind of working together – if it was only the teacher telling them then the kids might wait until the last minute to do.

I: Would you feel that you could call the teacher at any time?
FP: Well, for one thing, I would do it anyways.

Student comment: Sometimes my Mom quizzes me on stuff and it's really neat.

Case 6

I'm a parent who is in their face all the time . . .
and to me that's just part of my being a mother.

FP: I wished I didn't have to do it and he was just as smart as a whip and did his homework all the time and picked it up like that, but life's not like that way. I'd love to have more time to myself, but like most parents I don't and that's priority and so I do it.
FP: I try to always be on top of his homework. Our school has made it really good because everybody has to carry a Planner now, so the homework is supposed to be written in the Planner. I've told him that I don't care if he has no homework he still has to bring that Planner home so that I can look and sign it . . . . I make him sit down and do his homework and tend to check it over and see whether it's properly done and try and make him correct the spelling mistakes and punctuations, which he says isn't necessary, but I say is necessary because I'm his mother and I can't stand reading it.

FP: Oh, I often stop in just to chat. Especially if there has been any big discipline problems, that's usually the only things I'm down there for. . . . I'm a parent who is in their face all the time and they know that I'm there and to me that's just part of my being a mother. The school teaches but I am nosy and I want to know what they are teaching and how it is going. . . . How's he doing, are you noticing any improvement and that kind of stuff. . . . Oh, yeah, it's an exceptional school.

Student comment (on parents helping): I enjoy it when they do, but sometimes when it is something that I don't really understand, it's sort of boring until I get, she teaches it a different way.

Case 7

[On receiving a call about bad grades on the report card]:
I would have preferred to know if D. needed help in something . . . and to know that earlier.

I: When he does get a poor grade is he concerned or anxious about improving it?
FP: No. (laughter) Well, I think he is trying harder now than he was and I hope he does.
I know D. can do better, I don't expect him to do straight As or whatever.
I: Does he ever talk about the future?
FP: He says he is not going to school, he is not going to university, he is going to Valley Driving School and he is going to be a truck driver. His dad is a truck driver.
FP: D.'s teacher doesn't notify us of what is happening in his class, like what they are doing. . . . I had gone to see him previously, earlier in the year, and on few occasions and we

talked about things, but nothing came up about say D.'s work and then come report card I get a phone call, you know he calls and says, 'We're supposed to call the kids with lower grades, and we are warning parents that your child's getting a lower grade.' and I was like, 'What! Why wasn't this talked about', you know.

I: Could you describe ways in which you and D.'s teacher work together in his education?

FP: I guess to notify me if, like I would have preferred to know if D. needed help in something, you know and to know to take that, initiate that earlier. Call to me and say 'D. is not doing.' because previous to that it was, 'Oh, yeah, D. has got no problems in school' type of thing and then you get to Grade Four when you get letter grades. So I would like to know that if D. needs help in some areas and I would like to know that so I can help him. Be given extra work or whatever. I don't mind that.

Student comment: if I don't understand something then she will like ask me a question that makes sense and actually catch on more with it and then she asks me another and I catch on more and more.

Case 9

I picked this school before I picked the house . . .
it just felt right. I saw what was going on and I liked it.

FP: He's doing quite well. He's getting good grades right now so, I think the set-up they have is working quite well with him.

FP: My philosophy is as this is his first intermediate year and a lot of stuff, reports and essays and stuff, is new to him so, and with a learning disability, I hope that by giving him structure and direction and staying on top of it now, he will pick up some of these skills himself and I'll be able to back away from it. He will be able to be more self-motivating and that's my goal.

I: And, so do you enjoy the experience of helping your son with his homework, his school work?

FP: Yes, I do. I find learning interesting first of all . . . the ability to learn and the ability to analyze and the ability to put things together – I find it interesting to watch that develop in both of them.

FP: I picked this school out, I picked this school before I picked the house.

I: How did you choose the school?

FP: I knew somebody who was attending this school first of all and just going down and talking to the personnel and principal, the teachers and stuff and it just felt right. I saw what was going on and I liked it.

[On the teacher] FP: Uh, ya, I think that we both want the best of J. and that we're both encouraging of him doing his best but not pushing, but just encouraging.

Student comment (on parents helping): it's easy working with my parents.

Case 11

I just esteem him [teacher] so highly.

FP: We are very fortunate that he has a really good attitude. He realizes that a paper is due each month and it kind of surprised me in one of the news letters this month . . . that 11 students didn't do a book report. I guess when I grew up you did what is expected of you and I thought, wow, you know, here they are in grade six and already they are not taking their responsibility in learning.

FP: Well I find I learn things just from helping J. do his homework, even when you are helping him, you know what's going on, you know where he is at with math or language arts, social studies.

FP: There was that time where I just felt that they were being bombarded with a lot of homework so I actually did go. . . . I am all for homework . . . but there was just a time there when he was coming home and he was, you know, even at nine o'clock his homework wasn't finished . . . and so I did go and I just questioned, you know, 'am I the only mother' and he said 'no, there was someone else in' and her son as well had been doing four hours of homework the night before.

I: Are there things the teacher could do to make it easier for you to help your child?
FP: Well, how he has made it easy for me, and maybe that is why I just esteem him so highly, is because of the criteria. [a teacher grading system carefully explained to students/parents]

FP: Well, there's just such a good rapport between the principals, teachers, students, parents. I mean it is just like our own little community here . . . I think highly of the school.

Case 12

> Partly it's my fault, I should be asking her all the time if she has something;
> if I don't ask her, I don't know. She doesn't offer the information to me.

FP: Oh, definitely. She is getting way better marks this year.
FP: Sometimes she's very good. Sometimes she is a little bit irresponsible. Not so much this year.
FP: She wants to go to college. She is not sure what she wants to do yet. . . .
FP: And now I always tell her, like you do not wait. If you want me to help you, I will help you but be a little more responsible in the way that you give me time to do it . . . don't leave it until Sunday night at 9 o'clock . . . and say, 'well you know I've got something that has to be in in the morning', well that's your tough luck. You have early in the morning again.
FP: A few years ago when she was doing a project, she would just hand it in, not very full of information and not very neat, . . . but I think now with me, actually sitting down and helping her do it, she is finding it is a little better to do a little extra, extra and your grades go a little bit better.
FP: I think for me, I'm the one that has to start participating a little more, like you know if S. doesn't, like start reminding her, like do you have any notes or newsletters or whatever.

FP: I just find her very easy to talk to. . . . I feel free if I wanted to go in there, if I figured that there was. . . Like I said she hasn't had any problems this year, so I'm sure if there was a problem, Mrs M. probably would have got ahold of me . . . I find them pretty good because they tell you what they are basically covering for the year and as long I get them and take the time to read them, which I don't always do, so I'm guilty too.

Student comment (on parents): I like to get good marks because when I get good marks my Mom is like really proud of me and I like that.

Case 13

> My kids are bright enough, they are going to survive in the real world.
> I know people that were straight A students that couldn't make it in the real world.

FP: I want him to work hard and do his best but I am not that concerned about the grade because he is learning and he is happy and he's doing what he is supposed to be doing.
FP: I have no idea what they are being taught . . . . My kids are bright enough, they are going to survive in the real world. I know people that I grew up with that were straight A students that couldn't make it in the real world. So to me what you learn in school isn't just what is taught in the books it is all the rest, real life. And that's what is going on when they are sitting their desks trying to learn fractions.
I: Does he ask you to help him?
FP: No, not really, he doesn't really bring much homework home either.
I: What about studying for an exam?
FP: I don't think he does that. I have never seen him study. I don't know if they have exams.
I: Okay, so could you describe things you do to help M. learn?
FP: Nag him until it's done. Just nag him until it's done.
FP: She is fair, you know, like when things are going on with kids some teachers don't see everything and this one has eyes in the back of her head so it is really good that she is fair. . . . Ya, they are not pulling any fast ones on her . . . When there is something happening she phones. She is very good, she is very communicative and very good.

Student comment (on parent's advice): stay in school because he quit and he has a crappy job and now he hates it, he has to get up at 5.00 am and stuff. So stay in school.

Case 14

I get her to tell me if she has any problems with anything or anybody.
We talk out solutions to those things

FP: I'm blessed and D. is a very good student, so she doesn't really need a lot to help, she just does it.
I: What's put that desire in her?
FP: In some ways she has always been that way. . . . A very fast learner, you'd tell her something once and she would remember things. . . . If she doesn't get a good mark on something, she will always resolve to do better the next time and she does that on her own rather than us getting upset with her. She wants to have good marks, she wants to do really well and she wants to learn from her mistakes. . . . Oh, she is very conscientious about her homework. She'll stay up, if she happens to have forgotten that she has homework and she remembers, she'll either stay up until it's done or she'll get up early the next day and do it. One time when she forgot, she was more hard on herself than anybody else could be.
I: What would she like to do?
FP: She wants to do something with music. A career in music. . . . she wants to go to university. I don't think she quite knows how she gets into music. . . . She saw me graduate because I didn't get my Bachelor of Ed until two years ago. . . . She saw the cap and the gown.
FP: I get her to tell me about what she has been doing and I get her to tell me if she has any problems with anything or anybody. We talk out solutions to those things.
FP: Mrs J. is pretty good about sending what they have been doing in class.
I: Have there been times when you felt that you had to stand up for your child interests at school?
FP: No. I make her stand up for herself.

Case 15

I try and explain to him that it is important to care
about what you are doing and make an extra effort.

FP: Sometimes he will get right on task and get doing it and other times I will have to, you know, make sure that he is getting in and doing it, because he doesn't really tell me he has homework because he knows I am going to make him do it and he wants to go outside.
I: Do you think he is slowly starting to mature in that area?
FP: I think he was better at it before.
I: Does he want to do better in school, does he want to get good grades?
FP: Yes he does but I don't know how much harder he is willing to work at it to get them. When we get the report card, of course, then it's I wish I had gotten a better mark on that, I only got this. . . . We talk about when he graduates or when he is in high school, and he doesn't seem to think he needs to go past high school. He knows what he wants to do . . . he wants to be a mechanic like his Dad of course, but he knows, we have told him, that Dad had to go to college to do that.
FP: I don't know if he isn't listening properly to instructions or maybe she hasn't explained it clearly enough. Sometimes I find he doesn't know exactly what he is supposed to be doing. . . . I try to encourage him to put more effort into things so then he will get a better grade because he will tend to just kind of throw it together and then it is done. But I try and explain to him that it is important to care about what you are doing and make an extra effort.
FP: I have had some concerns lately with my son and so I have stopped in and talked to her about it and she has no problem with that . . . I find that in the whole school, all the teachers I've had contact with . . . I don't feel like I shouldn't be there or I feel I can drop in. I don't want to disrupt them during their lesson or whatever but I can pretty much any time.

CHAPTER 4

Samples of the scales and the items which make up the scales were shown in the Appendix.

Table 4.1 shows the class-by-class distribution of mean scores on each of the most important scales. The large Standard Deviation in some cases suggests that there is

Table 4.1   Class-by-class distribution of mean scale scores

	PARSC 1 M 2.50	RA	PARSC 3 M 3.03	RA	PARSC 5 M 2.05	RA	PARSC 7 M 1.58	RA	STSC B M 2.17	RA	STSC E M 1.94	RA	OVERALL RANK
ANOVA p =	SD 0.80 >.05		SD 0.84 >.1		SD 0.61 >.1		SD 0.51 >.05		SD 0.63 >.05		SD 0.59 >.1		
CL 1/1	2.87	1	3.26	3	2.18	2	1.53	8	2.61	1	2.01	5	3.33
CL 1/2	2.78	3	3.21	4	2.29	1	1.65	5	2.18	6	2.11	2	3.50
CL 1/3	2.59	4	3.30	2	2.08	7	1.70	3	2.41	3	2.07	3	3.67
CL 1/4	2.40	7	3.10	5	2.10	6	1.31	12	2.24	4	1.99	6	6.67
CL 1/5	2.55	5	2.70	10	1.81	12	1.35	11	2.00	9	1.92	8	9.17
CL 1/6	2.29	9	3.05	7	1.83	11	1.69	4	2.18	5	1.82	11	7.83
CL 1/7	2.29	8	3.01	8	1.95	9	1.55	7	1.94	12	1.64	12	9.33
CL 2/1	2.27	10	2.46	12	1.89	10	1.98	1	2.02	8	2.13	1	7.00
CL 2/2	2.00	12	3.05	6	2.14	4	1.57	6	1.94	11	1.83	10	8.17
CL 2/3	2.13	11	2.63	11	1.96	8	1.53	9	2.46	2	2.02	4	7.50
CL 2/4	2.42	6	3.00	9	2.17	3	1.36	10	1.98	10	1.91	9	7.83
CL 2/5	2.80	2	3.34	1	2.11	5	1.83	2	2.15	7	1.93	7	4.00
hi/lo	2.87/		3.34/		2.29/		1.98/		2.61/		2.13/		
range	2.00		2.46		1.81		1.31		1.94		1.64		

considerable discrepancy in parent opinion within the classroom. This should be reflected in the interview data.

In selecting classrooms for the hi-lo analysis, the choice of classrooms 1/1 and 1/2 seems clearcut. They are lowest in overall rank and rank low on both the key scales, Parent Scale 5 and Student Scale E. Similarly classroom 2/5 is low on three of the parent scales. Classroom 1/4 is midrange on several scales, and interesting from that perspective. Classroom 1/6 although not highest overall is high on both the key scales. But there are sharp discrepancies which overall is high on both the key scales. But there are sharp discrepancies which prevent clear-cut choices on purely quantitative grounds.

CHAPTER 5

1. The surveys used were similar to those already given in the Appendix. (Student Scale H is new; it is given in full.) The Alphas given in Table 5.1 are again measures of internal consistency. An Alpha of around .80 or better indicates a well-constructed scale.

Table 5.1 Surveys – analysis of scales

PARENT SURVEY T3: Analysis of Scales

Scale 1. perception of student/teacher communication. 'Alpha': .84.
Scale 2. perception of student/parent communication. 'Alpha': .84.
Scale 3. perception of teacher/parent communication (instruction). 'Alpha': .84.
Scale 4. perception of teacher/parent communication (general). 'Alpha': .82.
Scale 5. perception of teacher concern about parent involvement. 'Alpha': .85.
Scale 6. perception of parent/school communication. 'Alpha': .83.
Scale 7. parent values schooling. 'Alpha': .77.
Scale 8. perception of school climate. 'Alpha': .82.
Scale 9. perception of parent efficacy 'Alpha': .71.

STUDENT SURVEY T3: Analysis of Scales

Scale A. communications with parents. 'Alpha': .79.
Scale B. student values school. 'Alpha': .73.
Scale C. perception of school/home communication. 'Alpha': .83.
Scale D. perception of personal efficacy. 'Alpha': .78.
Scale E. perception of student/teacher collaboration. 'Alpha': .84.
Scale F. perception of parent valuing school. 'Alpha': .72.
Scale G. perception of peergroup values. 'Alpha': .61.
Scale H. perception of school climate. 'Alpha': .90.

Scale H is new scale for t3. Items with item-scale correlation given (centrally important items in bold):

.42 24. This school is a better place for students than others I know about.
.75 36. I feel proud of my school.
.30 43. I feel safe in this school.
.67 46. I believe that the teachers in this school really care about how well I do in school.
.72 64. Teachers in this school treat the students with respect.
.70 65. Rules in this school are fair.
.77 66. Teachers treat students fairly in this school.
.61 67. Everyone in this school, including teachers, is involved in learning.
.52 68. The principal and the teachers in this school treat each other with respect.
.72 69. If I had a choice, I would choose to go to this school

Table 5.2   Descriptive statistics – Scales, Times 3, 4

Time 3	N	MEAN	MEDIAN	TRMEAN	STDEV	SEMEAN
Scale 1	188	2.2878	2.2500	2.2789	0.5946	0.0434
Scale 2	188	1.9270	2.0000	1.8919	0.6243	0.0455
Scale 3	188	2.7099	2.7258	2.7038	0.6856	0.0500
Scale 4	188	2.4572	2.4286	2.4504	0.6136	0.0448
Scale 5	188	1.9122	2.0000	1.8920	0.5517	0.0402
Scale 6	188	1.9648	1.8828	1.9278	0.5881	0.0429
Scale 7	188	1.6273	1.6250	1.6092	0.4463	0.0326
Scale 8	188	1.9423	2.0000	1.9356	0.4761	0.0347
Scale 9	188	2.2470	2.2196	2.2408	0.5240	0.0382
RatingPt	188	7.3462	7.0000	7.4475	1.2564	0.0916
Scale A	188	1.8485	1.8000	1.7960	0.6734	0.0491
Scale B	188	1.7062	1.6000	1.6680	0.4945	0.0361
Scale C	188	2.5472	2.5361	2.5375	0.7796	0.0569
Scale D	188	1.6989	1.6000	1.6470	0.6134	0.0447
Scale E	188	2.1646	2.0909	2.1190	0.6635	0.0484
Scale F	188	1.8749	1.7778	1.8427	0.5404	0.0394
Scale G	188	2.1226	2.0000	2.0826	0.7044	0.0514
Scale H	188	2.0845	2.0000	2.0440	0.7567	0.0552
RatingSt	188	6.9780	7.0000	7.0880	1.5890	0.1160

Time 4	N	MEAN	MEDIAN	TRMEAN	STDEV	SEMEAN
Scale 1	159	2.2897	2.2500	2.2660	0.6566	0.0521
Scale 2	159	1.9617	2.0000	1.9399	0.6025	0.0478
Scale 3	159	2.8349	2.7500	2.8304	0.8023	0.0636
Scale 4	159	2.5422	2.4286	2.5350	0.6914	0.0548
Scale 5	159	1.9489	2.0000	1.9183	0.6125	0.0486
Scale 6	159	2.0416	2.0000	2.0229	0.5838	0.0463
Scale 7	159	1.6513	1.6250	1.6339	0.4591	0.0364
Scale 8	159	2.0268	2.0000	2.0120	0.5288	0.0419
Scale 9	159	2.2170	2.1429	2.2003	0.5629	0.0446
RatingPt	159	7.1720	7.0000	7.2470	1.2840	0.1020
Scale A	159	1.8477	1.8000	1.8125	0.5913	0.0469
Scale B	159	1.7033	1.6000	1.6813	0.4197	0.0333
Scale C	159	2.7671	2.6667	2.7410	0.8104	0.0643
Scale D	159	1.6390	1.6000	1.5972	0.5704	0.0452
Scale E	159	2.1497	2.0909	2.1060	0.6503	0.0516
Scale F	159	1.8446	1.8750	1.8185	0.4913	0.0390
Scale G	159	2.1257	2.2500	2.1135	0.5878	0.0466
Scale H	159	2.2006	2.1000	2.1825	0.6884	0.0546
RatingSt	159	6.7960	7.0000	6.8850	1.5170	0.1200

2. Descriptive statistics for Time 1 and Time 2 were given in the Appendix. Table 5.3 gives the descriptive statistics for Times 3 and 4.

3. The interventions were simple: at introductory meetings in the school year, teachers were given some materials to facilitate collaboration with the home, and some rationale for their use. At various sessions during the year, there were discussions with small groups of teachers about the various materials and practices suggested which included accounts by teachers of successes and failures. These after-school dinner sessions were quite well attended, and practices were generally reported on with some enthusiasm. The student planners, a daily log which students carried home as a record of school activities and homework assignments, and which parents were asked to sign and return, were particularly well received. Student Work Folders, which students took home for parent perusal about twice a month, were also popular, as were 'Good News' phone calls. Teachers reported parent amazement at receiving a call that did not signal trouble for student and parent.

Table 5.3 Testing between classroom differences, by ANOVAs
(p = or < .05 considered significant)

T1/T2 ANOVAS N=162 (12 classes)	T1	T2
PARENT SCALES		
1 (student/teacher communication)	NS	0.021
2 (student/parent communication)	NS	NS
3 (teacher/parent communication [instruction])	NS (0.053)	0.000
4 (teacher/parent communication [general])	NS	0.007
5 (teacher concern about parent involvement)	NS	0.007
6 (parent/school communication)	NS	0.006
7 (parent values schooling)	0.029	NS
8 (school climate)	0.001	0.000
9 (personal parental efficacy)	NS	NS (0.059)
Rating of School	0.021	0.031
STUDENT SCALES		
A (communication with parents)	0.015	NS
B (student values schooling)	0.033	NS (0.058)
C (school/home communication)	0.000	0.001
D (personal efficacy)	NS	NS (0.059)
E (student/teacher collaboration)	NS	0.006
F (parent values schooling)	0.043	0.042
G (values of peers)	NS	NS
Rating of School	NS	0.035
T3/T4 ANOVAS N=159 (20 classes)	T3	T4
PARENT SCALES		
1 (student/teacher communication)	NS	0.031
2 (student/parent communication)	NS	NS
3 (teacher/parent communication [instruction])	NS	0.025
4 (teacher/parent communication [general])	NS	0.027
5 (teacher concern about parent involvement)	NS	NS
6 (parent/school communication)	0.047	NS
7 (parent values schooling)	NS	0.047
8 (school climate)	0.048	NS
9 (personal parental efficacy)	NS	NS
Rating of School	NS	NS
STUDENT SCALES		
A (communication with parents)	NS	NS (0.068)
B (student values schooling)	NS	NS
C (school/home communication)	NS	0.001
D (personal efficacy)	NS	0.050
E (student/teacher collaboration)	0.000	0.002
F (parent values schooling)	NS	NS
G (values of peers)	NS	NS
H (school climate)	0.046	0.030
Rating of School	NS (0.053)	0.036

4. Student and parent surveys which measured these attitudes used Likert-type scales. The lower the scale score the more positive the attitude. Mean scale score differences between Time 2 and Time 1 (Time 2 minus Time 1) that are mathematically negative therefore indicate more positive attitudes. The final question of the survey asked respondents to rate the school on a 9-point scale (1=very poor, 9=excellent). In this case mean score differences between Time 2 and Time 1 that are positive indicate a more positive rating of the school and mean score differences between Time 2 and Time 1 that are negative indicate a less positive rating of the school.

ANOVAs were conducted for each of the scales as well as for parent and student rating for Time 1, 2, 3, and 4. ANOVAs measure only differences between the classrooms

Table 5.4 Testing changes from fall to spring, by T-TESTS

		LESS POSITIVE	
CLASSROOM	SCALES	T VALUE	P VALUE
23	1	3.68	0.005
	3	2.97	0.016
	G	3.27	0.010

		MIXED RESULTS	
CLASSROOM	SCALES	T VALUE	P VALUE
21	3 (−)	3.20	0.010
	C (−)	2.63	0.025
	7 (+)	−3.30	0.008
	D (+)	−2.44	0.035
25	5 (−)	2.87	0.011
	6 (−)	2.45	0.025
	9 (−)	2.19	0.043
	7 (+)	−2.68	0.016

		MORE POSITIVE	
CLASSROOM	SCALES	T VALUE	P VALUE
16	4	−3.20	0.010
	7	−3.31	0.008
	8	−3.21	0.009

regardless of the nature or number of those differences. Especially strong or weak scores from only one classroom can be powerful enough to create a significant ANOVA. (See Tables 5.3 and 5.4.)

T tests were run on the Time 1/Time 2 (Year 1) and Time 3/Time 4 (Year 2) differences between the scores for all scales and the rating of the school (for each classroom individually for both parents and students) to determine whether there were any changes in attitude (more positive or less positive) that were significant (p = or < 0.05).

CHAPTER 6

Table 6.1 Time 1 and 2 ANOVAs for parent and student scales

Parent scales		T1	T2
1	Student–teacher communication	*	*
2	Student–parent communication	*	*
3	Teacher–parent communication (Instruction)	*	0.000
4	Teacher–parent communication (General)	*	0.007
5	Teacher concern for parent involvement	*	0.007
6	Parent–school communication	*	0.006
7	Parent values school	*	*
8	School climate	0.001	0.000
9	Parent efficacy	*	*
	Rating of School	*	*
Student scales			
A	Communication with parent(s)	*	*
B	Student values school	*	*
C	Home–school communication	0.000	0.001
D	Student efficacy	*	*
E	Student–teacher collaboration	*	0.006
F	Parent values school	*	*
G	Peer values	*	*
	Rating of School	*	*

Notes: ●F-values significant at the noted level of probability.

CHAPTER 7

Creating portraits

We first examined and tallied all the frequency counts, by classroom, into summary tables. For each classroom, there were two triads, a and b. The teacher is common to both triads, so the teacher codes were the same. Naturally, pa21 identified the parent(s) of sa21. For a specific code, the following conventions were used: the initiator of the collaboration was given first, so that 'st p coll topic' means that the activity was initiated by the student and involved some form of collaboration or assistance between student and parent with respect to a particular topic, for example mathematics homework. The assistance might be mutual. That is to say the student might be helping the parent to understand what was required in an assignment. The cell in which the item appears identified the reporter of the collaboration – generally for collaboration between parent and student that will be one of those two parties, although not invariably – the report might be given by a teacher – thus 'I gave Mrs H. some materials on how to help J. and she used them I know'. Categories were often combined for convenience – for example, in 'barr' to collaboration are combined barriers and problems, that is to say perhaps 'parent working during the day' with 'don't like him, can't talk to Mr Jones about my child', which would be coded with a 'tone negative' code. Since 'barriers' were so prevalent in the minds of some triad members, we thought it appropriate to balance positive and negative comments by arriving at net totals; this provided a more accurate representation of attitudes and practices than simply examining positive statements. The summary tables allowed us to further summarize the data.

CHAPTER 8

1. The quantitative analysis

For this particular analysis, we sought triads for which complete survey data were available (i.e. parent, student, and teacher); the year 1 student n = 143; the year 2 n = 111. This subset of our original data set was analyzed separately.

The Cronbach Alpha scores, showing the internal reliability of the attitude scales, for the various scales for Time 4 (as illustration) are shown in Figure 8.4. Scale scores for each participant on each scale were derived. The relationships between these scale scores and student responsibility for Times 2 and 4 are shown in correlation matrices, Tables 8.1 and 8.2. (Basic descriptive data have already been given.)

TIME 4 ANALYSES	
STUDENT SCALES/ALPHA (n=111)	PARENT SCALES/ALPHA (n=103)*
Sc. A .75	Sc. 1 .90
Sc. B .67	Sc. 2 .82
Sc. C .85	Sc. 3 .91
Sc. D .78	Sc. 4 .85
Sc. E .87	Sc. 5 .88
Sc. F .71	Sc. 6 .77
Sc. G .46	Sc. 7 .80
Sc. H .85	Sc. 8 .84
	Sc. 9 .74

Figure 8.4   Scale Alphas for parents and students, Time 4
*(Some parents had more than one child in sample)

Table 8.1   Simple correlations for parent and student attitude scales, Time 2

	SR1	SR2	SC1	SC2	SC3	SC4	SC5	SC6	SC7
SR1	1.0000	.6510**	.2299**	.2912**	.1895	.1394	.1239	.1258	.1713
SR2	.6510**	1.0000	.2044	.3394**	.2065	.1699	.1332	.1401	.2234**
SC1	.2299**	.2044	1.0000	.3591**	.4116**	.4595**	.6149**	.4359**	.2876**
SC2	.2912**	.3394**	.3591**	1.0000	.1217	.1121	.1250	.1780	.4996**
SC3	.1895	.2065	.4116**	.1217	1.0000	.8036**	.6534**	.6517**	.2361**
SC4	.1394	.1699	.4595**	.1121	.8036**	1.0000	.7280**	.7244**	.2211
SC5	.1239	.1332	.6149**	.1250	.6534**	.7280**	1.0000	.7230**	.2622**
SC6	.1258	.1401	.4359**	.1780	.6517**	.7244**	.7230**	1.0000	.4534**
SC7	.1713	.2234**	.2876**	.4996**	.2361**	.2211	.2622**	.4534**	1.0000
SC8	.0842	.1399	.6078**	.0761	.6290**	.7022**	.7621**	.5746**	.2701**
SC9	.2149	.2616**	.3340**	.4167**	.3980**	.3950**	.4486**	.4597**	.4484**
SCA	.3021**	.5521**	.1499	.4385**	.1018	.1228	.0811	.1260	.2954**
SCB	.5615**	.8666**	.1356	.2590**	.2197	.2009	.1293	.1489	.1593
SCC	.0170	.1378	.3193**	.0513	.4398**	.4008**	.3812**	.3689**	.1950
SCD	.1996	.5209**	.1959	.3814**	.1015	.1156	.0634	.0824	.2969**
SCE	.2390**	.3064**	.4722**	.1691	.2702**	.3190**	.3400**	.2139	.2203**
SCF	.1352	.3332**	.1761	.2555**	.2525**	.2945**	.2394**	.2248**	.2360**
SCG	.2725**	.4792**	.0792	.2415**	.0569	.0846	.0516	.0107	.0930
SRATE	-.2190**	-.2885**	-.2396**	-.1467	-.2322**	-.1901	-.1947	-.1725	-.1515

** – Signif. LE .01 (2-tailed). SCALES(STUDENTS): SR1 student responsibility, fall; SR2 student responsibility, spring; SCA student/parent communication; SCB student values school; SCC home/school communication; SCD student efficacy; SCE student/teacher collaboration; SCF parent values school; SCG peer attitudes to school; SCH school climate. SCALES(PARENTS) SC1 student/teacher communication; SC2 student/parent communication; SC3 teacher/parent communication – instruction; SC4 teacher parent comunication – general; SC5 teacher concern re parent involvement; SC6 parent/school communication; SC7 parent values school; SC8 school climate; SC9 parent efficacy.
(Note: relationships considered practically significant [as opposed to statistically significant| in BOLD.)

Table 8.1 Simple correlations for parent and student attitude scales, Time 2 (cont.)

	SC8	SC9	SCA	SCB	SCC	SCD	SCE	SCF	SCG	S.RATE
SR1	.0842	.2149*	.3021**	.5615**	.0170	.1996*	.2390**	.1352	.2725**	-.2190**
SR2	.1399	.2616**	.5521**	.8666**	.1378	.5209**	.3064**	.3332**	.4792**	-.2885**
SRDIF	-.0822	-.0791	-.3349**	-.4251**	-.1512	-.4166**	-.1062	-.2568**	-.2788**	.1047
SC1	.6078**	.3340**	.1499	.1356	.3193**	.1959*	.4722**	.1761*	.0792	-.2396**
SC2	.0761	.4167**	.4385**	.2590**	.0513	.3814**	.1691	.2555**	.2415**	-.1467
SC3	.6290**	.3980**	.1018	.2197*	.4398**	.1015	.2702**	.2525**	.0569	-.2322**
SC4	.7022**	.3950**	.1228	.2009*	.4008**	.1156	.3190**	.2945**	.0846	-.1901*
SC5	.7621**	.4486**	.0811	.1293	.3812**	.0634	.3400**	.2394**	.0516	-.1947*
SC6	.5746**	.4597**	.1260	.1489	.3689**	.0824	.2139	.2248**	.0107	-.1725*
SC7	.2701**	.4484**	.2954**	.1593	.1950	.2969**	.2203**	.2360**	.0930	-.1515
SC8	1.0000	.4241**	.1579	.1316	.3987**	.2209	.4242**	.2111	-.0003	-.2103*
SC9	.4241**	1.0000	.2639**	.2059	.2700**	.2963**	.2605**	.2508**	.1306	-.1652
SCA	.2954**	.1579	1.0000	.4664**	.2320**	.5985**	.3399**	.5604**	.3816**	-.1399
SCB	.1593	.1316	.2059	1.0000	.1905	.4776**	.3328**	.3369**	.6361**	-.3346**
SCC	.3987**	.2700**	.2320**	.1905	1.0000	.1815	.3717**	.3638**	.1053	-.2481**
SCD	.2209*	.2963**	.5985**	.4776**	.1815	1.0000	.3128**	.4379**	.4142**	-.2468**
SCE	.4242**	.2605**	.3399**	.3328**	.3717**	.3128**	1.0000	.2946**	.3542**	-.3456**
SCF	.2111	.2508**	.5604**	.3369**	.3638**	.4379**	.2946**	1.0000	.2411**	-.1456
SCG	-.0003	.1306	.3816**	.6361**	.1053	.4142**	.3542**	.2411**	1.0000	-.2752**
S.RATE	-.2103	-.1652	-.1399	-.3346**	-.2481**	-.2468**	-.3456**	-.1456	-.2752**	1.0000

** – Signif. LE .01 (2-tailed). SCALES(STUDENTS): SR1 student responsibility, fall; SR2 student responsibility, spring; SCA student/parent communication; SCB student values school; SCC home/school communication; SCD student efficacy; SCE student/teacher collaboration; SCF parent values school; SCG peer attitudes to school; SCH school climate. SCALES(PARENTS) SC1 student/teacher communication; SC2 student/parent communication; SC3 teacher/parent communication – instruction; SC4 teacher parent comunication – general; SC5 teacher concern re parent involvement; SC6 parent/school communication; SC7 parent values school; SC8 school climate; SC9 parent efficacy. (Note: relationships considered practically significant [as opposed to statistically significant] in BOLD.)

Table 8.2 Simple correlations for parent and student attitude scales, Time 4

	SR3	SR4	SC1	SC2	SC3	SC4	SC5	SC6	SC7
SR3	1.0000	.5753**	.3127**	.1596	.1635	.1325	.1038	.0745	.2195
SR4	.5753**	1.0000	.3014**	.2113	.0839	.1565	.1492	.0138	.2465
SC1	.3127**	.3014**	1.0000	.3673**	.6629**	.6890**	.5793**	.4380**	.3579**
SC2	.1596	.2113	.3673**	1.0000	.3286**	.4046**	.3585**	.2845**	.4968**
SC3	.1635	.0839	.6629**	.3286**	1.0000	.8814**	.7200**	.5989**	.2643**
SC4	.1325	.1565	.6890**	.4046**	.8814**	1.0000	.7994**	.6805**	.2456
SC5	.1038	.1492	.5793**	.3585**	.7200**	.7994**	1.0000	.6182**	.1841
SC6	.0745	.0138	.4380**	.2845**	.5989**	.6805**	.6182**	1.0000	.2359
SC7	.2195	.2465	.3579**	.4968**	.2643**	.2456	.1841	.2359	1.0000
SC8	.2220	.2682**	.5041**	.2405	.3860**	.4455**	.4671**	.3460**	.4332**
SC9	.3069**	.3074**	.4997**	.4783**	.4132**	.3978**	.4203**	.2979**	.4933**
SCA	.3605**	.4357**	.1922	.4079**	.1865	.2121	.2439	.1165	.3820**
SCB	.5447**	.8655**	.2995**	.2298	.0729	.1290	.0733	-.0047	.2403
SCC	.1918	.3661**	.4451**	.1501	.5082**	.5037**	.4326**	.2600**	.1318
SCD	.3740**	.6097**	.2240	.2558**	.0569	.0694	.1517	.0121	.2956**
SCE	.3383**	.5592**	.6111**	.2580**	.4675**	.5172**	.4733**	.3455**	.2429
SCF	.2908**	.4703**	.2247	.1648	.2302	.2088	.2936**	.2707**	.2986**
SCG	.2478**	.3763**	.1654	.0937	.0521	.0304	-.0004	-.0531	.1358
SCH	.3010**	.5303**	.3026**	.1651	.2046	.2742**	.2534**	.2215	.1761
S.RATE	-.2528**	-.3417**	-.1106	-.1796	-.0598	-.1069	-.0505	-.0418	-.3317**

** – Signif. LE .01 (2-tailed). SCALES(STUDENTS): SR3 student responsibility, fall; SR4 student responsibility, spring; SCA student/parent communication; SCB student values school; SCC home/school communication; SCD student efficacy; SCE student/teacher collaboration; SCF parent values school; SCG peer attitudes to school; SCH school climate. SCALES(PARENTS) SC1 student/teacher communication; SC2 student/parent communication; SC3 teacher/parent communication – instruction; SC4 teacher parent comunication – general; SC5 teacher concern re parent involvement; SC6 parent/school communication; SC7 parent values school; SC8 school climate; SC9 parent efficacy.
(Note: relationships considered practically significant [as opposed to statistically significant] in BOLD.)

Table 8.2 Simple correlations for parent and student attitude scales, Time 4 (cont.)

	SC8	SC9	SCA	SCB	SCC	SCD	SCE	SCF	SCG	SCH	S.RATE
SR3	.2220	.3069**	.3605**	.5447**	.1918	.3740**	.3383**	.2908**	.2478**	.3010**	-.2528**
SR4	.2682**	.3074**	.4357**	.8655**	.3661**	.6097**	.5592**	.4703**	.3763**	.5303**	-.3417**
SC1	.5041**	.4997**	.1922	.2995**	.4451**	.2240	.6111**	.2247	.1654	.3026**	-.1106
SC2	.2405	.4783**	.4079**	.2298	.1501	.2558**	.2580**	.1648	.0937	.1651	-.1796
SC3	.3860**	.4132**	.1865	.0729	.5082**	.0569	.4675**	.2302	.0521	.2046	-.0598
SC4	.4455**	.3978**	.2121	.1290	.5037**	.0694	.5172**	.2088	.0304	.2742**	-.1069
SC5	.4671**	.4203**	.2439	.0733	.4326**	.1517	.4733**	.2936**	-.0004	.2534**	-.0505
SC6	.3460**	.2979**	.1165	-.0047	.2600**	.0121	.3455**	.2707**	-.0531	.2215	-.0418
SC7	.4332**	.4933**	.3820**	.2403	.1318	.2956**	.2429	.2986**	.1358	.1761	-.3317**
SC8	1.0000	.4597**	.1593	.2503	.1918	.2483	.4225**	.2049	.1408	.3467**	-.3231**
SC9	.4597**	1.0000	.3750**	.3220**	.2536	.3202**	.3856**	.2239	.1487	.2212	-.2809**
SCA	.1593	.3750**	1.0000	.3854**	.3478**	.5254**	.3594**	.6538**	.3107**	.3571**	-.2387
SCB	.2503	.3220**	.3854**	1.0000	.3242**	.6100**	.4540**	.4753**	.5254**	.5791**	-.3377**
SCC	.1918	.2536	.3478**	.3242**	1.0000	.2307	.6798**	.3350**	.2013	.4171**	-.1544
SCD	.2483	.3202**	.5254**	.6100**	.2307	1.0000	.3799**	.6351**	.5237**	.5012**	-.2933**
SCE	.4225**	.3856**	.3594**	.4540**	.6798**	.3799**	1.0000	.3923**	.3247**	.4954**	-.2534**
SCF	.2049	.2239	.6538**	.4753**	.3350**	.6351**	.3923**	1.0000	.4013**	.4927**	-.2087
SCG	.1408	.1487	.3107**	.5254**	.2013	.5237**	.3247**	.4013**	1.0000	.3704**	-.2814**
SCH	.3467**	.2212*	.3571**	.5791**	.4171**	.5012**	.4954**	.4927**	.3704**	1.0000	-.6096**
SRATE	-.3231**	-.2809**	-.2387	-.3377**	-.1544	-.2933**	-.2534**	-.2087	-.2814**	-.6096**	1.0000

** – Signif. LE .01 (2-tailed). SCALES(STUDENTS): SR3 student responsibility; SR4 student responsibility, spring; SCA student/parent communication; SCB student values school; SCC home/school communication; SCD student efficacy; SCE student/teacher collaboration; SCF parent values school; SCG peer attitudes to school; SCH school climate. SCALES(PARENTS) SC1 student/teacher communication; SC2 student/parent communication; SC3 teacher/parent communication – instruction; SC4 teacher parent comunication – general; SC5 teacher concern re parent involvement; SC6 parent/school communication; SC7 parent values school; SC8 school climate; SC9 parent efficacy. (ote: relationships considered practically significant [as opposed to statistically significant] in BOLD.)

2. The qualitative analysis

The selection process yielded 10 triads for T1/2, and 7 for T3/4. Within these triads, 10 of the student responsibility scores actually declined; 7 increased. Each of the triads was analyzed separately. Two analysts worked independently on the data; the first analyzed the T3/T4 data and the second the T1/T2 data, without comparing notes with respect to emerging codes and categories of data.

The original set of codes was far too specific for our purpose here. Codes were combined and/or eliminated with the effect of reducing the number of codes and broadening them so that they had more general reference across and between triads. Once the code list was established, frequency counts were used (cautiously) to reveal general patterns, beginning with the student data on acceptance of responsibility. The subsequent process consisted of a careful and repeated scanning of a set of triad interviews in order to identify those general connections between student responsibility and such issues as attention to homework, attendance, participation in school and class activities, relationships with teachers and peers, activities outside school, and general instructional relationships with parents which existed in the minds of the three triad members.

During the process, the analysts were not aware of the direction of the shift in student responsibility score for each case being analyzed, although it would be naive to claim that the changes in the student's attitudes were not immediately apparent from the interview data. As well, familiarity with the data (these analysts also conducted many of the interviews), and with previous analyses of these and other project data, was such that truly emergent themes were unlikely at this stage.

CHAPTER 9

1. Quantitative analyses

Various cohorts of grade 5, 6 and 7 students and their teachers and parents were the subjects of this analysis. They constitute the second and fifth-year populations of the larger study. The interview data from year 2 of the study were drawn from 57 student cases in 10 classrooms in 2 schools. The interview data from year 5 of the study were drawn from 25 student cases in 7 classrooms in 5 schools. (As in other analyses, our numbers were limited by missing data.)

The regression analyses
The quantitative procedures involved the use of SPSS to conduct multiple regressions. Table 9.1 shows the basic statistics on the scales used; Table 9.2 shows simple correlations, together with scale labels and illustrative items from the scales.

Table 9.1   Basic statistics for student scales

	MEAN	MEDIAN	SD	RANGE	MIN.	MAX.
SCL.A	1.65	1.50	0.50	3.25	1.00	4.25
SCL.B	1.64	1.50	0.56	3.40	1.00	4.40
SCL.C	2.47	2.43	0.74	4.00	1.00	5.00
SCL.D	1.92	1.75	0.60	3.25	1.00	4.25
SCL.E	2.13	2.10	0.63	3.50	1.10	4.60
SCL.F	1.60	1.50	0.42	2.00	1.00	3.00
SCL.G	2.28	2.30	0.58	3.25	1.00	4.25
SCL.H	2.09	2.00	0.75	3.90	1.00	4.90
SCL.J	2.09	2.00	0.67	3.60	1.00	4.60
SCL.K	1.81	1.80	0.75	4.00	1.00	5.00
S. RATE	6.90	7.00	1.78	8.00	1.00	9.00

Note: lo = positive for scales (1–5); hi = positive for rating (1–9)

Table 9.2 Scale intercorrelations (Time 10)

	SCL.A	SCL.B	SCL.C	SCL.D	SCL.E	SCL.F	SCL.G	SCL.H	SCL.K	SCL.J	S.RATE
SCL.A	1.0000	.5179**	.1729**	.4017**	.4204**	.4578**	.3990**	.4223**	.4194**	.4631**	−.2040**
SCL.B	.5179**	1.0000	.2919**	.5882**	.4365**	.5689**	.5809**	.6406**	.5846**	.6070**	−.4025**
SCL.C	.1729**	.2919**	1.0000	.1868**	.5729**	.3822**	.3933**	.4247**	.5311**	.3503**	−.2246**
SCL.D	.4017**	.5882**	.1868**	1.0000	.3651**	.4799**	.4613**	.4803**	.4493**	.5861**	−.2936**
SCL.E	.4204**	.4365**	.5729**	.3651**	1.0000	.5027**	.4679**	.6215**	.7180**	.4591**	−.3007**
SCL.F	.4578**	.5689**	.3822**	.4799**	.5027**	1.0000	.4354**	.5327**	.5079**	.4130**	−.2072**
SCL.G	.3990**	.5809**	.3933**	.4613**	.4679**	.4354**	1.0000	.5368**	.4947**	.5513**	−.2860**
SCL.H	.4223**	.6406**	.4247**	.4803**	.6215**	.5327**	.5368**	1.0000	.7310**	.4627**	−.6359**
SCL.K	.4194**	.5846**	.5311**	.4493**	.7180**	.5079**	.4947**	.7310**	1.0000	.4837**	−.4576**
SCL.J	.4631**	.6070**	.3503**	.5861**	.4591**	.4130**	.5513**	.4627**	.4837**	1.0000	−.2747**

* – Signif. LE .05   ** – Signif. LE .01   (2-tailed)

LEGEND: Scales with key item (item-scale correlation):
SCL.A Communication with Parents. (.58) 17. I feel comfortable talking to my parents about schoolwork.
SCL.B Student Values School. (.60) 27. I don't stay home from school unless I have a really good reason.
SCL.C Percep. Home/School Comm. (.65) 4. My teacher lets my parent(s) know about our work in class.
SCL.D Percep. of Personal Efficacy. (.64) 50. I feel that I have the ability to do well in school if I want to.
SCL.E Percep. of S/Tchr Collab. (.62) 15. My teacher gives us opportunities to make suggestions about activities in the classroom.
SCL.F Percep. of P. Valuing School. (.47) 35. My parents expect me to get my homework done.
SCL.G Percep. of Peer Group Values. (.54) 71. My friends think that school is important to their futures.
SCL.H Percep. of School Climate. (.72) 66. Teachers treat students fairly in this school.
SCL.K Percep. of Teacher Caring. (.75) 78. My teacher treats me with respect in the classroom.
SCL.J S. Accepts Responsibility. (.42) 75. I take pride in the work I hand in to my teacher.

The relationships in Table 9.2 were scanned; previous relationships seemed to hold in the new data set. We then tested some possible relationships between the other scales and Scale H, paying particular attention to those strongly correlated with H; Scales B, E and K were of interest.

First we tried to assess whether Scale B (student values school) was primarily a home or a school-related variable. Table 9.3 shows the results – with Scale B as the dependent variable.

Since the three home-based scales A, D, and F accounted for close to 50% of the variance in this measure, and our most powerful in-school variable, Scale K, added only an additional 5%, we concluded that for these students Scale B largely measures home influences.

Our next step was to assess the relative influence of Scale B, as a summary of home influences, in conjunction with the strong in-school variables E and K, upon Scale H, our measure of school climate (see Table 9.4).

Table 9.3 Contributions of home-based student attitudes to variance in Scale B (student values school)

	BETA	CORREL (R)	MULTIPLE R	ADJUSTED R squared	R squared INCREMENT
SCALE A	0.24	0.52	0.52	0.27	–
SCALE D	0.35	0.59	0.66	0.44	0.17
SCALE F	0.29	0.57	0.71	0.49	0.06
SCALE K	0.27	0.58	0.74	0.54	0.05

Signif. of T (probability) < .001 in all cases

Table 9.4 Contributions of student attitudes to variance in Scale H (student perception of school climate)

	BETA	CORREL (R)	MULTIPLE R	ADJUSTED R squared	R squared INCREMENT
SCALE B	0.32	0.64	0.64	0.41	–
SCALE K	0.41	0.58	0.77	0.60	0.19
SCALE E	0.19	0.42	0.79	0.62	0.02

Signif. of T (probability) < .001 in all cases

Here we concluded that although Scale B is the strongest influence, in-school elements play their part. However, Scale K (perception of teacher caring) is the more important. Scale E (perception of student/teacher collaboration), although it is strongly correlated with Scale K, does not seem to be independently important as a predictor. In previous analyses we have found this a critically important explanatory measure in our set of relationships.

When student rating of school is treated as a dependent variable, Scales B, E, K, and H together account for 42% of the variance; however, Scale H alone accounts for 40%. Thus Scale H is the catchall measure that incorporates most of the attitudinal influences which we have identified upon student rating of school. (There are obviously other things, attitudinal and practical, which affect this rating.)

2. The individual scores

Our procedure with the individual scores was to sort the scales of interest (K and H) into high-low patterns. The subgroups comprised those cases which fell more than one standard deviation from the mean. We will focus upon the positive ends of these distributions. Table 9.5 shows the distribution of students by classroom.

Table 9.6 shows student scores for the positive end of Scale K, and related scale scores.

Table 9.5 Distribution of students by classroom

CLASSROOM	NO. OF CASES	CLASSROOM	NO. OF CASES
11	4	43	8
12	6	44	9
13	9	61	7
14	7	62	3
15	5	64	25
16	5	65	15
17	8	66	14
18	5	67	15
21	1	68	16
31	8	81	7
32	7	82	8
33	6	83	6
34	8	84	10
35	3	85	13
36	3	86	6
37	3	87	11
41	9	92	9
42	13	93	6
totals		36	298

Table 9.6 Scale scores sorted by Scale K (high)

ST. ID	SCLK	SCLE	SCLB	SCLH	RATE	ST. ID	SCLK	SCLE	SCLB	SCLH	RATE
13301	1.00	1.30	1.40	1.00	9	68301	1.00	1.30	1.40	1.20	7
13302	1.00	1.50	1.30	1.50	9	68302	1.00	1.80	1.10	1.00	8
13306	1.00	1.70	1.10	1.30	9	68308	1.00	1.80	1.10	1.10	9
13308	1.00	1.90	1.00	1.00	9	68312	1.00	1.70	1.20	1.40	8
13309	1.00	1.20	1.60	1.00	7	68313	1.00	1.90	1.10	1.40	8
13310	1.00	1.60	1.40	1.30	7	68316	1.00	1.40	1.60	1.40	9
13311	1.00	1.50	1.30	1.10	8	68318	1.00	1.90	1.10	1.20	9
15302	1.00	1.70	1.30	2.70	4	81309	1.00	1.50	1.20	1.50	8
17310	1.00	1.80	1.20	1.20	8	83301	1.00	1.20	1.00	1.00	9
18306	1.00	1.80	1.00	1.20	7	83302	1.00	1.20	1.10	1.20	8
34301	1.00	2.10	1.10	2.00	7	83304	1.00	1.10	1.20	1.70	6
34309	1.00	1.20	1.10	1.10	9	83308	1.00	2.30	1.40	1.90	5
42304	1.00	1.10	1.40	2.10	1	84301	1.00	1.60	1.30	1.10	9
42312	1.00	2.70	1.70	2.70	6	84305	1.00	1.10	1.00	1.50	7
42313	1.00	1.50	1.50	2.70	5	84306	1.00	1.30	1.40	1.40	8
43306	1.00	1.90	1.00	1.70	7	84308	1.00	1.20	1.80	2.00	7
44301	1.00	2.20	1.10	1.30	7	84309	1.00	1.30	1.60	1.10	9
61304	1.00	1.20	1.10	1.20	9	84310	1.00	1.10	1.20	1.00	9
61305	1.00	1.80	1.40	1.50	8	84311	1.00	1.70	1.70	1.60	9
64323	1.00	1.70	1.60	1.80	5	85301	1.00	1.10	1.00	1.80	7
64395	1.00	1.30	1.20	2.40	9	85303	1.00	1.90	1.00	1.00	9
65304	1.00	2.20	1.40	1.80	7	85308	1.00	1.90	1.70	1.10	8
65307	1.00	2.60	1.10	2.00	7	85311	1.00	1.70	1.20	2.10	4
65309	1.00	1.50	1.30	2.00	7	85313	1.00	1.60	1.30	1.00	9
65315	1.00	1.20	1.40	1.30	5	85322	1.00	1.50	1.20	1.40	8
66311	1.00	1.20	1.20	1.40	9	85323	1.00	1.60	1.10	1.10	9
66313	1.00	2.00	1.30	1.60	7	86302	1.00	1.90	1.30	2.00	5
67311	1.00	2.00	2.80	2.20	3	86306	1.00	1.60	1.20	1.50	8
67312	1.00	1.80	1.10	1.80	7	86307	1.00	1.50	1.50	1.70	8
						87301	1.00	2.10	1.20	1.40	8
						87304	1.00	1.20	1.80	1.50	8
						87311	1.00	1.60	1.10	1.30	6

The key points about this table are that:

1. These scores represent student choices of response 1, STRONGLY AGREE, **for all 5 items in the scale** - these are clearly strongly held opinions.

2. Amongst this group, only 4 of the 60 cases have scores for Scale H worse than the mean, illustrating that **student perception of teacher caring predicts a positive perception of school climate.** (The converse procedure works equally well – when ranked by Scale H, only 3 of the 43 most positive cases show scores for Scale K worse than the mean).

3. 20 of the 36 classrooms are represented here, illustrating the extent to which **this student perception is individualized and widely distributed.**

4. On the other hand, when the number of respondents by classroom is considered (Table 9.5 above) only classrooms 13, 83, 84, and 85 have an absolute majority of students in this positive group, although 68 and 86 come within one case. **These 6 classrooms are not the same ones which stand out in the qualitative analysis,** demonstrating again how dangerous it is to generalize from interview data – indeed classroom 13 contained the unique negative case (teacher violence) used as illustration. Even this strikingly circumstantial account is not sufficient evidence of a bad classroom, in isolation.

CHAPTER 10

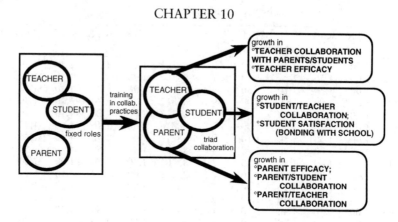

Figure 10.1   Anticipated attitudinal consequences of increased collaboration

The survey data were drawn from 23 classrooms in 7 schools. We also interviewed a subset of the parents and students from each classroom; Table 10.1 lists interviewees by classroom, and all the teachers involved. Because of the focus on teacher practices, the classroom is the appropriate unit of analysis (most of the previous analyses have been family-specific).

From teacher interviews, measures of teacher efforts to improve student/parent and teacher/parent collaboration during the school year were derived. A variety of missing data limited our analysis to only 12 classrooms. However, this yielded some 800 pages of transcripts to scrutinize; a minimal number of cases for quantitative analysis is a huge task for qualitative analysis.

We began by coding teacher, student and parent interviews. Then frequency counts and judgments about the interviews were used to rank-order classrooms with respect to teacher practices. In Step 3 the same process was carried out with the parent and student interviews. Finally, the resulting patterns were compared with quantitative analyses (conducted independently of the coding and analysis of the interviews) to provide some estimate of the reliability of the qualitative findings.

Table 10.1   Interviews available for analysis, listed by classroom

CLASS	PARENT INTS		STUDENT INTS	
22100	22201	22205	22301	22305
25100	25201	25205	25301	25305
28100	28201	28216	28301	28316
29100	29204	–	29304	–
62100	62203	62207	62303	62307
63100	63204	63208	63304	63308
72100	72204	72207	72304	72307
73100	73204	73206	73304	73306
74100	74204	74211	74304	74311
77100	77205	77208	77305	77308
78100	78202	78210	78302	78310
79100	79204	79207	79305	79307

CLASSROOM NUMBER	TRIAD INVOLVEMENT	T/STUDENT COLLAB	PRAC CHANGE	TOTALS /RANK
22100	t helps p, 10 p help, 8 p efficacy, 1 p t collab, 12 p inv instr home, 11 **42**	st choice/ dec, 3 t respects/ reaches st, 8 **12**	3 way confer, 3 good news calls/ planner use, 2 **t prac change, 19**	73 / 03
25100	t helps p, 2 p help, 2 p t collab, 8 p inv instr home, 3 **15**	st choice/ dec, 7 t respects/ reaches st, 3 **15** st resp growth, 5	good news calls/ planner use, 12 **t prac change, 13**	43 / 07
28100	t helps p, 4 p help, 7 p efficacy, p t collab, 16 þ inv instr home, 5 **32**	st choice/ dec, 7 t respects/ reaches st, 5 **20** st resp growth, 8	3 way confer, 3 good news calls/ planner use, 2 **t prac change, 17**	69 / 04
29100	t helps p, 11 p help, 5 p t collab, 7 p inv instr home, 1 **24**	st choice/ dec, 4 t respects/ reaches st, 2 **6**	 **t prac change, 4**	34 / 10
62100	t helps p, 7 p help, 12 t calls p, 8 p t collab, 18 p inv instr home, 3 **48**	st choice/ dec, 4 t respects/ reaches st, 13 **27** st resp growth, 10	3 way confer, 2 good news calls/ planner use, 2 **t prac change, 5**	80 / 02
63100	t helps p, 2 p help, 5 p t collab, 9 p inv instr home, 7 **23**	st choice/ dec, 4 **10** st resp growth, 6	good news calls/ planner use, 2 **t prac change, 4**	37 / 08
72100	t helps p, 2 p help, 4 p t collab, 9 p inv instr home, 3 **18**	st resp growth, 3 **3**	good news calls/ planner use, 1 **t prac change, 13**	34 / 11
73100	t helps p, 19 p help, 10 t calls p, 3 p t collab, 17 p inv instr home, 3 **52**	st choice/ dec, 7 t respects/ reaches st, 2 **21** st resp growth, 12	3 way confer, 2 good news calls/ planner use, 10 **t prac change, 8**	81 / 01
74100	t helps p, 4 p t collab, 7 t calls p, 1 p help, 3 p inv instr home, 1 **16**	t respects/ reaches st, 2 **5** st resp growth, 3	 **t prac change, 8**	29 / 12
77100	t helps p, 4 p help, 4 t calls p, 2 p t collab, 13 **23**	st choice/ dec, 4 t respects/ reaches st, 4 **17** st resp growth, 9	3 way confer, 1 good news calls/ planner use, 2 **t prac change, 5**	45 / 05
78100	t calls p, 4 p help, 4 p efficacy, 1 p t collab, 14 p inv instr home, 4 **27**	st choice/ dec, 1 t respects/ reaches st, 10 **15** st resp growth, 4	good news calls/ planner use, 1 **t prac change, 2**	44 / 06
79100	t helps p, 1 p help, 4 t calls p, 3 p t collab, 10 p inv instr home, 1 **19**	st choice/ dec, 4 t respects/ reaches st, 2 **15** st resp growth, 9	good news calls/ planner use, 1 **t prac change, 2**	36 / 09

Figure 10.2   Counts from teacher interviews for topics relating to student commitment

CLASSROOM	PARENTS PTC+	PTC-	PSC+	PSC-	STC+	STC-	PARENT COLLAB.	STUDENTS SPC+	SPC-	STC+	STC-	PTC+	PTC-	STUDENT COMMIT.	RANKING P/S
22100 A	24	6	14	6	11	4	33	35	13	61	13	10	0	92	4 / 2 HI
22100 B	11	1	10	11	5	0	14	26	1	20	22	7	0	18	
22100 summary	35	7	24	17	16	4	47	61	14	81	35	17	0	110	
25100 A	17	22	15	0	16	4	8	19	1	10	14	15	0	14	11/12 LO
25100 B	12	6	13	5	3	5	16	28	4	18	28	2	2	22	
25100 summary	29	28	28	5	19	9	24	47	5	28	42	17	2	36	
28100 A	16	6	6	9	7	2	0	13	6	18	9	9	0	36	10/7 LO
28100 B	21	7	15	7	7	7	30	24	5	35	11	7	2	40	
28100 summary	37	13	21	16	14	9	30	37	11	53	20	16	2	76	
29100 A	30	3	27	2	10	0	57	35	6	24	11	11	0	35	1 / 4 HI
29100 ● (B)	30	3	27	2	5	9	57	24	14	59	20	10	4	59	
29100 summary	60	6	54	4	15	9	114	59	20	83	31	21	4	94	
62100 A	16	2	7	1	2	0	18	14	5	53	15	4	5	58	7 / 3 HI
62100 B	11	3	13	7	5	0	25	27	3	38	5	9	0	42	
62100 summary	27	5	20	8	7	0	43	41	8	91	20	13	5	100	
63100 A	9	2	12	8	7	0	20	16	3	64	15	13	0	44	12/5 MOD
63100 B	0	1	2	0	7	8	3	23	6	34	15	3	0	39	
63100 summary	9	3	14	8	14	8	23	39	9	98	30	16	0	83	
72100 A	15	2	7	0	6	0	18	11	2	17	5	6	0	9	6/9 MOD
72100 B	11	9	15	1	6	8	27	26	8	51	0	3	0	53	
72100 summary	26	11	22	1	12	8	45	37	10	68	5	9	0	62	
73100 A	18	11	13	0	12	3	36	37	1	26	0	10	0	59	2 / 1 HI
73100 B	18	2	4	2	7	3	26	18	1	35	10	7	0	61	
73100 summary	36	13	17	2	19	6	62	55	2	61	10	17	0	120	
74100 A	22	3	8	2	14	0	35	35	5	75	0	15	0	33	5/8 MOD
74100 B	10	1	3	2	7	1	11	24	4	18	8	3	0	36	
74100 summary	32	4	11	4	21	1	46	59	9	93	8	18	0	69	
77100 A	19	3	8	4	4	3	24	38	5	20	11	9	0	36	8/10 LO
77100 B	10	0	4	3	3	4	10	11	0	11	1	7	1	23	
77100 summary	29	3	12	7	7	7	34	49	5	31	12	16	1	59	
78100 A	19	5	7	7	5	5	17	30	4	21	6	16	0	20	9/11 LO
78100 B	9	3	7	0	3	0	16	13	2	15	8	5	0	21	
78100 summary	28	8	14	7	8	5	33	43	6	36	14	21	0	41	
79100 A	13	5	16	0	5	0	29	19	6	29	10	9	0	52	3/6 MOD
79100 B	10	5	8	0	5	0	18	23	0	24	4	7	2	26	
79100 summary	23	10	24	0	10	0	47	42	6	53	14	16	2	78	

Figure 10.3 Frequencies of references from interviews for various aspects of collaboration

Qualitative analyses

The initial coding of the teacher data was based on grounded theory principles already described. Then we focused on teacher reports of (1) attempts to strengthen parent involvement in instructional activities (TRIAD); (2) instances of teacher/student collaboration (T/ST COLL); and (3) instances of practice change (PR CHANGE) judged likely to affect student commitment. Some two hundred codes were reduced to these categories (Figure 10.2). Although not all the practice changes we count are directly attributable to the project, they are all commensurate with the coproduction principles (some non-specific claims of practice change were coded/counted).

The frequency counts in Figure 10.2 reveal some patterns – for example, high levels of teacher student collaboration (20+ instances, col. 3) coincide with relatively high levels of triad involvement. The reverse is also true. This relationship between parent involvement and student readiness to collaborate with teachers has already been demonstrated in previous chapters.

Classrooms 22, 28, 62 and 73 emerge as the stronger group in a simple 2-way comparison in the set of 12 classrooms. But the practice change measure does not coincide with the overall ranking, suggesting that these classrooms were different before the commencement of the project.

In the next chart (Figure 10.3) somewhat similar data for parents and student perceptions is presented. Parent/teacher collaboration is defined simply as any comment by a parent suggesting either that this relationship is facilitated or that it does occur; for example, good relationships between parents and teachers are often said to exist – these do not themselves constitute collaboration but do facilitate it. The same is true of parent/student collaboration and student/teacher collaboration.

Both positive and negative instances are recorded, since in some interviews there are many of the latter, and it seems misleading to ignore them. There are relatively high numbers of negative comments in some interviews – for example, in classroom 25 (both respondents A; also student respondent B). There are also occasional discrepancies between respondents in the same classroom (classroom 28, 63, and 74, parents A and B); and the occasional discrepancy between parent and student rankings (classrooms 62 and 63).

Note that perceptions may be based in part on issues beyond the control of the teacher. Classroom 78 provides a good illustration: the parent has overriding concerns about the school's failure to report adequately on student progress, but that failure is not attributable to either the teacher or the school; it is a feature of the Year 2000 philosophy adopted province-wide. When the focus of parent response is on teacher 78 activities of other kinds, the tone is more positive.

In general the counts shown in these tables are far less useful than the quotations themselves, illustrated in the main text. However, the 800 pages of transcripts must be summarized somehow, and the tables reveal two important elements – the relative weight of various categories of commentary, and the relationships between various codes.

Quantitative analyses

After the completion of the qualitative work, we examined the quantitative data to see whether the classroom differences emerging from the qualitative analysis were confirmed by the surveys. The reliability of the various attitude scales was assessed using Cronbach's Alpha. (Table 10.2; these are remarkably consistent with those from previous years, in different schools.)

Table 10.2   Scales, with reliabilities (Cronbach's Alpha)

Parent perceptions of	Student perceptions of
Sc 1. student/teacher communication Alpha .87	Scale A. communications with parents. Alpha .75
Sc 2. student/parent communication Alpha .87	Scale B. student values school. Alpha .77
Ac 3. teacher/parent communication (instruction) Alpha .93	Scale C. school/home communication. Alpha .85
Sc 4. teacher/parent communication (general) Alpha .85	Scale D. personal efficacy. Alpha .78
Sc 5. teacher concern about parent involvement Alpha .93	Scale E. student/teacher collaboration. Alpha .83
Sc 6. parent/school communication Alpha .91	Scale F. parent valuing school. Alpha .67
Sc 7. parent values schooling Alpha .76	Scale G. peer group values. Alpha .79
Sc 8. school climate Alpha .86	Scale H. school climate Alpha .90
Sc 9. parent efficacy Alpha .74	

CHAPTER 11

The most recent versions of our surveys are given here, since the scales were slightly improved over time. Items in bold are considered central to the scale – focusing on these items will help teachers to interpret the significance of the scale scores.

I suggest that each school construct surveys for students and parents, using the items from the scales. Retaining the item numbers we used (the second number) might be useful when interpreting the results. (It also mixes the scales up in the survey – a technically desirable strategy.) A sample page from our surveys is given below, with advice on scoring and interpretation.

PARENT SURVEY Analysis of Scales

Scale 1. Perception of student/teacher communication. (11 ITEMS; ALPHA = .91)

.65 16. My child's teacher(s) makes sure my child understands homework assignments.

.69 23. My child feels comfortable approaching teacher(s) with schoolwork questions or concerns.

.57 43. My child feels that her/his learning is important to the teacher(s).

.70 46. My child feels comfortable asking the teacher(s) for help.

.60 48. My child feels comfortable making suggestions for classroom improvement to the teacher.

.48 62. My child's teacher spends time helping students after class.

.58 64. My child's teacher encourages students to give their own opinions in class.

.81 65. **My child feels that he/she can get help from the teacher when s/he needs it.**

.67 73. My child's teacher cares about how well s/he does.

.80 74. **My child's teacher treats him/her with respect.**

.65 75. My child's teacher treats all students fairly.

Table 10.3 Ranking of classrooms combining interview and survey analyses

STUDENT PERCEPTIONS

CLASS	FROM Chart 3 SCOMM	SCC	SCE	SCH	SRATE	CLASS ORDER	HI/LO PLACES
73	HIGH	62 HIGH	73 HIGH	73 HIGH	73 HIGH	73	4 OF 12
22	HIGH	73 HIGH	78 HIGH	78 HIGH	78 HIGH	78	3 OF 12
62	HIGH	77 HIGH	63 HIGH	62 HIGH	63 HIGH	62	2 OF 12
29	MOD	78 MOD	62 MOD	63 MOD	62 MOD		
63	MOD	63 MOD	77 MOD	72 MOD	74 MOD		
79	MOD	29 MOD	79 MOD	77 MOD	22 MOD		
28	MOD	79 MOD	29 MOD	74 MOD	77 MOD		
74	MOD	22 MOD	22 MOD	79 MOD	79 MOD		
72	MOD	74 MOD	72 MOD	28 MOD	72 MOD		
77	LOW	28 LOW	28 LOW	22 LOW	28 LOW	28	3 OF 12
78	LOW	25 LOW	74 LOW	29 LOW	29 LOW	29	2 OF 12
25	LOW	72 LOW	25 LOW	25 LOW	25 LOW	25	4 OF 12

PARENT PERCEPTIONS

CLASS	FROM Chart 3 PCOLL	SC2	SC1	SC8	PRATE	CLASS ORDER	HI/LO PLACES
29	HIGH	79 HIGH	73 HIGH	73 HIGH	29 HIGH	79	3 OF 12
73	HIGH	78 HIGH	79 HIGH	79 HIGH	72 HIGH	73	2 OF 12
79	HIGH	28 HIGH	78 HIGH	29 HIGH	62 HIGH	78	2 OF 12
22	MOD	73 MOD	22 MOD	62 MOD	73 MOD		
74	MOD	72 MOD	29 MOD	78 MOD	77 MOD		
72	MOD	77 MOD	62 MOD	72 MOD	22 MOD		
62	MOD	29 MOD	77 MOD	22 MOD	79 MOD		
77	MOD	62 MOD	72 MOD	28 MOD	74 MOD		
78	MOD	74 MOD	74 MOD	74 MOD	78 MOD		
28	LOW	22 LOW	63 LOW	63 LOW	63 LOW	25	4 OF 12
25	LOW	25 LOW	28 LOW	77 LOW	28 LOW	63	4 OF 12
63	LOW	63 LOW	25 LOW	25 LOW	25 LOW	28	2 OF 12

Scale 2. Perception of student/parent communication. (8 ITEMS; ALPHA = .86)

.63 3. My child keeps me informed about classroom activities.
.45 8. My child talks to me about his/her plans for schooling in the future.
.70 12. My child lets me know when s/he is having problems in the class.
.65 13. My child usually discusses homework with me.
.62 17. My child keeps me informed about school activities.
.67 45. My child lets me know when he/she doesn't understand a homework assignment.
.59 55. My child lets me know when he/she needs help with a homework assignment.
.54 57. My child usually shows me the work he/she has done in class.

Scale 3. Perception of teacher/parent communication (instruction). (12 ITEMS; ALPHA = .92)

.74 5. My child's teacher(s) provides information about instructional programs so that I understand my child's schoolwork.
.76 6. My child's teacher(s) keeps me informed about classroom activities.
.71 7. My child's teacher(s) keeps me informed about homework assignments.
.69 10. My child's teacher(s) gives me useful ideas about how I can help my child learn at home.
.79 15. My child's teacher(s) keeps me informed about what my child is learning in the classroom.
.64 19. My child's teacher(s) informs me when my child is doing well in class.
.56 20. I feel free to contact my child's teacher to ask about my child's progress in school.
.53 33. My interviews with my child's teacher(s) give me good information about my child's progress.
.64 34. My child's teacher(s) usually lets me know how my child is doing before report card time.
.62 35. My child's teacher(s) usually sends home a list of projects to be completed in the coming months.
.70 53. My child's teacher(s) gives me information which allows me to help my child with homework.
.59 58. My child's teacher(s) usually gives me monthly previews of what my child will be learning.

Scale 5. Perception of teacher concern about parent involvement. (9 ITEMS; ALPHA = .92)

.83 27. I am sure that my child's teacher(s) will contact me about my child's work in class, if necessary.
.84 29. I am sure that my child's teacher(s) will contact me about my child's homework, if necessary.
.79 31. I am sure that my child's teacher(s) will contact me about my child's behaviour, if necessary.
.64 37. My child's teacher(s) makes me feel part of a team.
.72 39. My child's teacher(s) seems interested in hearing my opinions about my child.
.52 40. Parents find teachers easily approachable at this school.
.80 44. My child's teacher(s) makes time to talk to me when it is necessary.
.71 56. I am sure that my child's teacher(s) will ask me to help my child with schoolwork if necessary.
.72 61. I find my child's teacher(s) easily approachable.

Scale 6. Perception of parent/teacher communication. (4 ITEMS; Alpha .90)

.81 **21. I feel free to contact my child's teacher(s) about my child's work in class.**

.80 25. I feel free to contact my child's teacher(s) about my child's behaviour in class.

.74 67. I feel free to contact my child's teacher(s) when I think my child is having difficulty.

.78 69. I feel free to contact my child's teacher(s) about my child's homework.

Scale 7. Parent values schooling. (8 ITEMS; ALPHA = .76)

.41 1. I talk to my child about school events/activities.

.45 4. I encourage my child always to do his/her best work in school.

.50 11. I really want my child to do well in school.

.51 14. I set high expectations for my child's school achievement.

.47 41. I expect that my child will go on to post-secondary education after high school.

.60 **42. It is important to me that my child does a good job on his/her homework.**

.38 59. I talk to my child about schoolwork quite a lot.

.51 **68. Success in school is important to my child's future.**

Scale 8. Perception of school climate. (7 ITEMS; ALPHA = .83)

.66 **24. Students are excited about learning in this school.**

.46 26. Students in our school have the necessary ability to achieve well in basic skills.

.64 28. The academic emphasis in our school is challenging to students.

.66 **30. Students are proud of our school.**

.62 32. Our school reflects the values of the community in which it is located.

.50 36. Teachers make schoolwork interesting for students.

.46 47. Our school makes visitors feel welcome.

Scale 9. Perception of parent efficacy. (5 ITEMS; ALPHA = .74)

.49 38. My own education prepared me well to help my child with schoolwork.

.62 **49. I usually feel able to help my child with homework.**

.55 52. I am able to make a strong contribution to how well my child does in school.

.53 54. Our family has strengths that help my child to succeed in school.

.46 REVERSED 60. My child and I often find it difficult to work together on schoolwork.

Scale 10. Perception of student responsibility. (7 ITEMS; ALPHA = .82)

.70 2. My child is very conscientious about getting schoolwork done at home.

.44 22. My child tries hard to get to school on time.

.74 **66. My child takes a very responsible attitude towards schooling and schoolwork.**

.61 70. It bothers my child if s/he is late handing in assignments.

.34 71. My child doesn't stay home from school unless s/he has a really good reason.

.72 **72. My child takes pride in the schoolwork s/he hands in to the teacher.**

STUDENT SURVEY: Analysis of Scales

Scale A. Communications with parents. (8 items; Alpha .77)

.46 1. I let my parent(s) know about school events and activities.

.58 2. I would tell my parents if I was having trouble with schoolwork.

.35 3. I let my parent(s) know about things that happen in class.

.43 9. I would tell my parents if I was in trouble at school.

.48 11. I let my parent(s) know what homework I have.

.41 12. I would tell my parents if I was having a problem with my teacher(s).

.51 13. I feel comfortable asking my parents for help with my homework.

.58 **17. I feel comfortable talking to my parents about schoolwork.**

Scale B. Student values school. (10 ITEMS; Alpha .81)

.31 18. How well I do in school is mostly up to me.
.50 21. It is important to me that I graduate from high school.
.57 22. REVERSED School is a waste of time for me.
.60 27. **I don't stay home from school unless I have a really good reason.**
.59 28. **It's important to me that my teacher knows that I am doing my best in school.**
.53 32. It's important to me that my parent(s) know that I am doing my best in school.
.41 33. It bothers me if I am late handing in assignments.
.41 37. I do my homework without being reminded.
.61 REVERSED 41. I stay away from school whenever I can.
.56 73. School is important to my future.

Scale C. Perception of school/home communication. (7 ITEMS; Alpha .82)

.66 4. My teacher lets my parent(s) know about our work in class.
.64 5. My teacher lets my parent(s) know about what I am learning in the classroom.
.53 6. My teacher lets my parent(s) know about my homework assignments.
.67 31. My teacher lets my parents know about class projects that are assigned.
.50 34. My teacher lets my parents about how I am doing in school.
.50 38. My teacher lets my parents know about what we will be studying next in class.
.53 44. My teacher lets my parents know how they can help me with my schoolwork.

Scale D. Perception of personal efficacy. (8 ITEMS; Alpha .79)

.60 14. I am a good learner.
.58 42. When my teacher explains things in class I usually understand first time.
.49 45. When I do well on a difficult assignment it is usually because I worked hard.
.37 47. When I don't do well on an assignment, I usually feel that I can do better next time.
.52 48. When I make up my mind to do well in school I usually succeed.
.37 49. REVERSED I often have difficulty with my schoolwork.
.64 50. I feel that I have the ability to do well in school if I want to.
.51 51. I almost never have trouble doing my homework.

Scale E. Perception of student/teacher collaboration. (10 ITEMS; Alpha .83)

.37 7. My teacher spends time talking to me individually about my schoolwork when it is necessary.
.62 15. My teacher gives us opportunities to make suggestions about activities in the classroom.
.43 16. My teacher asks me to help other students with work in the classroom.
.55 20. It is important to my teacher that I understand my homework assignments.
.50 25. I feel comfortable making suggestions to my teacher about activities we could do in the classroom.
.60 30. My teacher is interested in hearing my opinions even when I disagree with her/him.
.50 39. My teacher sometimes asks students to take leadership in classroom activities.
.63 40. I know I can get help from my teacher when I need it.
.48 52. My teacher sometimes asks students to explain ideas in class.
.50 53. My teacher sometimes learns things from students in class.

Scale F. Perception of parent valuing school. (10 ITEMS; Alpha .69)

.37 8. My parent(s) want me to do well in school.
.51 10. My parent(s) want me to participate actively in all classroom activities.

.32 23. My parent(s) expect me to tell them when I am having problems with my schoolwork.

.47 35. My parents expect me to get my homework done.

.33 56. My parents often read books and magazines.

.46 57. My parents enjoy attending events at the school.

.24 58. My parents know my teacher.

.30 59. My parents make sure I have a quiet place to do my homework.

.30 60. My parents expect me to continue my schooling after graduation from high school.

.45 62. My parents believe that school is important to my future.

Scale G. Perception of peergroup values. (8 ITEMS; Alpha .67)

.33 19. When I am having trouble with something in class I feel free to ask my friends for help.

.37 26. It is important to my friends at school that they have their assignments done on time.

.46 29. My friends don't stay home from school unless they have a really good reason.

.35 43. When one of my friends is having trouble with schoolwork I help them. (old 39)

.43 63. REVERSED My friends think that school is a waste of time.

.22 70. REVERSED My friends often act up in class.

.54 71. My friends think that school is important to their futures.

.27 72. My friends participate in a lot of school activities.

Scale H. Perception of school climate. (10 ITEMS; Alpha .89)

.50 24. This school is a better place for students than others I know about.

.69 36. I feel proud of my school.

.67 46. I believe that the teachers in this school really care about how well I do in school.

.75 55. I feel safe in this school.

.62 64. Teachers in this school treat the students with respect.

.62 65. Rules in this school are fair.

.72 66. Teachers treat students fairly in this school.

.56 67. Everyone in this school, including teachers, is involved in learning.

.54 68. The principal and the teachers in this school treat each other with respect.

.58 69. If I had a choice, I would choose to go to this school.

Scale J. Perception of teacher caring/respect for individual student. (5 ITEMS; Alpha .87)

.67 74. My teacher cares about how well I do in class.

.70 76. My teacher makes sure I get a chance to participate in things in class.

.75 78. My teacher treats me with respect in the classroom.

.75 80. My teacher makes sure that everyone gets a chance to participate in things in class.

.67 81. My teacher treats all students fairly in class.

Scale K. Student responsibility. (5 ITEMS; ALPHA = .66)

.30 54. When I have a project to do I leave it until the last minute.

.40 61. I try to help out in the class so we can all learn.

.42 75. I take pride in the work I hand in to my teacher.

.55 77. I make sure I am well-prepared for tests in class.

.44 79. If I miss some days of school I ask the teacher about work I have missed.

STUDENT SURVEY

•PLEASE TRY TO ANSWER **EVERY QUESTION** BY CIRCLING THE MOST APPROPRIATE RESPONSE.

IT IS MOST IMPORTANT THAT YOU ANSWER EVERY QUESTION CAREFULLY.

	AGREE STRONGLY 1	AGREE 2	NOT SURE 3	DISAGREE 4	DISAGREE STRONGLY 5
1. I let my parent(s) know about school events and activities.	1	2	3	4	5
2. I would tell my parents if I was having trouble with schoolwork.	1	2	3	4	5
3. I let my parent(s) know about things that happen in class.	1	2	3	4	5
4. My teacher lets my parent(s) know about our work in class.	1	2	3	4	5
5. My teacher lets my parent(s) know about what I am learning in the classroom.	1	2	3	4	5
6. My teacher lets my parent(s) know about my homework assignments.	1	2	3	4	5
7. My teacher spends time talking to me individually about my schoolwork when it is necessary.	1	2	3	4	5
8. My parent(s) want me to do well in school.	1	2	3	4	5

The student surveys should be administered to students *anonymously*; they can be hand-scored in the classroom by students. Deriving scale scores can be taught in a few minutes. There are three steps:

1. Identify the items for a scale.
2. Sum those item reponses.
3. Divide the total by the number of items in the scale.

The result is the scale score for the individual. These are then collated for the classroom, again by a student. I would recommend this process in the classroom be supervised by someone other than the regular classroom teacher. A parent volunteer with mathematics skills sufficient to catch obvious errors would be suitable. Or colleagues could simply switch classrooms. Alternatively, the Principal could do the data collection in each classroom. This has the advantage of standardizing the process for each room.

Some scales are more useful than others. Amongst the parent scales (which could also be scored by students) I recommend using Scales 3, 5, 7, 8; amongst the student scales, try A, B, D, E, H, J, K.

Interpreting the results can be done for classroom, for school, or both. The sample scores given for various groups in the Chapter Notes for Chapters 1 and 4 give some idea of the typical range of scores to be expected. The following comments may be helpful:

1. Typically the classrooms within a school are quite diverse.
2. Changes in the scores from fall to spring are more important than one-time scores.
3. Parent scale scores will help one to understand student scores.
4. Look at the key items in the scale frequently, to re-focus your definition.
5. Parents and students in the fall express attitudes developed in earlier years.
6. *Remember, every teacher has difficulty in* **reaching all the students/parents.**

References

Atlas, J. (1997). Annals of parenthood: Making the grade. New York: *The New Yorker*, April 14.

Barlow, M. & Robertson, H-J. (1994). *Class Warfare*. Toronto: Key Porter.

Baskwill, J. (1989). *Parents and Teachers: Partners in Learning*. Toronto: Scholastic Press.

Battistich, V., Solomon, D., Kim, D., Watson, M., & Schaps, E. (1995). Schools as communities, poverty levels of student populations, and students' attitudes, motives, and performance: A motivational analysis. *American Educational Research Journal*, 32(3), 627–658.

Bentler, P. M. (1991). *EQS, A Structural Equation Program*. Los Angeles, CA: BMDP Statistical Software Inc.

Blase, J. J. (1987). Dimensions of effective school leadership: The teachers' perspective. *Educational Administration Quarterly*, 24(4), 589–610.

Bossert, S. T. (1988). School effects. In N. Boyan (ed.), *Handbook of Research on Educational Administration*. New York, NY: Longman.

Bossert, S. T., Dwyer, D. C., Rowan, B., & Lee, G. V. (1982, summer). The instructional management role of the principal. *Educational Administration Quarterly*, 18(3), 34–64.

Bridges, E. M. (1986). *The Incompetent Teacher: The Challenge and the Response*. Philadelphia, PA: Falmer Press.

Brophy, J. & Good, T. L. (1986). Teacher behavior and student achievement. In M. C. Wittrock (ed.), *Handbook of Research on Teaching* (3rd ed.). New York: Macmillan.

Bryk, A. S., Easton, J. Q., Kerlow, D., Rollow, S. G., & Sebring, P. A. (1994). The state of Chicago school reform. *Phi Delta Kappan*, 76, 74–78.

Cairns, S. A. (1994). *Now I belong: An investigation of factors affecting bonding between student and school at the secondary level*. Unpublished MA Thesis. Burnaby, B.C.: Simon Fraser University.

Caracelli, V. J. & Greene, J. C. (1993). Data analysis strategies for mixed-method evaluation designs. *Educational Evaluation and Policy Analysis*, 15(2), 195–207.

Chrispeels, J. (1992). *Purposeful Restructuring: Creating a Culture for Learning and Achievement in Elementary Schools*. Washington, DC: Falmer.

Chrispeels, J. (1996). Effective schools and home–school–community partnership roles: A framework for parent involvement. *School Effectiveness and School Improvement*. 7(4), 297–323.

Clark, R. (1983). *Family Life and School Achievement: Why Poor Black Children Succeed or Fail*. Chicago: The University of Chicago Press.

Cohen, D. K., McLaughlin, M. W., & Talbert, J. E. (1993) *Teaching for Understanding: Challenges for Policy and Practice*. San Francisco: Jossey-Bass.

Coleman, J. S. (1987a). Families and schools. *Educational Researcher*, 16(6), 32–36.

Coleman, J. S. (1987b). The relations between school and social structure. In M. Hallinan (ed.) *The Social Organization of Schools: New Conceptualizations of the Learning Process*. New York: Plenum.

Coleman, J. S. & Hoffer, T. (1987). *Public and Private High Schools: The Impact of Communities*. New York, NY: Basic Books.

Coleman, P. (1984). Towards more effective schools: Improving elementary school climate. *Administrator's Notebook*, *31*(4).

Coleman, P. (1992). Quality assurance: A case study of the work of Local Education Authority inspectors and advisers in England. *School Organisation, 12*(2) 201–235

Coleman, P. (1994). *Learning about Schools: What Parents Need to Know and How They Can Find Out*. Montreal, Quebec: Institute for Research on Public Policy.

Coleman, P. & Collinge, J. (1991). In the web: Internal and external influences affecting school improvement. *School Effectiveness and School Improvement, 2*(4), 262–285.

Coleman, P. & LaRocque, L. (1990). *Struggling to be 'Good Enough': Administrative Practices and School District Ethos*. London: Falmer Press.

Corwin, R. G. & Borman, K. M. (1988). School as workplace: Structural constraints on administration. In N. Boyan (ed.), *Handbook of Research on Educational Administration*. New York, NY: Longman.

Cyster, R., Clift, P. S., & Battle, S. (1979). *Parental Involvement in Primary Schools*. Windsor, Berks, England: NFER.

Davis, G. A. & Thomas, M. A. (1989). *Effective Schools and Effective Teachers*. Boston, MA; Allyn & Bacon.

DeVellis, R. F. (1991). *Scale Development: Theory and Applications*. Newbury Park, CA: Sage.

Dye, J. (1989). Parental involvement in curriculum matters: Parents, teachers and children working together. *Educational Research*, *31*(1), 20–33.

Dryden, K. (1995). *In School: Our Kids, our Teachers, our Classrooms*. Toronto, Ont.: McLelland & Stewart.

Elmore, R. (1990). Introduction. In Richard Elmore & Associates (eds.), *Restructuring Schools: The Next Generation of Educational Reform*. San Francisco, CA: Jossey-Bass.

Epstein, J. L. (1985). A question of merit: Principals' and parents' evaluations of teachers. *Educational Researcher*, *14*(7), 3–10.

Epstein, J. L. (1986). Parents' reactions to teacher practices of parent involvement. *Elementary School Journal*, *86*(3), 277–294.

Epstein, J. L. (1987). Parent involvement: What research says to administrators. *Education and Urban Society*, *19*(2), 119–135.

Erickson, F. & Shultz, J. (1992). Students' experience of the curriculum. In P. Jackson (ed.), *Handbook of Research on Curriculum*. New York, NY: Macmillan.

Finn, J. D. (1989). Withdrawing from school. *Review of Educational Research*, *59*(2), 117–142.

Fullan, M. (1991). *The New Meaning of Educational Change*. Toronto: OISE Press.

Fullan, M., Bennett, B. & Rolheiser-Bennett, C. (1989). *Linking classroom and school improvement*. Invited Address presented at the annual meeting of the American Educational Research Association, New Orleans, April.

Galassi, J. P., Gulledge, S. A., & Cox, N. D. (1997). Middle school advisories: Retrospect and prospect. *Review of Educational Research*, *67*(3), 301–338.

Garnier, H. E., Stein, J. A. & Jacobs, J. K. (1997). The process of dropping out of school: A 19-year perspective. *American Educational Research Journal*, *34*(2), 395–419.

George, P. S. & Alexander, W. M. (1993). *The exemplary middle school* (2nd edn). Orlando, FL: Harcourt Brace.

Goodlad, J. I. (1984). *A Place Called School: Prospects for the Future*. New York: McGraw-Hill.

Gray, L. & Maxwell, T. W. (1995). School accountability: Lessons from British Columbia. *Australian-Canadian Studies*, *13*(1), 109–127.

Hallinger, P., & Murphy, J. (1986, May). The social context of effective schools. *American Journal of Education*, *94*(3), 328–355.

Hanushek, E. A. (1997). Assessing the effects of school resources on student performance. *Educational Evaluation and Policy Analysis, 19*(2), 141–164.

Hargreaves, D. H. (1995). School culture, school effectiveness, and school improvement. *School Effectiveness and School Improvement, 6*(1), 23–46.

Haylow, L. & Coleman, P. (1991). *Building better schools through teacher collaboration: Planning for school improvement*. A paper presented at the Annual Meeting of the American Educational Research Association, Chicago.

Hesse-Biber, S., Dupuis, P., & Kinder, T. S. (1991). HyperRESEARCH: A computer program for the analysis of qualitative data with an emphasis on hypothesis testing and multimedia analysis. *Qualitative Sociology, 14*(4), 289–306.

Hoover-Dempsey, K. V., Bassler, O.C., & Brissie, J. S. (1987). Parent involvement: Contributions of teacher efficacy, school socioeconomic status, and other school characteristics. *American Educational Research Journal, 24*(3), 417–435.

Hoover-Dempsey, K. V. & Sandler, H. M. (1997). Why do parents become involved in their children's education? *Review of Educational Research, 67*(1), 3–42.

Hossler, D. & Stage, F. K. (1992). Family and high school experience influences on the postsecondary educational plans of ninth-grade students. *American Educational Research Journal, 29*(2), 425–451.

Hoy, W. K. & Hannum, J. W. (1997). Middle school climate: An empirical assessment of organizational health and student achievement. *Educational Administration Quarterly, 33*(3), 290–311.

Huberman, A. M., & Miles, M. B. (1984). *Innovation Up Close: How School Improvement Works*. New York: Plenum.

Hughes, M., Wikeley, F., & Nash, T. (1994). *Parents and their Children's Schools*. Oxford: Blackwell.

Hyman, H. H., Wright, C. R., & Reed, J. S. (1975). *The Enduring Effects of Education*. Chicago: The University of Chicago Press.

Hyman, H. H. & Wright, C. R. (1979). *Education's Lasting Effects on Values*. Chicago: The University of Chicago Press.

Katz, F. E. (1964). The school as a complex social organization: A consideration of patterns of autonomy. *Harvard Educational Review, 34*, 428–455.

Kellaghan, T., Sloane, K., Alvarez, B., & Bloom, B. S. (1993). *The Home Environment and School Learning: Promoting Parental Involvement in the Education of Children*. Boston: Jossey-Bass.

Krumm, V. (1994). Expectations about parents in education in Austria, Germany and Switzerland. In A. Macbeth & B. Ravn (eds.), *Expectations about Parents in Education: European Perspectives*. Glasgow: Computing Services (University of Glasgow) Ltd.

Kushman, J. W. (1992). The organizational dynamics of teacher workplace commitment: A study of urban elementary and middle schools. *Educational Administration Quarterly, 28*(1), 5–42.

Lareau, A. (1989). *Home Advantage: Social Class and Parental Intervention in Elementary Education*. London: The Falmer Press.

Lawton, S. B. (1995). *Busting Bureaucracy to Reclaim our Schools*. Montreal, Quebec: Institute for Research on Public Policy.

Levin, B. (1997). The lessons of international educational reform. *Journal of Educational Policy, 12*(4), 253–266.

Lightfoot, S. L. (1979). Families and schools. In W. Walberg (ed.), *Educational Environments and Effects*. Berkeley, CA: McCutchan.

Lightfoot, S. (1983). *The Good High School*. New York: Basic Books.

Little, J. W. (1982). Norms of collegiality and experimentation. *American Educational Research Journal, 19*(3), 325–340.

Little, J. W. (1990). The persistence of privacy: Autonomy and initiative in teachers' professional relations. *Teachers College Record, 91*(4), 508–536.

Livingstone, D. (1995). Popular beliefs about Canada's schools. In R. Ghosh & D. Ray (eds.) *Social Change and Education in Canada*. Toronto: Harcourt-Brace.

Lortie, D. C. (1975). *Schoolteacher*. Chicago, Ill: University of Chicago Press.

Louis, K. S. & Smith, B. (1992). Cultivating teacher engagement: Breaking the iron law of social class. In F. M. Newmann (ed.), *Student Engagement and Achievement in American Secondary Schools*. New York: Teachers College Press.

Macbeth, A. (1989). *Involving Parents: Effective Parent–Teacher Relations*. Oxford: Heinemann.

Macbeth, A. (1994). Expectations about parents in education in England, Scotland and Ireland. In A. Macbeth & B. Ravn (eds.), *Expectations about Parents in Education: European Perspectives*. Glasgow: Computing Services (University of Glasgow) Ltd.

MacGilchrist, B. & Mortimore, P. (1997). The impact of school development plans in primary schools. *School Effectiveness and School Improvement*. 8(2), 198–218.

MacGilchrist, B., Myers, K., & Reed, J. (1997). *The Intelligent School*. London: Paul Chapman.

Mackenzie, D. E. (1983). Research for school improvement: An appraisal of some recent trends. *Educational Researcher*, 12(4), 6–16.

McGeeney, P. (1980). The involvement of parents. In M. Craft, J. Raynor, & L. Cohen (eds.), *Linking Home and School*. London: Harper and Row.

McLaughlin, M. (1987). Learning from experience: lessons from policy implementation. *Educational Evaluation and Policy Analysis*, 9(2), 171–178.

McLaughlin, M. W. (1993). What matters most in teachers' workplace context. In J. W. Little & M. W. McLaughlin (eds.), *Teachers' Work: Individuals, Colleagues, and Contexts*. New York: Teachers College Press.

McLaughlin, M. W. & Pfeifer, R. S. (1988). *Teacher Evaluation: Improvement, Accountability, and Effective Learning*. New York: Teachers College Press.

McLaughlin, M. W. & Yee, S. M. (1988). School as a place to have a career. In A. Lieberman (ed.), *Building a Professional Culture in Schools*. New York: Teachers College Press.

Madden, N. A., Slavin, R. A., Karweit, N. L., Dolan, L. J., & Wasik, B. A., (1993). Success for all: Longitudinal effects of a restructuring program for inner-city elementary schools. *American Educational Research Journal*, 30(1), 123–149.

Marjoribanks, K. (1989). Environments, adolescents' aspirations, and young adults' status attainment. *Educational Studies*, 5(2), 155–164.

Marshall, C., Patterson, J., Rogers, D. L., & Steele, J. R. (1996). Caring as career: An alternative perspective for educational administration. *Educational Administration Quarterly*, 32(2), 271–294.

Martin, J. R. (1992). *The Schoolhome: Rethinking Schools for Changing Families*. Cambridge, MA: Harvard U. P.

Martinez, R.-A., Marques, R., & Souta, L. (1994). Expectations about parents in education in Portugal and Spain. In A. Macbeth & B. Ravn (eds.), *Expectations about Parents in Education: European Perspectives*. Glasgow: Computing Services (University of Glasgow) Ltd.

Marx, R., Grieve, T., & Rossner, V. (1988). *The Learners of British Columbia*. Vancouver, B.C.: British Columbia Royal Commission on Education.

Mayer, S. (1997). *What Money Can't Buy; Family Income and Children's Life Chances*. Cambridge, MA: Harvard U. P.

Metz, M. H. (1993). Teachers' ultimate dependence on their students. In J. W. Little & M. W. McLaughlin (eds.), *Teachers' Work: Individuals, Colleagues, and Contexts*. New York: Teachers College Press.

Miles, M. B. & Huberman, A. M. (1984). *Qualitative Data Analysis: A Sourcebook of New Methods*. Beverly Hills, CA: Sage Publications.

Mitchell, D. & Encarnation, D. J. (1984). Alternative state policy mechanisms for influencing school performance. *Educational Researcher*, 13(5), 4–11.

Mortimore, P., Sammons, P., Stoll, L., Lewis, D., & Ecob, R. (1988). *School Matters: The Junior Years*. Wells, Somerset, England: Open Books.

Muller, C. (1993). Parent involvement and academic achievement. In B. Schneider & J. S. Coleman (eds.), *Parents, their Children, and Schools*. Boulder, CO: Westview.

Newmann, F. M. (ed.) (1992). *Student Engagement and Achievement in American Secondary Schools*. New York: Teachers College Press.

Oakes, J. & Lipton, M. (1990). *Making the Best of Schools: A Handbook for Parents, Teachers, and Policymakers*. New Haven, CT: Yale University Press.

Parsons, T. (1959). The school class as a social system. *Harvard Educational Review, 29*, 297–318.

Plowden Committee (1967). *Children and their Primary School*. London: HMSO.

Power, T. J. (1985). Perceptions of competence: How parents and teachers view each other. *Psychology in the Schools, 22*, 68–78.

Prestine, N. & Bowen, C. (1993). Benchmarks of change: Assessing Essential School restructuring efforts. *Educational Evaluation and Policy Analysis, 15*(3), 298–319.

Purkey, S. D. & Smith, M. S. (1983). Effective schools: A review. *Elementary School Journal, 83*(4), 427–452.

Raddysh, J. (1992). *Fading out: Comparing the elementary school experiences of high school drop-outs and high school graduates*. Unpublished Master of Arts in Education Thesis, Simon Fraser University, Burnaby, B.C.

Ravn, B. (1994). Expectations about parents in education in Scandinavian countries. In A. Macbeth & B. Ravn (eds.), *Expectations about Parents in Education: European Perspectives*. Glasgow: Computing Services (University of Glasgow) Ltd.

Raywid, M. A. (1990). Rethinking school governance. In Richard Elmore & Associates (eds.), *Restructuring Schools: The Next Generation of Educational Reform*. San Francisco, CA: Jossey-Bass.

Redding, S. (1992). *Parent scale to measure the efficacy of strategies to enhance the curriculum of the home*. A paper presented at the Annual Meeting of the American Educational Research Association, San Francisco.

Roberts, N. (1985). Transforming leadership: A process of collective action. *Human Relations, 38*, 8–12.

Rosenholtz, S. J. (1989). *Teachers' Workplace: The Social Organization of Schools*. New York, NY: Longman.

Rudduck, J., Chaplain, R., & Wallace, G. (1996). Pupil voices and school improvement. In J. Rudduck, R. Chaplain & G. Wallace (eds.), *School Improvement: What Can Pupils Tell Us?* London: David Fulton Publishers.

Rutter, M., Maughan, B., Mortimore, P., & Ouston, J. (1979). *Fifteen Thousand Hours: Secondary Schools and Their Effects on Children*. Cambridge, MA: Harvard University Press.

Sammons, P. (1995). Ethnic and socioeconomic differences in attainment and progress: A longitudinal analysis of student achievement over 9 years. *British Educational Research Journal, 21*(4), 465–486.

Sammons, P., Thomas, S., & Mortimore, P. (1997). *Forging Links: Effective Schools and Effective Departments*. London: Paul Chapman.

Sarason, S. B. (1990). *The Predictable Failure of Educational Reform: Can We Change Course Before it's Too Late?* San Francisco, CA: Jossey-Bass.

Sarason, S. B. (1995). *Parental Involvement and the Political Principle: Why the Existing Governance Structure of Schools Should be Abolished*. San Francisco, CA: Jossey-Bass.

Scaparro, F. (1994). Expectations about parents in education: An Italian point of view. In A. Macbeth & B. Ravn (eds.), *Expectations about Parents in Education: European Perspectives*. Glasgow: Computing Services (University of Glasgow) Ltd.

Sedlak, M. W., Wheeler, C. W., Pullin, D. C., & Cusick, P. (1986). *Selling Students Short: Classroom Bargains and Academic Reform in the American High School*. New York, NY: Teachers College Press.

Sergiovanni, T. J. (1987). The theoretical basis for cultural leadership. In *Leadership: Examining the Elusive*. The 1987 Yearbook of the Association for Supervision and Curriculum Development. Washington, DC: ASCD.

Shedd, J. B. & Bacharach, S. B. (1991) Introduction: Professionals in bureaucracies. Chapter 2 in *Tangled Hierarchies: Teachers as Professionals and the Management of Schools*. San Francisco, CA: Jossey-Bass.

Sizer, T. R. (1984). *Horace's Compromise: The Dilemma of the American High School*. Boston: Houghton Mifflin.

Slavin, R. E., Sharan, S., Kagan, S., Hertz-Lazarowitz, R., Webb, C., & Schmuck, R. (1985). *Learning to Cooperate, Cooperating to Learn*. New York: Plenum.

Smit, F. & van Esch, W. (1994). Opportunities for parents to influence education in the Netherlands. In A. Macbeth & B. Ravn (eds.), *Expectations about Parents in Education: European Perspectives*. Glasgow: Computing Services (University of Glasgow) Ltd.

Smylie, M. A. (1988). The enhancement function of staff development: Organizational and psychological antecedents to individual teacher change. *American Educational Research Journal, 25*(1), 1–30.

Smylie, M. A., Lazarus, V., & Brownlee-Conyers, J. (1996). Instructional outcomes of school-based participative decision making. *Educational Evaluation and Policy Analysis, 18*(3), 181–198.

Solomon, J. (1994). Towards a notion of home culture: Science education in the home. *British Educational Research Journal, 20*(5), 565–578.

Stevens, R. J. & Slavin, R. E. (1995). The cooperative elementary school: Effects on students' achievement, attitudes, and social relations. *American Educational Research Journal, 32*(2), 321–351.

Stevenson, D. L. & Baker, D. P. (1987). The family–school relationship and the child's school performance. *Child Development, 58*(5), 1348–1357.

Sulloway, F. J. (1996). *Born to Rebel: Birth Order, Family Dynamics, and Creative Lives*. New York: Pantheon Books.

Swap, S. M. (1992). *Developing Home–School Partnerships: From Concepts to Practice*. New York: Teachers College Press.

Sykes, G. (1990). Fostering teacher professionalism in schools. In Richard Elmore & Associates (eds.), *Restructuring Schools: The Next Generation of Educational Reform*. San Francisco, CA: Jossey-Bass.

Talbert, J. E. & McLaughlin, M. W. (1993). Understanding teaching in context. In D. K. Cohen, M. W. McLaughlin, & J. E. Talbert (eds.), *Teaching for Understanding: Challenges for Policy and Practice*. San Francisco, CA: Jossey-Bass.

Teddlie, C., Kirby, P., & Stringfield, S. (1989). Effective versus ineffective schools: Observable differences in the classroom. *American Journal of Education, 97*, 221–236.

Tizard, B. & Hughes, M. (1984). *Young Children Learning*. London: Fontana.

Tomlinson, S. (1989). Ethnicity and educational achievement in Britain. In L. Eldering & J. Kloprogge (eds.), *Different Cultures Same School: Ethnic Minority Children in Europe*. Amsterdam: Hove, Lawrence Erlbaum.

Vincent, C. & Tomlinson, S. (1997). Home–school relationships: 'the swarming of disciplinary mechanisms?'. *British Educational Research Journal, 23*(3), 361–378.

Virgilio, I., Teddlie, C., & Oescher, J. (1991). Variance and context differences in teaching at differentially effective schools. *School Effectiveness and School Improvement. 2*(2), 152–168.

Walberg, H. J. & Wallace, T. (1992). *Family programs for academic learning*. Paper presented at the annual meeting of the American Educational Research Association, San Francisco, CA.

Wang, M. C., Haertel, G. D., & Walberg, H. J. (1993). Toward a knowledge base for school learning. *Review of Educational Research, 63*(3), 249–294.

Wehlage, G., Rutter, M., Smith, G., Lesko, N., & Fernandez, R. (1989). *Reducing the Risk: Schools as Communities of Support*. London: Falmer.

Weick, K. E. (1976). Educational organizations as loosely coupled systems. *Administrative Science Quarterly, 21*(1), 1–19.

Zeldin, T. (1994). *An Intimate History of Humanity*. New York, NY: Harper.

Subject Index

Author Index

215